BRIT...

Arthur Eperon is one of the mo... ...best-known travel writers in Europe. Since leaving the RAF in 1945 he has worked as a journalist in various capacities, often involving travel. He has concentrated on travel writing for the past twenty-five years and has contributed to many publications including *The Times*, *Daily Telegraph*, *New York Times*, *Woman's Own*, *Popular Motoring* and the *TV Times*. He has also appeared on radio and television and for five years was closely involved in Thames Television's programme *Wish You Were Here*. He has been wine writer to the RAC publications and a number of magazines.

He has an intimate and extensive knowledge of France and its food and wine as a result of innumerable visits there over the last forty years. In 1974 he won the *Prix des Provinces de France*, the annual French award for travel writing.

Also available in the Eperon French Regional Guide Series:

NORMANDY

LOT (QUERCY)

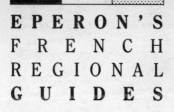

EPERON'S FRENCH REGIONAL GUIDES

BRITTANY

ARTHUR EPERON

PAN BOOKS
LONDON, SYDNEY AND AUCKLAND

First published 1990 by Pan Books Ltd
Cavaye Place, London SW10 9PG
9 8 7 6 5 4 3 2 1
© Arthur Eperon 1990
Illustrations © Mary Fraser 1990
Maps © Ken Smith 1990
ISBN 0 330 31219 7
Designed by Peter Ward
Photoset by Parker Typesetting Service, Leicester
Printed and bound in Great Britain by
Richard Clay Ltd, Bungay, Suffolk

This book is sold subject to the condition that it
shall not, by way of trade or otherwise, be lent, re-sold,
hired out, or otherwise circulated without the publisher's prior
consent in any form of binding or cover other than that in which
it is published and without a similar condition including this
condition being imposed on the subsequent purchaser

CONTENTS

KEY TO PRICES
vi

INTRODUCTION

How to Get There   1
Food and Drink   8
History   16

MAJOR TOWNS

St Malo   30
Brest   39
Rennes   44
Dinard   52
Nantes   55

PLACES
63

MAPS

Departments of France   vi
Finistère   269
Ille-et-Villaine   270
Loire-Atlantique   271
Morbihan   272
Côtes-du-Nord   274

INDEX
275

KEY TO PRICES

MEALS A = Under 75F   ROOMS A = Under 100F
             B = 75–90F   B = 100–150F
             C = 90–125F   C = 150–200F
             D = 125–150F   D = 200–250F
             E = 150–175F   E = 250–350F
             F = 175–225F   F = 350–450F
             G = over 225F   G = over 450F

Room prices per night for double room without breakfast. Meals include tax and service.

1   *Departments of France*

INTRODUCTION

HOW TO GET THERE

FERRIES
Portsmouth–St Malo (9 hours Brittany Ferries)
Plymouth–Roscoff (6 hours Brittany Ferries)
Cork (Ireland)–Roscoff (16 hours Brittany Ferries) (14 hours in summer).
Portsmouth–Caen in Normandy, 166km from St Malo (6 hours Brittany Ferries)
Poole–Cherbourg in Normandy, 185km from St Malo (4½ hours day, 6 hours night; end May to mid September – Brittany Ferries)
Portsmouth–Cherbourg (4¾ hours Sealink, P & O)
Weymouth–Cherbourg (4 hours Sealink)

AIR
Brest–Gatwick (Britair), Cork (Britair)
Nantes–Heathrow (Air France), Gatwick (Air Vendée), Cork (Britair)
Quimper–Gatwick (Britair)
Rennes–Gatwick (Britair)

Deep affection – that is the feeling people have for Brittany when they know it well. It may not inspire the same passionate devotion that many have for the breathlessly beautiful Dordogne, the awed respect for the mountains of the Savoie Dauphinée or the coquettish love which even the most loyal Parisians have for the dreamy, garden lands of the Loire. But the variety of Brittany's scenery and moods, the independence of its people and the very simplicity of its life lures a great variety of people to return again and again.

The sailors of old, on first seeing the coast of Finistère, with its fearsome rocky tips thrashed by Atlantic rollers, must indeed have wished to keep a respectful distance. The little creeks between offered scant hope of shelter. The long sand beaches loved by modern holidaymakers meant only a gentler shipwreck. Even from the coast those rocks look awesome, especially from the higher cliffs looking down. In winter the seas can look very frightening. It is from this coast that the tunny boats and trawlers still sail to Africa, Ireland, Iceland and the west coast of England. It has, too, one of the greatest natural harbours in Europe in the Rade de Brest which makes the port so important for the navy and for commerce. The little coves and beaches are the hideouts of connoisseurs of Brittany rather than the mass of tourists, though some little resorts like Morgat have been gradually discovered, and Tréboul has become the recognised haven for sailors and people learning to sail.

The north coast was where the Americans and British discovered holidays in Brittany last century, beginning with the big beach at Dinard and spreading to the big and small coastal villages like Perros-Guirec, still quite a fashionable resort with superb beaches for children, and Paimpol, known to yachtsmen

Rugged coastline of Brittany

and oyster-lovers. St Malo, the old port, is in a world of its own – still looking like the pirates' nest that it used to be, still important as a fishing and commercial port and ferry port for England. There are some truly delightful little places along this coast – small fishing villages, coves with tiny beaches, even a corniche road along the Bay of Lannion.

Today the south coast is a holiday playground for both French and British, with fine beaches like those at Bénodet, Quiberon and Beg-Meil; the medieval walled town of Concarneau with its modern fishing port; and small fishing ports like Loctudy, with good little family-run hotels, gîtes and plenty of good campsites. It has been disconcerting, perhaps, to old-time Brittany addicts to find places like Bénodet, Beg-Meil and Quiberon, once villages with empty beaches, so changed, but still, they can hardly be called 'Costa' resorts.

To most people, Brittany conjures images of the sea and the coast. The coastline is so jagged and indented that its twelve hundred kilometres would be less than half that length without its multitude of bays and coves. And the most vivid memories of Brittany are of reefs and islands; of scarred cliffs of red, grey or mauve and huge piles of rocks; of high headlands with wide seascapes which show why the west is called 'Finisterre' – the end of the world; of secretive inlets and long beaches of fine sand. There is Armor, 'the land next to the sea', as the Romans called it. But there is Argoat, too, the interior of Brittany which was called 'the land of the woods', for it was forested until the trees were felled for heating, building and especially for building ships.

The forests have vanished, though there are still wooded hillsides amid fields bounded by wooded banks, heaths covered in gorse and brush which look mysterious and melancholy in mists or rain, rocky slopes and little rivers which somehow open up into big estuaries. Inland Brittany is not only a land of granite but of sandstone.

It is here, in the hamlets, the villages and the little farms, that the old Celtic mystery and myths still thrive. It is here that legends of the old Breton saints survive – stories of dragon-slaying, of fighting sorcery and casting out devils and of instant miracles. Brittany is said to have seven thousand, seven hundred, seven score and seven saints – 7,847. Most of them seem to have been Cornish or Welsh monks who came over as the head of their people in the great emigration from Britain when the Celts were driven out by the Anglo-Saxons, from 460 AD for about two centuries.

To say that Brittany is the Wales of France is a cliché and, like so many clichés, largely true. The Bretons came from Wales and England from the fifth century, absorbing the old tribes, and brought their Celtic language with them. They called their new land *Cornouaille* after Cornwall, or 'Little Britain' and gradually dropped the 'little'. Some words have remained similar. *Aber* means estuary in both languages. An isle is *ynys* in Welsh, *enez* in Breton. A true Breton would, until very recently, have been as angry if you called him a Frenchman as a Welshman would be if you called him English. The anger has turned to mere annoyance with the growth of industry which has broadened horizons.

The Bretons were separate from France until the daughter of the Duchess Anne, Claude, married the future François I of France in 1515 and ceded her rights to Brittany to her husband. The French definitely treated Bretons as second-rate citizens for centuries – a subject people to be taxed, without rights, and a land to be milked without giving anything in return. This was especially true when Colbert was Louis XIV's minister and trying to pay for his unsuccessful wars against England and extravagances at home. Until quite recently you could hear jokes in France about the dumb Bretons as you could in England about the Irish – both equally untrue.

Perhaps the patriotic pride of the Bretons is best expressed by their attitude to the brilliant soldier Bertrand du Guesclin. Born in Brittany, he was at first a Breton hero but became Marshal of France and actually led a French invasion of Brittany. Many true Bretons still regard him as a traitor. The memorial stone to him at Dinard just describes him as 'sometime Constable of France whose body lies at St Denis in France'.

The revival of Breton folklore in a struggle to keep Breton culture alive began in the 1930s when the *Ar Falz* movement was started. Traditional dance groups were formed and Breton music became a folk fashion all over France. Old, local fêtes were revived or invented. The traditional 'pardons' were boosted into great local religious fêtes and tourist attractions. Pardons were basically pilgrimages or processions where pilgrims asked forgiveness for their sins. Most were started in the sixteenth century. The processions still take place and Mass is said. Many people still dress in their traditional Breton costumes. But after the service the fun begins – feasting, traditional and modern dancing. *Crêperie* stalls do big business – so, these days, do hamburger and pizza stalls in many places. Cider is consumed in vast quantities. It can be great fun and a good chance to hear the old music from bagpipes and *bombardes* (oboes), to see the old dances and, not least, the costumes and *coiffes* – those delightful head-dresses. You may well see the traditional Breton sport of wrestling. Before they start trying to throw each other, the wrestlers kiss each other loudly three times!

The people of Brittany were always religious even before the Celts brought in Christianity from Wales and Cornwall. They took Druidism very seriously. Statues of their saints are carried in pardon processions.

Celtic religious leaders became the patron saints of early bishoprics. Healing saints were always popular and are still invoked against various ailments. St Eugénie, for instance, cures headaches – even from hangovers. But the most popular is St Yves – the righter of wrongs and comforter of the poor. He was Yves Helon, born in 1253 in Minihy-Tréguier, son of a gentleman, who became a lawyer then a priest. At the bishop's palace in Tréguier he acted as a magistrate in one court and as a lawyer in the other. He always chose poor clients and became 'the poor man's lawyer' and was known as a magistrate for his justice and conciliation. He was canonised in 1347 and his cult as patron saint of lawyers has spread all over the world. Men of law from all parts of the globe join the pilgrims who attend the *Pardon des Pauvres* (the Blessing of the Poor) at Tréguier on 19 May.

The most famous pardon is that of St Anne-d'Auray on 26 July at Auray. The cult of St Anne was brought back by Crusaders, and possibly because of the very popular Duchess Anne of Brittany she became patroness of Brittany. She was reputed to be the mother of the Virgin Mary. An old local legend claims that she was a Breton woman who was whisked away to Nazareth to save her from a brutal husband.

My favourite is the saint of Dol, St Samson, a Welshman who seems to have practised magic more suited to the wizard Merlin or a Druid than a monk. One of his party tricks was to make a fiery dragon eat its own tail then tell it to drop dead, which it did. This would be an extremely useful gift when dealing with all dragons – animal, human or political.

The megaliths (great stones) which almost litter parts of Brittany were set up by the unknown tribes who lived here before the Gauls, sometime between 5,000 and 2,000 BC, and were almost certainly connected with religion, although the single menhirs, standing upright, are nearly always near a spring or tomb. Lines or other geometric formations of menhirs are said to be remains of religious symbols of worship of the sun or moon. Many are set astronomically, either by the points of the compass or in line with sunrise or sunset. A recent theory is that they helped the tribes to know when to plant crops by giving the moon's position in relation to stars.

As some weighed up to 350 tons, the mystery remains of how these tribes managed to set them upright. There are many in the Carnac area. The dolmens, in the form of rough stone chambers, are assumed to have been graves, as they are everywhere.

Brittany has been fairly free of fighting in modern wars – certainly compared with Normandy and the North of France. The bombing of World War II was almost completely confined to big ports – Brest, Lorient and Nantes – and the Americans coming down from the Cotentin peninsula of Normandy took Brittany very quickly, apart from St Malo and Brest. So a great number of old buildings have survived, especially churches, houses and even whole villages, from delightful Dinan to cosy little fishing ports.

A great deal of old domestic furniture survived, too. Twenty or thirty years ago you could often see superb old furniture even in the humblest cottages. People were rightly proud of it, for most pieces were heirlooms, and they were delighted if you told them how beautiful it was. Alas, many have been tempted to sell to antique dealers because their owners needed money so badly.

The farmers of Brittany suffered considerably from low prices in the early days of the EEC, and were constantly at war with Paris over the low return for their land and labour. Prices have become more stable, industries have been encouraged, especially around Rennes, where Citroën has two factories. But if Brittany is more prosperous, the main reason is tourism.

The British were the first modern tourists in Brittany and are still the majority, although Parisian families have discovered its beaches and its sailing and fishing ports. This is a double blessing, for they have also discovered that Bretons are people, like themselves.

In fact, the seaside holiday business really started in Brittany at the fishing village of Dinard, which was discovered by Americans in the 1850s. The British followed fast and by 1906 Dinard, with a casino and *grand* hotels, was being described in Paris as one of the most elegant and fashionable resorts in Europe. Later, British families moved in. It was an easy place to reach from England by the old Southern Railway ferry to St Malo, and there were good enough sand beaches to keep children out of the wind or too much sun. Sunbathing was *not* fashionable.

After World War I a lot of Britons moved to Brittany, especially to Dinard and Dinan. Artists, writers, retired people, non-working 'gentlemen' with smallish incomes could live there more cheaply and better than in the Home Counties. Many went back to Britain very grudgingly in 1940.

With the holiday boom in the 1950s the British returned, spreading further along the south coast. Then came the boom in camping, on-site caravan holidays and cheap sailing dinghies and Brittany's holiday industry really took off.

Boating holidays on the Vilaine and other rivers and the canal de Nantes, right into the heart of the countryside, are delightful. They were started some fifteen years ago by a British company.

La Baule thrived through all this, from the 1880s on, and remains fashionable even in the age of long haul jet travel.

Technically La Baule has been outside Brittany since 1965 when the French bureaucrats thought fit to invent Pays Loire, as a sort of link with the Vendée. After the Revolution this area had already been turned into a new département called Loire-

Atlantique (*see* History, page 16). But it would be quite ridiculous to write a book on Brittany without including this area of La Baule, Grande Brière and Nantes itself, which was, for a long time, capital of Brittany. All France regards this land as being Brittany except the bureaucrats and the people of the Loire. Even the very 'establishment' Green Michelin guide includes it in Brittany.

FOOD AND DRINK

A Parisian-trained restaurant-owner was being interviewed in front of me about Breton cuisine by an English girl who had read Gault-Millau and that was about her limit.

'What great contribution has Brittany made to French gastronomy?' she asked.

He looked very uncomfortable. 'Well ... fresh fish and pancakes, I suppose.' He said *crêpes*, of course, for *crêpes* are different.

Basically, he was right. There are some very good chefs indeed in Brittany – chefs who can invent fine versions of sauces, cook lighter versions of classical dishes, and who can even,

though grudgingly, turn beautiful fish into a sort of fish blancmange called *mousse* to please their visitors carrying the Gault-Millau guide. But even the best of Breton chefs are at their *very* best when they keep their cooking simple. Raw ingredients are so superb that it would be extremely arrogant for anyone but a genius to elaborate the dishes too much.

Brittany has just about the best fish I have tasted, in such variety and so consistently good. I admit that I like cold-water fish more than the fish of the Mediterranean beloved in Provence and by TV cooks.

What are luxuries in Paris and London are everyday ingredients in Brittany. Superb oysters and mussels, succulent fleshy crabs, *langoustines*, turbot, sole, bass, *lotte* (monkfish), fresh scallops, *palourdes* (very fresh clams) – they all abound and are very cheap compared with prices in Paris or London. Lobsters, though not cheap, are much cheaper than any Briton or Parisian has to pay. Strawberries from Daoulas and Plougastel, fresh young vegetables (especially carrots, potatoes, artichokes and cauliflowers), *pré-salé* lamb from salt marshes are all superb. Salmon and carp still live in unpolluted rivers. Butter and cream are excellent, and if the Bretons do not use as much of them in their cooking as the Normans still do, it is because the people of Normandy have been much richer through the centuries. But cider and apples are used almost as extensively as in Normandy and there are almost as many pork sausages and pâtés. Brittany is the biggest producer of pork in France.

Shellfish are quite superb. *Homards* (the big lobsters) are meatier and slightly more flavoursome than the smaller *langouste*; so are *langoustines*, those pink shellfish – like very small lobsters or very large prawns with long, thin claws, which are really not like either.

If you see *araignée* on a menu that means spider crab, which has a lovely flavour. Stuffed clams (*palourdes*) are delicious – try them especially at the delightful Ti al-Lannec Hotel at Trébeurden (*see* page 255 – you will have to book). A simple stuffing is of chopped shallots, garlic and herbs mixed with butter, then grilled.

The great controversial dish is Lobster *à l'Armoricaine*. Some call it 'à l'Americaine', which is wrong. But, then, how can it be a true Breton dish with tomatoes and oil in the sauce? The excuse for the *Americaine* tag is especially complicated. It was said to have been created from an old recipe by a young Breton who opened a restaurant in America, and it then returned to France via Paris. But the story I have always believed is that it was named *Armoricaine* in honour of Armorica (Brittany) but was invented by the chef in the Breton pavilion at the Great Paris Exposition of 1867, and changed to *Americaine* by a chef who didn't read the name properly.

Anyway, the sauce is basically made with cream, wine, onions, garlic, tomatoes and herbs, though some chefs put in something like vinegar or lemon juice to make it more piquant. The lobster is usually sautéed in oil and flambéed in brandy. The sauce is used on other fish these days and can be delicious or ghastly. The most delicious I have had was cooked by Emile Hardy at Hotel Hardy at Coutainville – in Normandy. The worst example of *Armoricaine* sauce came from a tin in a French supermarket from a shelf marked *Sauces Gourmets*.

A true Breton dish is the fish stew *Cotriade*, which is often described as a northern bouillabaisse, which it isn't. It does not have the same fish in it, it does not have saffron or any truly spicy herbs. It varies according to the chef and the catch, but mostly it is of simple, cheaper white fish such as whiting, mackerel, often eel, with mussels, scallops, potatoes, onions, perhaps celery and carrot, often white wine, sorrel and cream. The vegetables are usually served on a separate plate.

Oysters are farmed at Cancale and Morlaix in the north and in the river estuaries of the Bélon and Peneurf. Disease hit the Brittany oyster beds in the early 1970s and stock was brought in from Portugal and Japan, but the true Breton belon oyster is back to its best. To sit on the quayside outside a restaurant in Cancale eating a dozen oysters straight from the beds you can see in front of you with a bottle of Muscadet is one of the joys of life. The best scallops come from Brest, St Brieuc and Quiberon Bay. Mussels are farmed between the Rance estuary and Cap Fréhel.

Apart from St Malo, the big fishing ports are on the south coast - Concarneau (also good for mussels), Lorient, Douarnenez, Camaret, Quiberon, St Guénolé. St Malo is the port for cod. Tunny and sardines are landed in season, with sole, plaice, turbot and brill. Quimper has an excellent market for all food from sea and country. In Brittany haddock, called *aiglefin* elsewhere, is called *anon*. *Burbot*, a freshwater fish with a long tail and dorsal fins, is a Breton delicacy. Sometimes called *lotte de rivière* (river monkfish), it is cooked with mussels in Muscadet, with sliced leeks, onions, sliced potatoes, chives and cream. Rivers also offer perch, shad, eel and pike (*brochet*), all of which Bretons love and cannot understand why so few tourists will eat them. They are often served with *beurre blanc*. This sauce is used in France for fish likely to be dry. Nantes lays a strong claim to having invented it, and certainly makes it the local speciality. But so do chefs in Anjou and Touraine.

The simple way to make it is to chop three shallots in a small saucepan and boil them in six tablespoons of dry wine until reduced to two tablespoons of liquid. Cut 100 grams of unsalted butter into knobs, whisk it into the liquid knob by knob over a very low heat until a smooth cream forms. Season it. Some people use half wine, half wine vinegar, while others prefer to add a few drops of lemon juice. Salmon from the Odet and Aunis rivers, alas, are becoming rare and farmed or imported salmon is more frequent.

Fish and the sea are so dominant that you could forget that Brittany produces fine meat and dairy products. Butter from beef-dairy cattle is almost up to Normandy standards. *Pré-salé* lamb from sea-washed meadows, mostly around Mont-St-Michel bay, is delicious and pricey. Favourite lamb dishes are *gigot* or *épaule de pré-salé à la bretonne* (leg or shoulder of lamb with white haricot beans – *à la bretonne* nearly always means with white beans) and *côtes d'agneau à l'estragon* (lamb chops with tarragon).

Andouillette bretonne (pork chitterling sausage) tends to be fatter than elsewhere. Pork and smoked sausages are used in Breton hot-pot (*potée bretonne*). So are salted belly of pork, shin of beef, lots of vegetables, including heads of green cabbage, and chicken – making a fine old peasant dish kept on the fire to feed the family.

Brittany produces a third of France's home-produced chickens. Nantes area produces excellent duck and lately a lot of turkeys, which have become more popular all over France. But the special Nantes-bred duck has been 'exported' and *caneton nantais* is just as likely to come from around Challons in the Vendée. *Magret de canard aux cerises* (duck breasts in cherry sauce), beloved by nouvelle cuisine chefs, is by no means new and is traditional in Brittany (*caneton nantais aux cerises*).

Nantes is regarded very much as a gastronomic area, but it isn't technically in Brittany, although it was for a long time its capital. It is now capital of the département of Loire-Atlantique. But the Bretons still claim its culinary descriptions: *à la nantaise* (garnished with turnips, peas and potatoes), *sauce nantaise* for pork (vinegar, shallot and gherkin sauce), *potage nantais* (cream of potato soup), *coquilles St Jacques nantaises* (scallops with white wine sauce, mushrooms and mussels), *hareng à la nantaise* (herring fried with soft-roe butter), *lard nantaise* (pork chops baked on liver and other offal of pork), *rouget à la nantaise* (red mullet grilled with a sauce of the livers, shallots and white wine).

For centuries Brittany has been known for onions (from

around Roscoff) and lovely, early, kidney-shaped potatoes. The 'Roscoff Johnnies', the onion growers who came across to Britain with strings of onions on poles in autumn to sell them from door to door, have been replaced by Brittany Ferry boats from Roscoff to Plymouth bringing them in plastic nets. The onion growers and the EEC Brussels bureaucrats have been at war over prices and regulations for some years. I well remember a hazardous drive to catch a boat at St Malo, sliding, squelching and skidding over slimy onions which had been dumped by farmers on to the roads as a protest against low prices the EEC had forced upon their superb onions. The other hazard was thrifty townsfolk of St Malo rushing among the sliding cars with boxes, grabbing all the free onions they could gather.

Inland, behind Concarneau and Lorient, French beans and lovely peas are grown. Market gardens use the rich alluvial soil near St Malo and of the Loire north of Nantes to produce gorgeous young carrots and cauliflowers.

Roscoff-Morlaix area produces cauliflowers and superb large globe artichokes, which are simply boiled and eaten hot, leaf by leaf, dipped in melted butter or, cold in vinaigrette sauce.

Traditional vegetable dishes include *pommes petit salé* (potatoes boiled with onions, a piece of salt pork and butter). *Concombres farcis* are cucumbers split open, de-seeded and stuffed with cooked, chopped peas, carrots and hard-boiled egg. *Bardatte* is cabbage stuffed with boned rabbit or chicken, shallots, carrots, onions, garlic, parsley, bread and egg, wrapped in bacon slices and cooked in Muscadet wine. It is a bit of a bother to make but delicious. Find an old-style inn which serves it.

Crêpes (pancakes) are a Breton way of life. *Crêperies* are everywhere, some just beachside stalls, some big restaurants. Usually *crêpes* are made with sugar and served with fruit, jam or cream fillings. Bretons like to eat them with cider or lait baratté (buttermilk) around the late afternoon. Made with salt, they are filled with cheese, bacon, fried egg or a mixture of these, and become a snack lunch or supper. The original savoury version is made with buckwheat (*sarrasin*) flour and called a *galette*. You can buy *crêpes* in packets or by the dozen in *boulangeries* or *pâtisseries* and they can be reheated in butter or oil, but they are easy to make fresh, even if not as superbly as in some *crêperies*.

All *crêpes* are made on a special griddle or large flat *galetière* on which the batter is spread with a raclette, a device which scrapes the batter thinly over the surface.

Far, Breton pudding, is said to be an ancient form of food. In that case, Yorkshire pudding may also have been, for *far* is a sweet batter pudding with raisins in it, served hot or cold.

Gâteau breton is a flattish fruit cake.

CHEESES

Brittany does not produce cheeses with the same dedicated enthusiasm as neighbouring Normandy. Two very similar fresh cream cheeses are usually eaten as a dessert with fruit, jam or sprinkled with sugar. They are *crémets nantais* and *maingaux* (or *mingots*) *Rennais*, which is a combination of fresh and soured cream beaten together and sometimes used sugared in a sweet *crêpe*.

Nantais is a cow's milk cheese, soft and mild, with yellowish rind, made in factories these days. It is often called *Fromage du Curé* because it was invented in 1794 during the Vendée war by a priest trying to help combat famine.

Montauban de Bretagne, an uncooked cheese, was originally called Montalbanais after the village where it was produced. As with *Armoricaine* sauce, someone got careless with the name. It is difficult to find. So are *Jonchée de Bretagne*, a sheep's cheese made aromatic with bay leaves before being pressed into a covering of rushes, and *St Agathon*, a local Guingamp cow's milk cheese, small, round and available from October to July.

Three other cheeses are produced in abbeys. Abbaye de la Meilleraye produces a fine cheese (*Trappiste de la Meilleraye*) in May to February (large square slab with ochre rind; tangy and supple). A fresh cheese is produced at the Abbaye de Ty-Madeuc, not far from Loudéac on the Côtes-du-Nord. And the best and most easily attainable is produced by *les trappistes*, the nuns of the Abbaye de Campénéac, who took it over from the Abbaye de St Anne-d'Auray. It is a yellow, supple cheese rather like St Paulin, in large discs with yellowish rind. It is called *Campénéac* or sometimes *Trappiste*.

DRINK

Cider varies greatly in Brittany, from a light-alcohol apple juice to a version as strong as the best cider of Normandy or strong mature ciders of England. It was traditionally served in a *bol* or *bolette* (like a teacup without a handle) and that still happens in many farmhouses or *crêperies* aimed at tourists, perhaps served by a girl in traditional costume.

Cider is sparkling or still, sweet, dry or so dry that it seems to disappear on your palate without reaching the throat. *Cidre bouché* is very sparkling, corked like Champagne because it undergoes secondary fermentation in the bottle. It is fashionable and not in the same class as the strong still cider.

Bretons still regard Muscadet as their wine as it is produced in Coteaux de la Loire as well as Sèvre et Maine, all around Nantes and therefore once in Brittany. It is often called 'the wine of Abelard', who was a Breton. Rabelais wrote of it in 1530 but that was a very different wine. In 1709 the vineyards were destroyed by appalling weather and the *vignerons* got fresh vines from Burgundy called Melon de Bourgogne or Muscat, a grape no longer used in Burgundy itself. The wine was hardly drunk outside the Nantes area and Brittany and Normandy until 1929 when Parisian *sommeliers* discovered it and plugged it. It was actually used to 'stretch' Chablis when there was a shortage of the white Burgundy in the 1930s.

In 1956 a terrible frost almost wiped out the Chablis vineyards and Muscadet was used as a substitute, becoming more fashionable, dearer and some not so good as producers strove to meet the demand.

Muscadet should be light, fresh, bone-dry and drunk young. Now, in attempting to get rid of honest acidity to please people used to less aggressive tastes, some makers are producing bland, dull wine ('collapsed'). Sixty-five million bottles are produced every year. Only Beaujolais beats that.

It is worth paying a bit more for a good Muscadet. The best comes from around Vallet, Clisson and Le Pallet in Sèvre-et-Maine. Muscadet des Coteaux de la Loire is often heavier and uninteresting. Good domaines are Château Galissonière and its neighbours Château Jannière and Maisdonnière, Domaine des Quatre-Routes, and the Drouet wines. The Sauvion family have owned the historic Château de Cléray since Grandpa bought it in 1935. Now son Ernest, helped by his three sons, produces excellent wine – vital, lively, flowery and reliable. They are also *négociants* (wine merchants) and each year pick ten *Découvertes* (Discoveries) of outstanding Muscadet. A jury picks the top wine, called Cardinal Richard after a previous owner of the château, which has perfect wine-keeping caves. The château once belonged to the Malestroit family. Comte de Malestroit lives the other side of Vallet in the elegant Palladian-style Château Noë de Bel Air, built in 1838 to replace one burned down in the Revolution. The family have made good wine here since 1741.

Muscadet-sur-lie means that it has been bottled straight off its lees (pips, skins, etc.) after fermentation and not racked. This gives it more flavour, especially of fruit. In the Muscadet area (vaguely south, west and east of Nantes just past Vallet), Gros Plant is produced from a grape of the same name. In good years when the grapes ripen well, it is light, dry and fruity and some Frenchmen prefer it to Muscadet with shellfish. In many years it is tart and acidic.

HISTORY

The story of the Bretons is of a fight for independence and individuality which has only diminished quite recently, in the face of encroaching industry and the increasing power of the EEC.

The Celts from Wales and Cornwall came to the land they called 'Little Britain' in the 5th and 6th centuries to keep their independence from the Anglo-Saxons who had taken their country. They bequeathed to their descendants their independent spirit.

Before that, the unknown tribes who left behind the mysterious stone megaliths which still puzzle scholars were overrun by another Celtic people, the Gauls, who were divided into tribes. It was one of these, the Veneti, from what is now Vannes, who were defeated by Brutus in a naval battle on what is now the

Marais Salants but was then a sea. They were then viciously wiped out by Julius Caesar.

The Romans landed in the year 1 BC, called the country Armor and stayed for four centuries. When they were forced to return to defend Rome itself from tribal attacks, Brittany was overrun by the barbarous Franks who destroyed what culture the Romans had built up.

The Celts who came from Britain brought their Christianity with them. The Bretons have kept their intense evangelical religious faith to this day, even if most of their saints'-day pardons – religious processions and festivals – have become a lot more secular and touristy. Legend tells us that the monkish leaders of the Celts had supernatural powers and many became Breton saints. They came across not only in boats, but, according to legend, on stones or floating on leaves!

Charlemagne, King of the Franks and emperor of much of western Europe, sent his general Roland on a punitive expedition in 778 because the local Breton counts would not pay taxes, and by the early 9th century he had established his hold on the peninsula. When Charlemagne died, his empire was divided among his sons and Louis the Pious, who inherited Brittany, decided to strengthen his hold on the area by supporting one of the local counts, Nominoë, Count of Vannes. Nominoë defeated all his rivals, conquered the whole province and became Duke of Brittany, technically owing allegiance to the King of the Franks. When King Louis died, Nominoë, who had always dreamed of independence, defeated Charles the Bald, the new King of the Franks, near Redon in 846 and threw off the Frankish allegiance.

But the people of West and East Brittany could not readily agree and this left the door open for invasion and pillaging by the Normans, the Norsemen who had settled in Normandy. In 939 Alain Barbe-Torte, who had been a refugee in England, returned, became Duke and drove out the Normans. He chose Nantes as his capital, which the people of Rennes did not like.

Though the dukes, under the feudal system, paid homage to the kings of France, they did exactly as they liked, as did the counts of Toulouse, the very powerful dukes of Burgundy and the even-more powerful dukes of Aquitaine who, after Henry

Plantagenet had married Eleanor of Aquitaine, were also kings of England. It was Henry, as Henry II of England, who gained influence over Brittany in the 12th century. Breton nobles were stirred into rebellion by France, so the Duke of Brittany, Conan IV, asked for aid from England. Henry II gave it to him on condition that Conan's daughter, Constance, should marry Henry II's son Geoffrey.

When the childless Duke Jean II died in 1341, the Breton War of Succession broke out. The French claimed the Duchy for Jean III's niece, Jeanne de Penthièvre, wife of Charles de Blois and the English-backed Jean III's brother, Jean de Montfort. The war ruined Brittany. Finally Charles de Blois, though backed by the great Breton commander du Guesclin, was beaten and killed at the Battle of Auray in 1364 and Jean de Montfort became Duke Jean IV. Bertrand du Guesclin was taken prisoner and ransomed for 100,000 crowns. This was the beginning of du Guesclin's switch of allegiance to France. He actually invaded Brittany at the head of French troops for Charles V in 1373 and forced Jean IV to flee temporarily to England. But when Charles V threatened to annexe Brittany in 1379, Jean returned in triumph. Once more Charles sent du Guesclin to invade Brittany but as he crossed the border most of his army deserted. They were Bretons who did not mind fighting the English or Spanish but drew the line at fighting their fellow countrymen. Charles sent du Guesclin elsewhere to fight the English and he was killed in the Siege of Châteauneuf-de-Randon, near Le Puy.

Under the Montforts, Brittany was restored and had the greatest period of its history. The arts flourished, too.

Louis XI of France was determined to bring Burgundy and Brittany under French rule. A patient but cunning and ruthless man, he tried to get important Bretons on his side whilst attacking Brittany, to the detriment of the peasants. When Louis died in 1483, his son Charles VIII was only thirteen and his elder sister Anne de Beaujeu, governed France as Regent. Power groups were formed, one by Louis, Duc d'Orléans, who had been forced against his will at the age of fourteen to marry Louis XI's religious, kind, almost saintly but physically unattractive younger daughter, Jeanne de France. Louis d'Orléans was so unpopular with Anne the Regent that he had to flee to Brittany, where he and a group of disgruntled expatriate Frenchmen made trouble for Duc François II.

A year earlier François had betrothed his five-year-old daughter Anne to the Hapsburg Emperor Maximilian, a widower whose own daughter Margaret was betrothed to Charles VIII of France. These weddings of young children were sanctioned by church and state. The children were just pawns in a power game of politics.

This alliance between Brittany and the powerful Hapsburg Austrian Empire was very dangerous to France, so Anne the Regent took action. In May 1487 a French army of 15,000 men invaded Brittany, but after some early defeats the Bretons drove the French out. So next year the French sent a more powerful army under Général Louis de la Trémoille. At St Aubin-du-Cormier, between Fougères and Rennes, the Bretons were totally defeated. Louis d'Orléans was taken prisoner and many prisoners were killed.

Three weeks later Duc François II was forced to sign a humiliating treaty with Charles VIII of France at Château de Vergers, near Angers. An important clause was that François could not marry off his daughters without the consent of the French king. Less than two months later, François died of exhaustion. Anne, his eleven-year-old daughter, was Duchess of Brittany. Two advisers were appointed under the terms of François' will but the precocious and strong-willed Anne was soon making her own decisions. Her advisers did not want her to marry her betrothed, Maximilian of Austria. To keep Brittany independent and to keep the Breton nobles' hold on it, they tried to make her marry one of them, Alain d'Albret. He was nearly fifty, spotty-faced and ill-tempered. Anne would have none of it. In 1489 she left Nantes, the capital, for Rennes, breaking with her advisers, and was crowned Duchess in Rennes cathedral. She had the support of the English and the Spaniards. The following year she married Maximilian by proxy.

D'Albret was so angry that he handed over Nantes to the French. Charles VIII invaded Brittany on the excuse that Anne's proxy marriage had broken her father's treaty of Verger.

The French took all the important places except Rennes,

where Anne was besieged. In the face of pleas from her starving subjects, Anne was forced to make peace.

Charles was determined to marry her to ensure that Brittany became part of France. Within four days of signing the treaty she agreed to marry him – the man who had just wrecked her country. He was a keen jouster and horseman, dreaming of conquest. A chronicler of his day wrote that he was 'a puny man with very little sense'. Another wrote that he was small, ill-formed and ugly. She was bright, wilful but not a beauty. She was small, thin and had one leg shorter than the other. She was fourteen. He was twenty-one. They married at the Château at Langeais on the Loire. Her wedding dress was decorated with 160 sable furs.

Anne de Beaujeu had a hand in the wedding contract. It stipulated that, if she were widowed, she must marry the next king of France. The French were determined to hang on to Brittany.

The Emperor Maximilian was furious. He had lost a wife and a hold on Brittany, and his daughter, who had been betrothed to Charles, had lost her chance of being Queen of France.

Charles and Anne's four children all died in infancy. Then the couple were walking round the château at Amboise inspecting some new building work when he hit his head on a corner stone. Though dazed he seemed to be all right and watched a tennis match in the courtyard. Suddenly he collapsed and died.

The new king was none other than Louis d'Orléans – now Louis XII. And according to Anne's contract she had to marry him. But he had already been made to marry poor Jeanne de France, Louis XI's daughter. And the heir was François, Duc d'Angoulême, who was only four years old, hardly a marriageable age!

Louis saw a wonderful opportunity to get rid of his deformed, deeply religious wife Jeanne. Perjuring himself, he stood up in court and swore that the marriage had never been consummated because Jeanne was too deformed and that she could never have children. Jeanne was subjected to the most brutal and disgusting cross-examination but she kept her temper and dignity. Louis got his annulment from the notorious

Pope Alexander VI of the Borgia family in return for favours to the Pope's son Cesare Borgia. Cesare himself presented Louis with the decree in December 1498. Jeanne retired to found a religious order. In the New Year Anne and Louis were married at the château at Nantes. The wedding contract was in Anne's favour. If she died before the King, the Duchy would go to her heirs. Her second son or daughter would succeed her as Duchess of Brittany. The Brittany parliament was to continue to sit, with power to levy taxes. Bretons could only be tried in courts of their own country. Breton nobles did not have to do military service outside their country.

In fact Louis stuck to his bargain and did not take a *sou* in taxes from Brittany. She had a guard of one hundred Breton gentlemen.

In 1499 a daughter named Claude was born to the couple. Still determined to keep Brittany's independence from France, she had Claude betrothed to Charles of Luxembourg, grandson of Maximilian. Charles later became the Emperor Charles V.

Louis was angry. In 1505, when Claude was six, he made a will making sure that Claude married the heir to the French throne, François d'Angoulême, and not a foreign prince. Anne died in 1514. In the same year Claude was married to François. Louis XII was married for a third time to a very sprightly girl of eighteen – Mary, sister of Henry VIII of England. He was fifty-two. He died the next year. Brantôme, the amusing court chronicler, wrote: 'A most beautiful princess, young and too much for him, which was bad luck on him.' So François was King of France.

In 1524 Claude died, bequeathing Brittany to François. He immediately explained to the Breton noblemen the advantages of union with France – and what would happen to them if they refused! They met at Vannes in 1532 and sent François a request for union. He granted their request, promising to respect old rights and privileges.

France immediately started to Frenchify Brittany. French was made the language of all legal and official documents, although the people of Brittany still went on using the Breton language for everything else for the next hundred years.

In the Wars of Religion, Brittany was mostly Catholic, but

the excesses of the Governor of Brittany, the Duke of Mercoeur, who was a leader of the extremist Catholic League, led to a revolt. Typical of his methods was the hanging of all the garrison of Châteaugiron, irrespective of creed, after he had taken it.

Gangs of soldiers of the League, or posing as League members, roamed Brittany, pillaging, looting, raping, killing and burning houses. The worst brigand was Fontanelle (*see* Île de Tristan, page 97), who laid waste whole areas of Brittany just for the loot, killing peasants, looting their houses and farms and then burning them down. People hid in forests or anywhere else they could go to avoid these gangs and many starved. In 1590 Fontanelle's thugs attacked the fishing community of the Penmarch peninsula in South Finistère, burned down 2,000 houses, killing the people, and filled 300 boats with loot to take back to his fortress on Île de Tristan.

The French kings were taxing Brittany into destitution and giving nothing in return. Colbert, Louis XIV's minister, was trying to pay for the King's wars and court extravagances such as Versailles. Among other taxes, he put a huge stamp duty on all legal documents, then re-imposed the duty on tobacco and pewter vessels, which were essential to every household which could not afford silver. Brittany had already paid two million livres to Paris to take over these taxes. In 1675 the Bretons revolted. Called the Revolt of the Bonnets Rouges, it started at Rennes, where the Breton Parliament sat, and spread quickly. But the French army put it down ruthlessly, hanging many Bretons, and the Breton Parliament was forbidden to sit again until 1690.

Then in 1762, the King's appointed Governor, the Duc d'Aiguillon, clashed with the Breton Parliament over the Jesuits. The Jesuits had great power in Brittany through their big colleges and the Breton Parliament voted to throw them out. Aiguillon ordered them to reverse their decision. They refused. Louis XV sent for the leaders at Versailles, ordered them to obey the Governor and sent three leaders into exile. The members of Breton Parliament resigned. The King had La Chalotais, their leader, arrested and the rest were banished from Brittany. Then the Paris Parliament backed the Breton Parliament. Aiguillon resigned and the Royal power slumped in Brittany.

The Bretons welcomed the French Revolution – at first. But they soon changed their minds. The reign of terror was too much for them, especially the drowning of thousands of people in Nantes by the sinister Jean-Baptiste Carrier (*see* Nantes). The persecution of priests upset the fervently religious Bretons. Brittany was plundered of food by requisition. Taxes were increased. Conscription was brought in. But the greatest blow was that Brittany and the Breton language were literally wiped off the map by the new Revolutionary bureaucrats in Paris. They divided France into five new départements. The word Brittany disappeared from all maps and legal documents. Worse still, the Breton language was banned. All citizens must be equal and alike – and speak the same language.

At first only the peasants revolted. They fought like a Resistance movement, hiding in forests and hills. Because they signalled to each other by making the noise of screech-owls –

chat-huant – they were called Chouans. But they were joined by royalists, aristocrats on the run, and by fellow counter-revolutionaries in Vendée (*see* Fougères, Nantes and Auray). Unfortunately, too, they were joined by exiled aristocrats who had fled to England, and an expeditionary force from England landed near Carnac on 27 June 1793. There were two commanders, both aristocrats, who could not agree on a plan of campaign. They were also at odds with the Chouans. The royalists wanted their privileges back. The Chouans wanted Breton independence. They were defeated by the brilliant young Général Hoche and despite his protests, the Revolutionary Tribunal had all the prisoners shot. Six years later the Chouans were defeated in a fresh campaign. And when Napoleon became First Consul and started to win battles, nationalistic fervour overcame Breton patriotism.

Paris continued to treat Brittany as a colony to be milked. It was still poorer and more backward than the rest of France well into this century. The losses of Bretons in the 1914–18 War were out of proportion to the population compared with other parts of France and the loss was felt deeply on farms and at sea.

The Breton language was being ruthlessly stamped out. From the late 19th century, children were punished by the state schoolteachers for speaking Breton. One punishment was to make them stand in class all day with a clog tied round their necks. Poor parents were so afraid that their children would be at a disadvantage if they spoke Breton that they would try to prevent them learning the language to save them from handicap and humiliation.

In World War II the Bretons applied themselves with courage and vigour to resisting the Germans, and the number of Bretons shot or deported was very sad indeed. The first German reprisals of shooting hostages to discourage the Resistance took place in Brittany at Châteaubriant and Nantes. Excavations at the citadel of Port-Louis near Lorient in 1945 revealed three ditches containing the bodies of sixty-nine Resistance men who had been tortured and mutilated by the Germans before death. A boy baker's apprentice, who made bread for the Maquis, was thrown alive into his own oven. Eight men of Pluvigner had their legs and backbones broken by iron bars to the music of a dance played on an accordion. Not only the Germans carried out these atrocities, but also Russians from Georgia who had changed sides and were sent to Brittany.

Robert Aron in his book *Histoire de la Libération de la France* says that on D-Day there were more than 19,000 combatant Resistance fighters in Brittany, of whom half were under arms. By the end of July the total was 31,500, of whom 13,750 were armed.

Morbihan's Maquis was very highly organised, with 7,000 men mobilised on D-day and another 8000 Reservists immediately called up. Some Free French Army troops from Britain were parachuted in under the renowned one-armed Colonel Bourgoin. The Germans heard about him and arrested every one-armed man in the Morbihan – except him!

On 18 June 1944 a battle took place between the Morbihan Resistance and a whole German Division at St Marcel, 3km west of Malestroit. The Resistance men had to disperse against such odds but they had killed 560 German front-line troops for the loss of 250 French. A similar battle took place on 28 June in the Saffré forest, south of Châteaubriant.

In Côtes-du-Nord, the Resistance not only killed 2,500 German troops and captured 200 vehicles, ambushing 50 convoys, but actually took St Brieuc prison and released 32 Bretons condemned to death by the Gestapo.

Small groups, called Jeds, were parachuted in from Britain to link up Resistance operators. Each group had a French officer, a British officer and a radio operator.

The Resistance did so much damage to German equipment, communications and morale that General Patton's army had a much easier path through Brittany than the Allies had in Normandy. He reached Brest from Avranches in about six days but left many German troops to escape through little roads. The siege of Brest lasted six weeks. It was defended by one of Hitler's most Nazi generals, Ramcke, who ordered his men to fight to the death. The American attack was not helped by the fact that Patton and the Free French commander, Colonel Eon, obviously fell out, especially after the Americans accidentally bombed Telgruc, nearby, killing more than a hundred Bretons. Eon was particularly annoyed at the way the Americans were 'stuffing

German prisoners with food' while his Resistance units were half-starved.

The Resistance in Brittany had to watch for the Milice, the traitorous French militia whose major job was to try to infiltrate the Resistance and report to the Gestapo. Then there were the ardent Breton nationalists. One group were openly pro-Nazi. A nationalist leader, Célestin Lainé, formed a Breton army called Bezenn Perrot to drive out the French. The Germans were at first fooled into believing that Brittany could be lured to their side to get rid of the hated French, just as they tried to do later with French-Canadian prisoners and succeeded in doing with many Ukrainians. But their success in Brittany was negligible. The Bretons even refused their offer to teach the Breton language in schools.

The most remarkable story was the way *all* the able-bodied men of the isle of Sein – 130 of them – sailed to England to join the Free French (page 251).

After the war, Breton leaders tried to get devolution. The Assembly set up in 1972 is just a rubber-stamp body indirectly elected. The French Government has been a little more tolerant of Breton and other regional languages since the 1960s and Giscard d'Estaing declared 'a cultural charter for Brittany' at Ploërmel in 1977, but most Bretons realised that it was mere vote-catching. At least the Breton language is allowed as an alternative subject in the Baccalauréat school examinations and can be taught up to three hours a week in state lycées. In most lycées though, it isn't because there are no teachers. Schoolteachers can be moved from school to school under the French state education system and those who say they want to teach Breton are liable to find themselves posted to another part of France. One brave pupil wrote all his 'bac' papers in Breton except the French-language paper. The Education Ministry in Paris did its nut but had to accept because of Giscard d'Estaing's promise.

There is now a chain of private schools where only Breton is spoken, but as the older people who spoke it are dying off, the people speaking Breton tend to be young intellectuals. They have especially an interest in old Breton music and songs, with groups playing the *bombardes* and bagpipes, played at a *fest-noz* –

fête of music and dancing. These became fashionable in the 1970s, but have tended to be replaced by a sort of 'folk pop' music, mixing the old and modern. Glenmor, the Breton singer, sold millions of records around the world in the 1970s and early 1980s. The Pan-Celtic annual folk festival at Lorient draws huge crowds, with Irish and Welsh groups taking part.

The ups and downs of the French economy have been especially difficult for Brittany in recent years because it had a lot of catching up to do. Industrialisation has been very patchy. Rennes has done well from it. The population has risen from 95,000 to over 250,000 since World War II, with work in two Citroën factories leading the way to expansion. Many followed – electronic equipment, telephones and other modern industries. Young technicians and scientists have come from Paris and Grenoble, young peasants have come in from farms which have been mechanised enough to make them overmanned. Rennes seems too lively to be the old Breton town we remember. But there is a now an air of foreboding because of Europe's recession. The new factories are branches of other, bigger factories in Paris, Toulouse or elsewhere, and in a recession it is the branches which are closed. That has already happened to some.

Brittany's agriculture has boomed. For centuries it was mainly fringe farming by poor peasants. The days when gluts of vegetables, especially potatoes and onions, knocked the bottom out of the market are over. Now Brittany is one of Europe's major food exporting areas and food processing is beginning to boom.

A lot of the credit for this goes to Alexis Gourvennec, once a farmer, who persuaded Paris to put up the money for a deepwater port at Roscoff and persuaded farmers to help set up Brittany Ferries. Originally, the ferry company was intended to take Breton vegetables to Plymouth. It was soon also a successful tourist route and the boats made money bringing back fish from Cornwall to France. The old St Malo run from Portsmouth was re-opened. The Southern Railway ran boats from Weymouth to St Malo until about 1934 but gave up the route because of tidal problems. Modern boats can handle the high tides and are infinitely more stable in rougher seas.

The St Malo service is very popular with tourists and truck drivers, although the newer Brittany Ferries route, Southampton to Caen (Ouistreham) in Normandy, is taking some business away from Brittany.

The Bretons gambled on Britain joining the Common Market and won. And the opening of the ferry services coincided with a big change in British holiday habits. A lot of Britons had tired of Spanish Costa crowds and airport delays and were turning to the freedom of getting into their cars and touring or just wandering to their holiday destination. They had also taken to caravans and tents waiting on site. Finally, the French opened their gîtes to foreigners. Gîtes are country rented holiday homes which can be anything from an old barn to a castle, or a new bungalow. The French Ministry of Agriculture gave small farmers big subsidies to convert these gîtes to help keep them on the land. At first foreigners could not hire them. Now they have become a way of holiday-life to an enormous number of families, especially the British. And Brittany is quite well off for them. The boom in British tourists has meant more accommodation, better hotels, cafés and restaurants, and more entertainment, and this has attracted more Parisian families, Germans and Belgians, and has made devolution even less likely, for Brittany is fast becoming as much part of Europe as part of France.

A wandering motor route round Brittany with places to see, hotels and restaurants appears in *The Complete Travellers' France* by Arthur Eperon (Pan Books, £5.99).

MAJOR TOWNS

St Malo

[MAP 3, page 270]

We owe a deep debt to the people who decided to rebuild St Malo after World War II, for they chose to rebuild much as it had been from the 15th century, when its corsair captains roamed the world's seas, to the fortnight in July 1944 when the Americans tried to dislodge the Germans and free it. St Malo was left in utter ruins. Now, just as in the 1930s, you can roam its narrow streets and walk the sea-washed ramparts of its inner walled town, Intra Muros, and pretend that you are in another age. True, some of the shops are boutiques and souvenir shops, tourists pack the streets and the pavement cafés and pour through Porte St Vincent in droves from the car and coach park outside the walls. But, as the sun goes down and the day-trippers leave, when the people move inside the cafés and restaurants, you can stand on the ramparts near Tour Bidouane looking towards the rock called Grand-Bé island, where the great Châteaubriand chose to be buried, and swear that you see sails moving towards the harbour to find sanctuary before night comes, and that you can hear the snarling and barking of *les Guets*, the fierce mastiff dogs which for five hundred years were let out at nightfall to discourage any Englishmen from sneaking up and taking the town by stealth, to be recalled at dawn by a trumpet blast. Or you can sit cosily on a late autumn or winter night in the warmth of one of the tiny restaurants huddled under the wall, the little Porte St Pierre, perhaps, or the Auberge des Chiens du Guet itself, and eat the super local mussels, the cod landed that morning and the lamb from the salt marshes with draughts of Muscadet and listen to the wind and the sea beating against the walls and you will be very glad that they were rebuilt so sturdily after the Americans freed the town. I have done all those things – and hope to do them again. St Malo is for dreamers. You don't need much imagination to evoke its turbulent past, to see the ghosts of bloodthirsty corsairs carousing in the inns which are now restaurants, celebrating another successful 'course' against the hated English or the capture of another Portuguese galleon carrying gold and treasure from the New World. The English called St Malo 'the Pirates' Nest'. It is incredible to think that almost all around you is so new – rebuilt after the 1944 destruction.

Technically, few of St Malo's pirates were actually called 'pirates'. They were 'corsairs', licensed by the king of France as Drake and Hawkins were licensed by Queen Elizabeth I. They were supposed to obey set rules and attack only enemy ships or those taking goods to the enemy; they were supposed to capture ships and crews and take them into port, where they and their cargoes were sold. A tenth of the price would go to the king, and of the rest, two thirds would go to the *armateurs* (ships' owners),

The walled ramparts of St Malo

while the remaining third would be divided between captain and crew. Thus there was little incentive to bring a ship back, and the corsairs would loot it, sink ship and crew and sell the loot in another port for gold. Furthermore, it was academic to their victims whether they had their throats slit by a 'licensed' corsair or a pirate. Still, in the end the armateurs got rich and built fine houses, whereas the corsairs mostly died violently or in poverty.

The two most notorious corsairs were very different. René Duguay-Trouin, son of an aristocrat-turned-shipowner, was educated for the priesthood but preferred wine, gambling and women to chastity and prayer. He maintained his aristocratic courtesy even towards prisoners. When in 1711 he captured Rio de Janeiro from the Portuguese to release its French prisoners, he stopped his men pillaging the town and executed eighteen of them for looting a church – remarkable. He was a corsair captain from 1692 to 1712 and in twenty years sank or captured eighty-five English ships, including ten Royal Navy boats and one hundred ships of other countries.

The English took him prisoner, but oddly he was allowed to wander around Plymouth (possibly because he was an aristocrat), so he persuaded the French wife of an English merchant to get him a boat to escape. When he died in 1736, he was Lieutenant-General of the French Navy, and for three hundred years warships have been named after him. The British captured one at Trafalgar, renamed it 'Implacable' and it was a Royal Navy training ship until it sank off Portsmouth in 1949. I believe that the current ship called Duguay-Trouin is a frigate carrying guided missiles.

Duguay-Trouin was a gallant dandy. Robert Surcouf, corsair in the Napoleonic Wars, was a courageous thug. He, too, was trained for the priesthood, but escaped from religious college to sea. The Royal Navy captured more than a thousand of Napoleon's corsair ships, but never Surcouf. He started as a slave trader, then became a corsair preying on the armed merchantmen of the East India Company in the Indian Ocean, using the French isles of Mauritius and Réunion as a base. With only eighteen men, he captured one merchant ship with twenty-six guns and 150 crew. He retired from the sea to become a shipowner and a backer of corsairs and slave traders. French guides do not usually point out that the British Royal Navy captured 1031 French privateers in the Napoleonic Wars alone, taking 69,147 prisoners.

St Malo's own greatest sailor was Jacques Cartier. In 1534 he sailed to look for gold in Newfoundland, discovered instead the mouth of the St Lawrence river, which he thought was in Asia, took possession of the land in the name of the King of France and called it Canada, which he thought was the Huron Indian name for the area but which really meant 'village'.

You can find interesting records of these sailors of St Malo in the castle-keep museum inside the old walled town (Intra Muros). Here, too, is an enlightening show of photographs of the devastation of 1944 before the rebuilding.

Unless you have a heavy suitcase to drop off at an hotel, don't drive into the old town. There is very little parking space, roads are narrow and crowded, and many are for pedestrians only. So leave your car outside in the big car park on esplanade St Vincent and join all the other visitors by walking through St Vincent Gate beside the castle.

The walk round the ramparts is stunning. They were begun in the 12th century, made bigger and stronger in the 18th century, and most survived the 1944 destruction.

You reach them from steps to the right as you come through St Vincent Gate. The sea views from them are best at high tide, which *is* high at St Malo (8–14 metres) and alters the seascape comprehensively. On the town side are interesting glimpses down the town's narrow streets.

The ramparts run above the quais of St Vincent and St Louis looking down on the busy port past Grande Porte (Grand Gate) to St Louis Bastion. The views are to the newer part of the town to the little resort of St Servan-sur-Mer.

From St Louis fort the ramparts skirt the houses of the *armateurs*, the rich shipowners of the old days. They were an independent lot, these men. Around 1588, when the extreme Catholic League were rampaging through Brittany trying to take it over, firing towns and villages and mass-murdering people, St Malo declared itself a republic for four years. The traditional boast of les Malouins, the people of St Malo, was and still is: *'Ni Français, ni Breton, Malouin suis'* ('I am neither a

Frenchman nor a Breton but a man of St Malo'). It has been expressed in more modern times as 'I am first Malouin, Breton perhaps, French if there is anything left over'. Perhaps its independence stemmed from its founder – a Welsh missionary bishop called Malo who settled in the Gallic-Roman town of Aleth, now part of St Servan, the resort next door. The people moved to the easily defended rock after attacks by Norsemen.

From this stretch of the ramparts you can see over the outer harbour to the Aleth rock, topped by the city fort, to the mouth of the Rance river, where the waves have been harnessed for hydro-electric power, and to the big beach of Dinard.

At the next corner is St Philippe bastion and the next stretch faces the open sea as far as Tour Bidouane and beyond. At Bastion de Hollande is a small public garden with statues of Surcouf pointing to sea, Jacques Cartier and Duguay-Trouin. You have fine views to the stretch of the Emerald Coast beyond Dinard, Dinard beach and to the islands near St Malo. To the right is Harbour island, then Grand Bé island to which you can walk at low tide, and Petit Bé island. In the background are Cézembre island and Conchée fort. You can see from here how easy it was to defend St Malo, and the rock and island hazards which still face ships' navigators.

The last stretch of ramparts from Bidouane Tower to St Vincent Gate gives you views of the important defence fort, Fort National, and of the great beaches sweeping towards Pointe de la Varde – Paramé, Rothéneuf and Le Minlhic. At the end of the ramparts, steps take you down close to Porte St Thomas (St Thomas's Gate) which opens on to the great beach of Paramé.

The castle stands above the beach. It was a ducal fortress, then royal when Brittany joined France. The smaller keep was built with the ramparts in 1395, the larger keep and corner towers in the 15th to 16th centuries. You can enter the courtyard and see the front of the town hall (a barracks from the 17th to 18th centuries), a well and the big keep.

The tower on the left wing of the castle is called Quic-en-Groigne. This comes from an inscription which the Duchess Anne had carved on it as a rebuke to the local bishop who objected to her marriage to Charles VIII of France. *Qui-qu'en-*

groigne, ainsi sera, car tel est mon bon plaisir ('Complain as you may, it will be thus because I wish it to be'). The tower is open from Easter to mid-September and contains reconstructions of historic scenes, with well-known people of St Malo represented by wax figures.

In the big castle keep is St Malo museum (closed Tuesday in winter). It, too, records the development and history of St Malo and its celebrities. Inevitably, Cartier, Duguay-Trouin and Surcouf figure highly. So do Châteaubriand, the writer Lamennais and the great Indies colonist Mahé de la Bourdonnais.

Félicité Robert de Lamennais (1782–1854) was born at St Malo. He returned with his brother, a priest, to their family estate – La Chesnaie – near Dinan, and wrote in 1808 *Réflexions sur l'État de l'Église* (Reflections on the State of the Church), which was suppressed by Napoleon. He fled to London until Napoleon disappeared to St Helena, then returned, became a priest, and wrote a religious work denouncing private judgement and tolerance, which Rome liked. Then he developed a fervour for popular liberty and he helped found the journal *L'Avenir* in 1830, which was banned the following year. More books brought about a complete break with the Church and a year's imprisonment from the State. He was active in the 1848 Revolution and was elected to the Assembly where he sat until the *coup d'état* by Napoleon III. He refused until his death to make peace with the Church.

The cathedral of St Vincent, started in the 11th century and enlarged in the 18th century, was much damaged in 1944. In 1972 it was restored and a tall granite spire added. A Renaissance and classical façade hides a 12th-century rib-vaulted nave. The 13th-century choir is set lower to follow the rock slope. It contains some delightful modern glass – magnificent sparkling windows by Jean le Moal, with bright and colourful windows by Max Ingrand. The restored 17th-century glass looks almost dull beside them.

The 12th-century tomb of the first bishop Jean de Châtillon is there and in a side chapel is a simple black marble slab covering a tomb with just the name 'Jacques Cartier'. No one in France – or Canada – would need to be told more.

Grand Bé is a strange island. At low tide you can walk to it by leaving Porte des Champs Vauverts and walking diagonally across the beach to a causeway. Many people go there in high summer yet it can be very isolated for the rest of the year.

On the seaward side you feel the loneliness more acutely and it is here that the writer Châteaubriand was buried at his own request. His grave is unmarked – an unnamed flagstone topped by a heavy granite cross. Most men would have preferred to be buried on the top of the island, from where you can see the entire Emerald Coast west of Dinard. But Châteaubriand was an introspective man who, despite having been an ambassador, was not very fond of his fellow humans, and his themes of sadness and loneliness still affect French literature.

François-René de Châteaubriand (1768–1848) was the tenth and last child of parents of a noble Breton family which fell on hard times. His father went to America to recoup his fortunes and made enough to set up as armateur in St Malo, where François-René was born. The apartment was reached from the courtyard of the old Hôtel France et Châteaubriand near Quic-en-Groigne tower. He wandered the port as a child and almost inevitably dreamed of the sea and travel. Then his father, a *vicomte*, took over the château at Combourg (page 106) and he moved there with his parents and sister Lucile. His father was a disagreeable man who alternated between lengthy silences and loud rage, and young Châteaubriand lived a lonely life, much of it spent in his bedroom in a turret. He studied at colleges at Dinan, Dol, Rennes and Brest, still dreaming of going to sea. In 1791 he sailed as ensign to North America on an eight-month voyage and wrote his first book, *Voyage in America*. After fighting for an émigré army against the Revolution and being badly wounded, he spent seven years as a refugee in London, teaching and writing so well that he was soon among France's best writers of the day. Then he became a diplomat in Rome, but refused to serve under Napoleon and started his wanderings again in the East, Greece, Palestine and Egypt. On the return of the monarchy he was made a peer and minister. He was still writing great books, including the epic *Les Martyrs*.

From 1822 to 1824 he was ambassador to the court in London. He was disappointed not to become prime minister and joined the Liberals. He became a Royalist again when Louis-

ST MALO

Philippe came to the throne and spent his time writing an eloquent six-volume autobiography, *Memoires d'outre-tombe*. He died in 1848 and asked to be buried on Grand Bé island.

Châteaubriand steak was invented by his chef Montmireil. It is a middle fillet, grilled in butter, with sauce of wine, shallot, tarragon and lemon. Some chefs now serve it with béarnaise sauce.

Fort National on the north edge of the old town peninsula was built by the great military architect Vauban in 1689 just in time to save St Malo from the Anglo-Dutch fleet in 1692. It was called 'Fort Royal' until the Revolution. You can reach it from Plage de l'Éventail at low-tide, walking across the sands (about eight to ten minutes). The view from its ramparts includes many of the islands to the Chausey islands in Normandy, off Granville.

Brittany Ferries boats from Portsmouth dock in a fairly new dock area on the road to St Servan. There are also ferries from St Malo to Dinard (page 52), Cap Fréhel (page 136), along the Rance estuary, to the isle of Cézembre, which has a fine sand beach, to the isles of Chausey off Normandy (uninhabited isles where they quarried the stone to build Mont-St-Michel), and to the British-owned Isle of Jersey.

St Servan-sur-Mer, on the Aleth peninsula, where St Malo himself settled and Fort de la Cité is built, used to be a fashionable, lively resort. It was made officially a suburb of St Malo in 1967. It has some nice houses with gardens, a main beach around Sablons Bay and little beaches along the Rance estuary. It is possible to walk across Sablons Bay at low tide. The town has three ports, too – the Bouvet bassin, used for trading and fishing boats, the old naval and military port of Solidor, and the port of St Père.

The walk round the Aleth Corniche from St Servan is splendid, offering magnificent views of St Malo, the islands and the Rance estuary and tidal power scheme.

The attractive Solidor tower which commands the estuary of the Rance was built in 1382 by Duc Jean III of Brittany during a siege of St Malo. It is really three towers joined together. It was used as a prison for some time but now houses the Musée International du Longcours Cap Hornier (International Museum of Cape Horn Vessels) – the story of the great sailors who rounded Cape Horn from the 16th to 20th centuries. It includes a model of the *Victoria*, first ship to sail round the world from 1519 to 1522. Its journey took 1084 days.

The City Fort was built by the Duc d'Aiguillon, Governor of Brittany, in 1759. He was the man who was forced into retirement by the Bretons, whose leaders had ordered the dissolution of the Jesuit Order in Brittany when he was backing it.

In World War II the Germans modernised City Fort and used it. In the inner court, where a theatre has now been built, they built a chain of blockhouses joined by underground passages which run for a mile under the town.

Paramé, at the northern end of St Malo, is now a suburb, too. It is a popular seaside resort with two magnificent beaches stretching for 2km and a splendid seafront promenade 3km long. It has a seawater thermal establishment.

TOURIST INFORMATION Esplanade St Vincent
(99.56.64.48)
MARKET Tuesday, Friday
FESTIVALS May – International Fair; 1 July to 15
August – Son-et-Lumière in castle courtyard

HOTELS

Central, 6 Grande-rue (99.40.87.70). Old-style hotel in convenient part of old town. English-style bar is former yacht club. ROOMS E–G. MEALS C–D. Shut January.

Elizabeth, 2 rue Cordiers (99.56.24.98). Nice bed and breakfast hotel in house built in 1600 in old town. Period style. ROOMS E–F. Open all year.

La Villefromoy, 7 Boulevard Hébert (99.40.92.20 – Rochebonne beach area). Second Empire mansion beautifully furnished. No restaurant. ROOMS E–F. Shut 15 November–15 March.

Porte Saint-Pierre, 2 place du Guet (99.40.91.27 – in old town). Sweet little old hotel of great character; don't go if you are an hotel snob! Old-style regional cooking – lots of choice. Good fish. ROOMS B–D. MEALS A–C. Shut 15 November–15 January.

Thermes et Restaurant Cap Horn, 100 boulevard Hébert, above

Rochebonne beach, very near the seawater spa (99.56.02.56). Very good cooking; diet dishes and classical. Seawater pool. ROOMS D–G. MEALS D–F. Shut January.

RESTAURANTS

Duchesse Anne, 5 place Guy La Chambre (99.40.85.33). Part of the old town scene, built into the ramparts, authentic 1920s. Same great classic dishes for years, especially fish. MEALS D–G. Shut Wednesday; December, January.

J–P. Delaunay, 6 rue Ste-Barbe (99.40.92.46). Excellent fish; was popular with younger smarter set but prices have risen; same high standards. In old town. MEALS C (weekdays), F–G. Shut Sunday evening, Monday; 3–28 November; 8–23 February.

Brest

[MAP 2, page 269]

Brest has such a magnificent natural harbour that it was destined to become a naval base, and that cost it complete destruction in World War II. It was one of the Germans' two top submarine bases (La Rochelle was the other), and it was bombed almost to extinction by Allied air forces. The Germans not only strengthened the port and expanded it but built new underground submarine shelters. The two German battleships *Scharnhorst* and *Gneisnau* were in Brest most of the war being repaired. They were bombed almost constantly by the RAF. In July 1941 aerial photographs of the port showed that they were still there. But the French Resistance leader 'Rémy' (in fact, one of the Renault car manufacturing family) reported that the *Scharnhorst* had slipped out of Brest, was at La Rochelle and preparing to raid shipping in the Atlantic. Spitfires of the RAF Photographic Reconnaissance Unit (PRU) flew low over both heavily armed ports. They got back safely and their pictures showed that the Resistance was right. Early next morning several squadrons of RAF Wellington bombers escorted by fighters bombed Brest docks. One of the fighters shot down was flown by Wing Commander Douglas Bader, the legless Battle of Britain ace. Meanwhile the new four-engined Halifax bombers of the handpicked No.35 squadron of the RAF, shortly to start the Pathfinder Force, flew to La Rochelle, painted black for night bombing, with no fighter escort because the target was too far. The *Scharnhorst* was defended by the port guns, the guns of many cruisers, destroyers and anti-aircraft ships, and twelve squadrons of Messerschmitt 109 fighters.

At dusk that evening, defended by the ships and fighters, the *Scharnhorst* steamed out of La Rochelle. Her bows were underwater. She was going back to Brest for still more repairs. As she left La Pallice a single Beaufort torpedo bomber came out of the dying sun and put a torpedo into her steering before crashing into the sea. The *Scharnhorst* did not leave Brest again for over two years. Of fifteen Halifax bombers, seven were shot down, which is why I spent the next four years in German prison camps.

When the Americans took Brest in 1944 the port was in complete ruins, anything the RAF missed having been blown up by the Germans before capitulating. But it had recovered completely by the late 1960s and is now the first French naval port and a very important commercial and industrial centre. It is a very different city from pre-war Brest, re-built on a geometric plan with main roads drawn in straight lines from the splendid place de la Liberté, which has an imposing vertical cenotaph. Rue de Siam, the widest road, joins it to the naval port (Port de Guerre).

One reminder of Old Brest is the 15th-century castle, built on the site of an early Roman fort. It was considerably enlarged in the 16th to 17th centuries. Though damaged in World War II, it has been much restored and is headquarters of the Préfecture Maritime – the Marine Police. But it is open to the public (except Tuesday).

From the Madeleine and Paradise towers you have views of the roadstead – the seaway leading to the port – showing just why Brest is so important. And in five rooms of Paradise Tower is a Naval Museum which shows paintings, models and many other items of naval history since the 16th century. There is plenty of naval history to depict.

Across the Penfeld estuary is the 16th-century Tour Tanguy, which houses the Musée de Vieux Brest (the museum of Old Brest). Dioramas by a local painter, Pierre Peron, show Brest's main historical events (open daily).

Overshadowing these two old buildings is the massive Pont de Recouvrance, over the Penfeld estuary, which is in keeping with the post-war Brest of concrete and glass. It is said to be the biggest drawbridge in Europe.

Of the modern buildings, the most impressive is the church of St Louis, built in St Louis Square in 1958. It is very large and upright with a very upright belltower. Most of it is in rough stone, but the belfry is in cement and so are the surrounds of the stained-glass windows. The modern stained glass is deliberately simple, to focus light on to the high altar. The brightest touch is in a side chapel, which has a modern tapestry with a yellow background by Olin.

Brest's museum was wiped out in World War II. Exhibits in the present museum in rue Emile Zola have mostly been bought since 1958 and many are 17th- to 19th-century paintings.

The good collection of 19th-century paintings inspired by Brittany include many of the local Pont-Aven school, including Schuffenecker, a colleague of Gaugin's on the stock exchange before they both gave up broking for a painting career, and Sérusier and Maurice Denis, founders of the Nabs group of painters in the 1890s, who rejected Impressionism and painted in flat areas of pure colour.

Brest is not really a holiday city but it is a fine place for yachtsmen – preferably with some experience. There are more than a hundred berths for yachts in the marina (Port de Plaisance du Moulin Blanc) and the bay (Rade de Brest) leads to two good sailing rivers, the Aulne and the Elfort.

The river Penfeld is a security zone with naval dockyards on both sides. Guided tours are restricted to French nationals – a familiar French rule which I find rather quaint, for France most surely has its unreliable extremists as does any other country. The Soviets do the same in Leningrad.

Brest was once occupied by the English. Just after the beginning of the Hundred Years War in 1337 the Duke of Brittany, Jean III, died. As successor the French backed his niece Jeanne de Penthièvre, wife of Charles de Blois. The English backed her brother Jean de Montfort (*see* History, page 18). Montfort asked the English to guard Brest. When he became Duke, he asked them to leave. They refused. He tried to drive them out with troops and failed. So did the King of France. They stayed from 1341 to 1397. Then Richard II of England, who had married Isabella, eldest daughter of the French King Charles VI, gave it back to the Bretons.

Henry VIII of England sent a fleet on St Laurence's Day, 10 August 1513, to attack Brest. The Bretons were holding a party and dance aboard a new ship, *Belle Cordelière*, which had been given to Brest by the Duchess Anne.

The ship put to sea with three hundred guests on board.

The commander of the Brest fleet panicked when the English attacked and fled back into the sound. *Belle Cordelière*'s captain, Hervé de Portzmugeur, covered the retreat. He fought a gun-to gun-battle with an English ship until the *Cordelière* was on fire. Then he told his crew and the three hundred guests: 'We shall now be celebrating the day of St Laurence, who died by fire.' Both ships were blown up.

Another famous Anglo-French battle off Brest took place in 1779 off the nearby Ile d'Ouessant (which the British call Ushant, *see* page 190). The Brest frigate *Surveillante*, commanded by Du Couëdic, fought a duel with the British frigate *Quebec*, commanded by George Farmer. After a tough fight, both ships were dismasted. But the *Quebec*'s sails fell across its hot guns and the ship caught alight. Du Couëdic ordered a rescue action. But the *Quebec* blew up, killing the wounded Farmer. Du Couëdic was hit in the head by two musket balls and hit in the stomach once. He died before reaching Brest.

Ile d'Ouessant is one of the places to which you can take a boat trip – a very rewarding one through the whole roadstead.

Ferries go daily across the Rade de Brest to Le Fret (¾ hr) where coaches connect with the resorts of Camaret, Crozon and Morgat. From June to September there are 1½ hr boat trips around the roadstead.

TOURIST INFORMATION 1 place de la Liberté
(98.44.24.96)
MARKET Monday, Friday
FESTIVALS mid-May – Commercial Fair

HOTEL

Voyageurs, 15 ave Georges-Clemenceau (98.80.25.73). Range of meals, from cheap menus in the grill to *dégustation* meals in the restaurant. Good 'fish of the day' dishes, excellent seafood platter. Bedrooms individual, soundproofed, some with sea views, some garden views. ROOMS B–E. MEALS A–B (grill), E–F (restaurant). Both shut 15 July–7 August; Monday. Hotel open all year.

RESTAURANT

Frère Jacques, 15 bis rue Lyon (98.44.38.65). Probably the best restaurant in Brest. MEALS D–F. Shut Saturday lunch, Sunday; 3–16 July.

Rennes

[MAP 3, page 270]

Rennes, capital of Brittany, has doubled its population since World War II by industrialising. It makes Citroën cars, railway equipment, electronic and communications equipment, and paper, and Rennes is the centre for transport, building and oil refining. Furthermore it has 27,000 students in its two universities and the national college of public health.

So it is a very different city from the tranquil provincial capital of the 1930s, and it has acute traffic and parking problems. But once you have parked, there are some fine things to see as you walk round.

The centre is elegantly 18th century, so dignified that people have called it 'cold'. Outside are the remains of the old city. The reason for this unusual arrangement is that the very centre was destroyed in a great fire of 1720 and the outer part survived. These are two parts of the city where people work in offices, go shopping, to the theatre and to restaurants. Over the Vilaine river a virtually new city has been built with hotels, sports stadium, and most of the houses and apartments. Around it all are the factories and more residential suburbs.

The fire of 1720 was a terrible accident. A carpenter got drunk and upset a lamp on to a pile of shavings. The wooden house went up in flames and the fire spread to a thousand more homes. The soldiers sent to put out the flames got drunk, too, and spent their time looting instead of fire-fighting.

Louis XV hired the well-known architect Jacques-Jules Gabriel to redesign the burned-out town, although it was started by a local architect – Robelin. Gabriel was the father of Jacques-Ange Gabriel who built Place de la Concorde in Paris. He needed to house the people as quickly as possible, so he built tall, classical apartment buildings in granite and sandstone, set in wide streets and spacious squares. The apartments were sold, not let – a new idea which became the norm in France, but did not spread across the sea to England until after World War II.

Rennes is a very old city. It was already an ancient Celtic town when the Romans built walls round it. Nantes was originally capital of Brittany, and residence of the Dukes, but Rennes was made capital in 1213 and the Duke came to Rennes to be crowned. It was near the borders of Brittany and France, and so had military as well as political importance.

When the popular Duchess Anne of Brittany married Charles VIII in 1491, she remained the ruler of Brittany and Rennes remained its centre of government. Even when France and Brittany were united in 1532 after Anne's daughter Claude married François I of France, Breton rights and privileges were maintained and in 1561 the Parliament of Brittany was established in Rennes. It lasted until the Revolution.

For a long time the Parliament met in the magnificent building which is now the *Palais de Justice* (Law Courts). It was built between 1618 and 1655, designed by Salomon de Brosse, who designed Luxembourg Palace in Paris and Louis XIII's hunting lodge at Versailles, the basis of Louis XIII's palace. Funds to build the *Palais de Justice* were raised by the Breton government by levying a duty of one *sol* on a litre of wine and a smaller amount on cider when a labourer's wages were about 7 *sols* a day. The façade was altered by Jacques Gabriel in the 18th century after fire damage, a huge double flight of steps at the courtyard entrance being replaced by an Ionic doorway. You enter through a room which leads to the *Salle des Pas Perdus* extending the full length of the main façade. Its wooden vaulted ceiling is painted in blue and gold, with the arms of Brittany and France in the centre. A fine double staircase sweeps down from the first floor, where rooms are very lavishly decorated by famous decorators, mostly employed by Louis XIV, including Jean Jouvenet, and members of the great Coypel family, including Noel, follower of Poussin, and his son Antoine, who painted the ceiling of Versailles' royal chapel.

The *Grande Chambre*, the parliamentary debating chamber and legal high court, has the most splendid decorations. The whole 20-metre-long ceiling is beautifully carved, panelled and painted, mostly in crimson and gold. There are delightful, well-decorated loggias from which important visitors listened to debates – like boxes at a theatre. Ten modern Gobelins tapestries show important events in Brittany's history.

As the *Palais de Justice*, this building was where the unlucky Dreyfus was tried for the second time in 1899. Dreyfus was the French army officer falsely accused of selling military secrets, found guilty on faked evidence and sent to Devil's Island. His retrial and final acquittal was a sensation of French history.

The people of Rennes are very proud of their *hôtel de ville* (town hall) which they regard as Gabriel's masterpiece. Built in 1734, it has a partly baroque façade and is basically an onion-dome clock-tower between two symmetrical wings. It has a central niche in which a statue of Louis XV stood until destroyed after the Revolution. In October 1911 the government in Paris set up a large statue there symbolising the union of Brittany and France in 1532. The statue showed Brittany kneeling before the statue of France, and predictably the Bretons were incensed, particularly, of course, the Breton Separatists, who called it the Monument of National Shame. In 1932 the secret society Gwenn ha Du (white and black, colours of the Breton flag) blew it up. Now there is a flagpole in the niche.

Inside the *hôtel de ville* is the Panthéon, a room listing the Bretons who have died for France, set up after World War I. The cornice of the *Salle des Fêtes* has a long succession of famous Bretons, ranging from the soldiers Du Guesclin and La Tour d'Auvergne to the ruthless Surcouf, the writer Châteaubriand and the great Dr René Laënnec of Quimper (1781–1825) who invented the stethoscope and did invaluable work on TB and chest diseases. Opposite the *hôtel de ville* is the graceful bow-fronted theatre.

The cathedral of St Peter is rather disappointing. It had to be virtually rebuilt after all the old cathedral except two classical towers collapsed in 1762. This one took fifty-seven years to build because of wars and revolutions, and was finally finished in 1884. It is over-decorated inside with gilding and massive polished brown columns of the sort you would expect to find in a 19th-century provincial wool market or bourse.

Of Rennes' multitude of churches, the most rewarding to me is St Sauveur nearby (17th to 18th centuries) with a graceful tower and a fine pulpit, made by a local ironworker in 1781. Much of the old town is, wisely, for pedestrians only and narrow, winding streets which escaped the great fire are well worth exploring unhurriedly. Many of the delightful 15th-to 16th-century houses have overhanging storeys and there are finer mansions with sculptured fronts around the cathedral. You could start in place St Sauveur and turn alongside the church into rue St Guillaume, where a lovely 16th-century house (No. 3), sculptured in wood and stone, is said to have belonged to Du Guesclin, which is helpful to the restaurant Ti-Koz which occupies it, though is somewhat unlikely as it seems to be too young. Rue de la Psalette, skirting the cathedral, is lined with

Église St Sauveur, Rennes

nice old houses. Rue de Chapitre has several fine houses, including a Renaissance house (No. 8) Hôtel de Brie and No. 6, Hôtel de Blossac, with a magnificent staircase which you can see from the courtyard. The courtyards of some of these houses are a delight. Rue des Dames is worth exploring, too.

Much of *place des Lices* (the Lists) is now covered by a 19th-century glass and iron meat-market. This was where the jousts and tournaments were held, scene of Bertrand Du Guesclin's first triumph. The man who was to become one of France's greatest soldiers was, in fact, born near Dinan in 1320 (*see* History, page 18). His father thought him rough and ugly and despised him. He sent him to be brought up by an uncle in the country. There he learned to fight with sword, spear and stick. Later when troubadours were telling of his exploits, he was described as 'scowling and stocky, hated so much by his mother and father that they wished him drowned'.

When he was seventeen, a great tournament was held in the Lists at Rennes to celebrate the wedding of Charles de Blois, a probable future Duke of Brittany, and Jeanne de Penthièvre. Bertrand turned up, borrowed a horse and armour which did not fit him properly from a cousin and challenged in the Lists without giving his name. He unseated one knight after another, still refusing to reveal his name. Then his own father challenged him, so he lifted his vizor. His father saw his face, recognised him and welcomed him back into the family. He was then able to follow his dream of a career as a soldier.

When the fight started for the dukedom between Charles de Blois, backed by the French, and Jean de Montfort, backed by the English, Bertrand got his own back on his mother by stealing her jewels to hire a band of thugs to harry the English mercenaries. He saved Rennes when the English were besieging it by capturing the English food wagons. But after Charles de Blois was beaten, Du Guesclin fought for the French, twice invading Brittany, and although he is a French national hero, he is by no means a hero to many Bretons. One famous Breton poem, *The Swan*, in La Villemarqués' collection called Barzaz-Breiz, calls for the curse of posterity on Bertrand Du Guesclin. And in the beautiful Thabor gardens in Rennes there used to be a memorial to him in the middle of the sunken lawn which is still called

Carré du Guesclin. It was destroyed by the Breton Separatists in 1946.

The Thabor gardens are a delightful example of French formalised garden design, with flowers planted in patterns, forming coats of arms, shapes of animals and symbolic designs. They are behind the interesting old abbey church of St Mélaine, on a high spot of the city. Among the ten hectares of peace and tranquillity are ponds rich in fish, a botanical garden which appeals to serious amateur gardeners, and an absolutely magnificent rose garden with scores of varieties of roses laid out in circles with paths between. Most of this was laid out about a hundred years ago but they were the gardens of the abbey back in the 11th century when the tower of St Melaine's church was built.

Sitting in the garden on a fine day, with the thriving city of Rennes below, it is difficult to imagine the city's turbulent history and its record of justified revolt. Perhaps the proudest record of Rennes was its revolt against the crippling taxation of Colbert and Louis XIV to pay for Louis' wars against England (*see* History, page 22). The Revolt du Papier Timbre may have ended with aims too idealistic to be thinkable in the 17th century but it did make the point to the French that Brittany was not a French colony, to be milked of its resources and left to rot.

Brittany's voice is heard loud and clear from Rennes these days, not least through the great newspaper *Ouest France*, founded as soon as Rennes was freed from German Nazi occupation in 1944 and now claiming to have the biggest readership of any provincial newspaper in France.

I find the Musée de Bretagne particularly interesting among French regional museums for its imaginative presentation of the life and history of Brittany, especially the furniture, costumes, farm implements, weavers' loom and other everyday objects. A vast room is given to Breton costumes of the 19th century.

The audio-visual displays are excellent. The technical presentation is kept up-to-date, as is the history of the Breton people in this century.

The museum is open every day except Tuesday and public holidays. The audio-visual is in French but easily followed if you have some small command. You much check times of the show

(½ hour) by telephone, 99.30.83.87. There are also fascinating work-it-yourself films on more specialist subjects.

The museum is in the Palais des Musées, 20 quai Emile-Zola, beside the Vilaine river. So is the Musée des Beaux Arts which has some most interesting pictures as well as some of very high quality, such as a lively picture of a *Tiger Hunt* by Rubens, and Veronese's *Perseus and Andromeda*; there are four lively, expressive pictures showing the dangers of travel around 1780 by P. J. de Loutherbourg, the Anglo-French painter who was well-known in theatrical circles as scene designer and painter for David Garrick at London's Drury Lane theatre. Equally interesting are the paintings of Jean Julien Lemordant, born in St Malo (1878–1968), who painted street scenes, pardons and festivals in Brittany at the start of the century. I think that he went to Paris and died there, but I have found none of his works outside Brittany. The 19th-century section has good pictures by Boudin, Sisley and Napoleon's official war painter, Baron Antoine-Jean Gros, who taught Géricault, Delacroix and Bonnington and was inevitably a highly dramatic painter working for a highly flamboyant military commander. The Pont Aven school is well represented, showing doleful scenes of Breton countryside and peasants of the late 19th century, summed up in Sérusier's *Solitude*. Gauguin, the master of this group, has a small still life called *Nature Morte à l'Orange*. Picasso livens things up a bit. (Open daily except Tuesday.)

Like most bigger cities in France, Rennes has a Maison de la Culture with a huge amphitheatre, theatre cinema and conference centre, and exhibition centre. But this one includes in its culture a disco! The building was designed by Calu, responsible for Chaillot Palace in Paris. Rennes also has some of those thirty storey blocks of apartments which were an essential part of every French city in the 1960s and 1970s. But altogether it is a rewarding city to explore once you have mastered the traffic.

Four kilometres nort-east is the Musée Automobile de Bretagne which has about eighty veteran and vintage cars, all in working order, with early-century fire engines, motorbikes, cycles and horse-drawn vehicles. The cars include an 1898 Hurtu (of which I had never heard) and a delightful 1899 De Bouton 'Vis-à-Vis' ('Face to Face') – a joy to amateurs like myself.

TOURIST INFORMATION Pont de Nemours
(99.79.01.98)
MARKET Daily in Les Valles; Tuesday in districts of
Cleunay, Maurepas and Thorigny-Landel; Wednesday
in Ste Thérèse; Saturday in Place des Lices; Friday,
Saturday in car park by esplanade De Gaulle
FESTIVALS Early March – Les Rigodailles (Fête du Pays
Gallo); end April–early May – International Trade Fair;
early June – Festival de la Création Breton; early
September – Rock Music Festival

HOTELS

Du Guesclin, 5 place Gare (99.31.47.47). No restaurant. A pity that Rennes' fine old classic hotel should have been modernised into dullness, but that can happen in a city devoted to business and industry. ROOMS E. Open all year.

Président, 27 av. Janvier (99.65.42.22). No restaurant. Elegant, stylish, well soundproofed. ROOMS E. Open all year.

RESTAURANTS

Piré, 18 rue du Maréchal-Joffre (99.79.31.41). Good balance between modern and classical cooking. Inventive. Choice of cheapish menus and excellent, pricier *à la carte* dishes. Charming old house with courtyard garden. MEALS B–F. Shut Saturday lunch, Sunday; 15–30 August; 23 December–6 January.

Palais, 7 place Parlement de Bretagne (99.79.45.01). Local ingredients cooked in a rather modern style which succeeds. Young chef Marc Tizon has possibilities of becoming very good indeed. MEALS C–F. Shut Sunday evening, Monday; 7–30 August.

Escu de Runfaô, 5 rue Chapitre (99.79.13.10). On its way up. 17th-century building, a patron who was *sommelier* at Le Fouquet's on Champs Elysées in Paris and young chef from the superb Tour Rose at Lyon. One cheap menu, one gastronomic. MEALS C–F. Shut Saturday lunch, Sunday.

Chouin, 12 rue d'Isly (99.30.87.86). The successful French formula of a shop piled high with beautiful fresh fish and simple restaurant next door cooking it well. Book. MEALS D–E. Shut Sunday, Monday; 30 July–21 August; 24 December–2 January.

Le Galopin-Gourmet, 21 ave Janvier (99.31.55.96). TV viewers in Britain will know where that title came from. Recovered from a bad patch. Good value cheaper menus. MEALS B–E. Shut Sunday; 24 July–15 August.

Dinard

[MAP 3, page 270]

Since Brittany Ferries reopened the ferry from England to St Malo, Dinard has once again become popular with British families (*see* Chapter I). It has been easy to reach from St Malo since the dam across the Rance estuary for the tidal-power electrical plant was built in 1965 with a big road across it.

When I was young Dinard was the place where many British children got their very first taste of 'abroad' and the sands were the place where we stuttered our first words of bad French to little French girls who did not know whether to laugh or run away. Meanwhile Mother got to like wine with meals and Dad discovered that although pastis tasted like lung tonic, it had a more interesting effect. I remember the old Grand Hotel with corridors so wide you could drive an Austin Seven down them. Some young 'blood' did in the 1920s. There was the Altaïr, the Lemenagers' family hotel where the pastry round the flans melted before it hit the back of your throat, and tiny La Paix bar and restaurant in the main square where the locally caught fish was delicious and meals were almost given away. They are all still there, including the Lemenager family.

Dinard may have lost some of its elegance and the people using the casino are certainly no longer the fashionable set, but it keeps its charm and is a wonderful place for children, with a choice of beaches, facing three ways, excellent sands and rock pools. There are water sports, too, and a good golf course nearby, and there are lovely water and road trips up and down the Rance river. I would still prefer to take younger children there than to the overheated Costa resorts of Spain. There is plenty for adults, including discos and night clubs and casino shows.

Hotels and the Casino line the main beach, plage de l'Écluse. From Pointe de Moulinet at the end are lovely coastal views to Cap Fréhel one way and St Malo the other. Round the corner begins the delightful promenade for pedestrians only, called Clair de Lune, and it was here in more elegant days that romances bloomed by moonlight. It has beautiful flowers and is nicely illuminated from June to September. It leads to Prieuré beach and beyond you can reach Pointe de la Vicomté, with views over the sea approaches to St Malo, the Rance estuary and the tidal electric-power dam and station.

Dinard's Aquarium and Marine museum has interesting souvenirs of Commander Charcot's Arctic expeditions in the 1930s (open Whitsun–mid-September). Dinard is a sailing centre.

The Rance dam, 750 metres long, encloses the estuary for the first plant to use tidal power to generate electricity. It was opened in 1966. The plant is in a tunnel 390 metres long. Generators of 240,000 kilowatts produce 550 million kilowatts a year. (Daily visits of half an hour.)

When the sluice gates are opened, it is quite a shock to see the waters burst out. I am told that it is not much fun for sailors just upriver, where the water goes down quite sharply. A friend told me that first time he experienced it he thought that someone had pulled out the plug and was emptying the river like a bath.

There are various sea boat trips from Dinard, including to the Chausey Isles in Normandy (*see* St Malo) and a superb trip to Cézembre isle, which has a magnificent beach of fine sand. The trip takes twenty minutes each way and you have 2½ hours on the isle (in season only). If you swim, watch the strong currents.

The trip along the Rance river to Dinan is superb. You can start it from St Malo. It takes 2½ hours, some between high wooded banks, and you pass little quays, old boatyards, mills and hamlets. On the quay at Dinan is a good simple restaurant (*see* Dinan, page 120) and a steep zig-zag path climbs to the old walled town. Because of tides you will get either eight hours in Dinan or a mere quarter-hour, so it is best to stay overnight as it is so delightful.

> TOURIST INFORMATION (Dinard) 2 boul. Féart
> (99.46.94.12)
> FESTIVALS July – tennis championships; 2nd fortnight of August – International Dance Academy

The waterfront at Dinan

HOTELS

Grand, et *Restaurant Georges V*, 48 ave George-V (99.46.10.28). True old Grand Hotel with gardens; lovely position. ROOMS F–G. MEALS D–E. Hotel shut 1 October–24 March; restaurant shut 1 October–20 April.

Altaïr, 18 boul. Féart (99.46.13.58). Patrick Lemenager, in the kitchen since he was fourteen, has made a few concessions to those who prefer modern cooking. Wide choice of menus and prices. Fine old Norman furnishings. ROOMS D–E. MEALS A–F. Shut Sunday except during French school holidays.

Dunes, 5 rue Clemenceau (99.46.12.72). Reopened; big improvement. Opposite main beach, good for families. ROOMS C–E. MEALS B–C. Shut 1 November–15 March; restaurant shut Tuesday.

Paix, 6 place République (99.46.10.38). *See above.* Simple, excellent value. ROOMS A–D. MEALS A–D. Shut Monday; 15 November–20 March.

Nantes

[MAP 4, page 271]

More prosperous, no doubt, perhaps more useful to the French economy, but Nantes is not the likeable, colourful old port we once knew, with old narrow streets which hinted at dirty deeds in the dark and of three Loire tributaries running through the town. Even the little trains which used to move goods from the quais and send impatient drivers mad have gone. But planners have still not solved the parking problem.

The new Nantes is best summed up by Le Corbusier's 'Living Unit' (Unité d'Habitation 1955) at Rezé.

After wartime damage, Nantes was reconstructed and reformed. In the great French national wave of aggressive 'technical progress' the city was torn apart to make way for high-rise buildings and wide, straight roads. The three Loire tributaries were hidden underground and two islands have been swallowed and covered with modern buildings. Much of its historic heritage has gone.

Nantes has a population of a quarter of a million and something in common with Liverpool, for it grew on the slave trade, cotton, sugar and rum. Even Voltaire, it is said, invested money in the 'ebony' trade (slaving). Most voyages made a two hundred per cent profit. But Nantes has kept its shipping trade and importance far more than Liverpool. The port, at the mouth of the Loire, is navigable by large vessels. The shipyards, with those of St Nazaire, make naval and commercial vessels, especially dredgers. The old industries, sugar refining and food-canning, have survived but added to them are factories producing electronics, refrigeration plants, oil-boring equipment, chemical products and ships' engines. The first ship's engine using nuclear energy was produced here. Blessedly, the city still distributes Muscadet and Gros Plant wines.

Nantes is an ancient town – Gallic, then Roman. During the Middle Ages it vied with Rennes as capital of Brittany. The Dukes of Brittany stayed in each alternately and squabbled with the French over Nantes until the Duchess Anne of Brittany married two French kings. Her father, Duc François II, had made Nantes virtually the sole capital. Rennes and Nantes are still great rivals.

The height of Nantes' prosperity was in the 18th century. The big shipowners and traders lived like aristocrats and built themselves mansions. A famous Nantais sailor was Cassard (1672–1740). His daring and skill, not to say his luck, in getting whole convoys through the tightest blockades has led to legends being woven around him. With the Revolution came disaster. Most Nantais were strongly religious Catholics, Royalist and against Revolution. Most of Brittany welcomed it, though loyalists (the Chouannerie) later opposed it (*see* History, page 23).

A terrible revenge was taken against the Royalists of Nantes. The prisons were already full of Royalists who had revolted in Vendée. Paris sent Jean-Baptiste Carrier, Deputy of the Cantal to the Convention, to 'purge the body politic of all the rotten matter it contains'. He was already notorious for executions elsewhere. He arrested priests, Royalists and suspects, but had no prison space left. So he put them into barges which were scuttled in the Loire opposite Chantenay. These executions were called *les noyades* (the drownings). One of his tricks was called *les marriages républicaines*. A man and woman would be stripped naked, tied to each other, and thrown in the river to drown. The Revolutionary Tribunal, which itself started the Terror, thought he had gone too far. He was recalled to Paris, then charged before the Nantes Revolutionary court, and guillotined. In Nantes he had killed 16,000 people in four months.

The Revolutionary Convention then banned the Slave Trade, a hard blow to Nantes' rich merchants. Then, under the Empire, home-grown French sugar beet was substituted for Antilles (French West Indian) sugar because of the British Navy blockade, and gradually ships became too big to reach Nantes. The town turned away from the sea to metal industries and food-canning for a living. Then in 1856 Nantes founded an outer-port at St Nazaire and in 1892 dug a lateral canal to the river.

New techniques allowed the dredging of the estuary in 1911 to take bigger ships and the canal was abandoned. Cargo ships up to 8¼ metres draught can dock at high tides. St Nazaire can still take much bigger ships, such as super-tankers over 500,000 tons and battleships and aircraft carriers.

The Château des Ducs in Nantes is a very severe fortress, but with some appealing touches, especially the Renaissance Tour de la Couronne d'Or with Italian-style loggias. It was begun in 1466 by François II and continued by Anne.

The court of the palace, part of the château, was used for jousting, and for performances of religious mystery plays and of farces. The Governor's Major Palace was rebuilt after a fire in 1684. It contained the prisons where many well-known people were held. One was Cardinal de Retz, the Archbishop of Paris, who plotted against Mazarin, Louis XIV's chief minister, and started the Fronde uprising in 1648. He escaped from Nantes to Spain and England but returned later to be made Abbot of St Denis. Another was Gilles de Rais. He was a Breton baron who fought beside Joan of Arc and became Marshal of France. He

Château des Ducs, Nantes

retired to his estates and is alleged to have indulged in the most appalling orgies. He kidnapped a hundred and fifty children and used them for his lusts and sorceries, killing them all. He confessed at his trial at Nantes, was hanged and burned. Another prisoner was Nicolas Fouquet, one of Louis XIV's finance ministers, who spent and distributed money so liberally that Louis guessed that he had his hand in the till and imprisoned him. His last rash act was to build a château (Château de la Vaux-le-Vicomte) more than fit for a king and throw one of the biggest and most lavish parties in history. A prisoner of the last century was the superbly eccentric and flighty Duchess of Berry, whose story I shall tell a little later.

Kings stayed more comfortably in the château. Louis XII married Anne of Brittany there. And there the newly-crowned Henri IV, gallant Protestant leader turned Catholic, issued his Edict of Nantes, giving the right of religious worship to the previously banned Protestants. Henri came to Nantes at the request of the ordinary people. They had been suffering sorely from the extremist Catholic League and from the separatist ambitions of its Governor, Philippe of Lorraine, Duke of Mercoeur, one of the League's leaders.

The château contains two museums. Musée d'Art Populaire Regional is a small favourite of mine. It shows typical interiors of old rural houses, furniture, costumes and *coiffes* from many parts of Brittany and the Vendée (like the castle, shut on Tuesday except in July and August). The other, Musée des Salorges, is a maritime museum with 18th-and 19th-century figureheads, models of 17th-and 18th-century boats, especially the slavers, and little models of Loire boats. The slave boats ran to the Guinea coast of Africa laden with brandy and goods to exchange for slaves. The slave run was to the West Indies where the wretched slaves who had survived were sold. On the return voyage they brought sugar, cotton, spices and rum. Also in this museum are the earliest preserving jars, 150 years old, containing vegetables and a large model of the famous Petit-Beurre biscuit factory (same opening times as Art Populaire).

Nantes cathedral, St Pierre, was begun in 1434, but not actually completed until 1893, only to be badly damaged in 1944 and by a fire in 1972. It has a dull, almost austere front but is impressive inside. The lines of its Flamboyant nave are superbly clean and effective. They soar to 37½ metres, compared with 33½ metres for the vaulting of Notre-Dame in Paris and 30½ metres for Westminster Abbey. Such heights are safe because it is built in limestone, not the heavy granite usual in Brittany. The tomb of Duc François II, carved around 1502–7 by da Fiesola and a Breton, Michel Colombe, is a beautiful work of Renaissance art. The Duke and Duchess lie on a white marble slab.

The Jules Verne museum (3 rue de l'Hermitage – shut Tuesday) in a 19th-century mansion, is devoted to the great writer of science fiction novels (*Around the World in Eighty Days* and *Journey to the Centre of the Earth*). He died in 1905.

The Beaux Arts museum gained after the Revolution when the French government redistributed works of art confiscated from churches and private collections and was later given works looted by Napoleon during his foreign campaigns. Although it has no really great works, it has many good ones to interest any amateur of art. They include paintings by Georges de La Tour (1593–1652), who was forgotten for three centuries but has been recently acclaimed. Mostly he painted religious subjects but his best here is *The Hurdy Gurdy Player*. There is also a Rubens taken from Tournai cathedral.

The Nantes adventures of the Duchess of Berry took place at Maison de Guigny, 3 rue Mathelin-Rodier, uphill from the castle, in 1832. This resourceful and attractive young widow was daughter-in-law of the deposed Bourbon King Charles X and her infant son the Duke of Chambord was heir to the French throne, which had been stolen by Louis-Philippe (the Citizen King), who had been appointed Regent for the infant.

The Duchess, in exile at Holyrood in Scotland, landed at Marseilles to rouse a rebellion. She went to Nantes hoping to obtain support from Royalist Vendée. She hid in this house, belonging to two sisters du Guigny, and for six months, with a small printing press and a staff of two men, she ran an opposition 'government' from an attic room, sending out proclamations and despatches to governments around Europe.

Nantes was thick with police and troops looking for her, and a million francs reward was offered for information leading to her arrest. A clerk, Deutz, working secretly for her, betrayed her. One evening her secretary saw the streets filling with soldiers. The Duchess, her maid and the two men just had time to hide in the secret place behind the attic fireplace. Unable to find the Duchess, the police left a heavy guard in the house for the night. Two policemen in the attic got cold and lit the fire. The four behind the chimney got warmer until the women's dresses caught alight. The Duchess wrote afterwards of how the gentlemen put out the flames – 'dispensing with ceremony'. The policemen slept, the fire died. But the policemen woke cold and relit the fire. This time the gentlemen failed in their duty. The Duchess put out the fire with her hands, but they were becoming asphyxiated and had to give themselves up. The Duchess was sent to prison but then admitted that she had made a second marriage with a Neopolitan marquis, thereby relinquishing her rights in France, so they released her as being politically finished. Anyway, Louis-Philippe was married to her sister, so she had some influence. Her son when he grew up showed little desire to take the throne as Henri V, though he had three chances. It was said of him that 'he passed forty years of blameless inertia' before dying in 1883 at the age of sixty-three.

Though most of the best Muscadet comes from Sèvre-et-Maine, south of the Loire, some quite good wines come from north-east of Nantes in the Coteaux de la Loire, north of the river. It is best in hot years, with less fruit than Sèvre-et-Maine but refreshing acidity. Gros Plant is produced there, too – the sharper, rougher wine which some Frenchmen prefer to Muscadet with shellfish. Red wines from Gamay grape (like Beaujolais) are produced at Ancenis, on the north bank of the Loire. They are drunk young – often chilled in summer.

You can get information and taste wine in Nantes at Comité Interprofessional des Vins du Pays Nantais, 17 rue des États (40.47.15.58), across rue des États from the Pont Levis of the château.

> TOURIST INFORMATION place du Commerce
> (40.47.04.51)
> MARKET Daily; bigger market Saturdays
> FESTIVALS February or March – Festival du Livre. Early June – Concours Hippique (Horse Trials). End June–early July – Jazz Festival. First fortnight of September – Carnival de Nantes

HOTELS

There is an enormous choice of hotels.

Pullman-Beaulieu, Ile Beaulieu, 3 rue Dr. Zamenhof (40.47.10.58). In commercial centre but good functional rooms and excellent cooking and good value in restaurant Le Tillac. ROOMS F–G. MEALS B–E. Open all year.

France, 24 rue Crébillon (40.73.57.91). Old hotel with classic rooms, modernised with taste. ROOMS D–G. MEALS B–E. Hotel open all year. Restaurant shut Saturday, Sunday lunch; mid-July–mid-August.

La Lande St-Martin at Haute-Goulaine, 11km east on N149 (40.06.20.06). Reliable, comfortable, modernised hotel in pleasant gardens away from Nantes industry and traffic. Good value; traditional cooking. Good Loire wines. ROOMS B–E. MEALS A–E. Restaurant shut Sunday evening.

Domaine d'Orvault, near Orvault, 7km north-west just off N137 (40.76.84.02). Relais et Châteaux hotel in gardens. Pricey but some of the best cooking around here. ROOMS E–G. MEALS E–G. Restaurant shut Monday lunch; February.

Abbaye de Villeneuve at Les Sorinières, 10km south by D178 (40.04.40.25). Another Relais et Châteaux hotel in superb 18th-century abbey; one of the excellent Savry family hotels. Beautiful restoration; peaceful park; pool. ROOMS G. MEALS D–G. Open all year.

RESTAURANTS

Le Colvert, 14 rue Armand-Brossard (40.48.20.02). Superb bistro in a charming street in old Nantes. Chef-patron, Didier Maconin, a Nantes man, was chef to the Aga Khan. Inventive dishes but not excessively modern. MEALS C–F. Shut Saturday lunch, Sunday; part February; mid-August–mid-September.

Les Maraîchers, 21 rue Fouré (40.47.06.51). Renowned for Brittany oysters. Pricey for delicately good cooking, MEALS E–G. Shut Saturday, Sunday.

Manoir de la Comète, at St Sébastien, 4km by D751 south-west 21 rue Libération (40.34.15.93). Fine simple cooking of the best local ingredients. MEALS C–G. Shut Saturday lunch, Sunday.

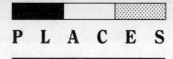

PLACES

LES ABERS
[N. Finistère]

The NW coast of Finistère, known as the coast of Legends, is broken up by estuaries called *abers* (Aber-Wrac'h, Aber-Benoit, Aber-Ildut), at their best at high tide. Aber-Benoit is especially attractive, with a bridge over it. Aber-Ildut, which has a village, is the theoretical division between the Channel and the Atlantic. It was in the Abers that the parasitic disease among oysters called Aber Disease was first found in 1970. It spread to all the oyster beds of southern Britanny, as far as Arcachon and northern Spain. Many beds were decimated and fresh stocks had to be brought in from Japan. Then the oil from the *Torrey Canyon* which broke upon nearby rocks in 1978, almost bankrupted the fishermen of Aber-Wrac'h.

ANCENIS
[Loire-Atlantique]

Very attractive old port on the Loire 38km upstream from Nantes. Once known for its sailcloth, now for its pig market and wine. Its houses rise in tiers above the river. The D751 just south of Ancenis across a suspension bridge is attractive and worth following to Nantes in preference to the N23 or A11 motorway.
    Tourist Information place Pont (40.83.07.44)
    Festivals June bi-annually – Fête Mediaevale;
    Autumn: dahlia show.

HOTELS
Val de Loire, at Jarrier d'Ancenis, 2km east by N23 (40.96.00.03).

New but fits into country surroundings. Air-conditioned bedrooms; garden. ROOMS C–D. MEALS A–E. Restaurant shut Saturday.

ANTRAIN
[ILLE-ET-VILAINE]

Attractive little steep streets in this market town overlooking farmlands. There are 15th- and 16th-century houses and an unusual church with a *porte des femmes* where women used to enter separately from men.

Nearby the Couesnon and Loisance rivers meet. Just to the south about 2 km along the Tremblay road is the 16th-century Château de Bonne Fontaine in a park of old trees. There the Duchess Anne used to dispense justice. The château was built as a feudal castle with battlemented round towers and turrets surrounding the main building. Much of its fortifications were dismantled last century. You can visit the park.

Château de Rocher Portail (10km south-east near Saint-Brice-en-Coglès) is a beautiful, dignified, classical house with a moat fed by an attractive pool. The left wing has a superb Renaissance gallery. Unfortunately you cannot go inside. It was built here in 1608 in the heart of the country by Gilles Ruellan, a pedlar who rose to be a councillor of state.

ARZON
[MORBIHAN]

The sailors of Arzon made a vow in 1673 to Ste Anne during a war and now they fulfil it by marching on Whit-Monday in the procession of Ste Anne-d'Auray. Arzon is near Port Navalo, on the seaside shore but only 1 km from the shore of the Gulf of Morbihan.

AUDIERNE
[S. Finistère]

A busy little fishing port at the mouth of the river Goyen, 15km from the westerly Pointe de Raz (*see* page 226). It is in a lovely setting at the foot of a hill and is also a popular resort. Boats bring in lobsters and langoustines and the hotel-restaurant Le Goyen in the port is the accepted place to eat them (*see* hotels, *below*).

Audierne has a superb beach of 900 metres of fine sands only one kilometre away, and there is a good choice of hotels and restaurants at port and beach.

There are seven miles of fine sands on fifteen beaches around this area. Fishing is good, too – sea and river (trout, some salmon). And it is the port from which to take a boat trip to the Isle of Sein (*see* page 251).

From quai Petletan along the corniche road you can see the great viviers where live lobsters and large crabs are kept in thirty tanks. Opposite these is La Chaumière, a thatched cottage with fine old furniture. In the church are modern stained-glass windows.

Tourist Information place Liberté, shut afternoon low-season (98.70.12.20)

Festivals Several pardons in July and August. Second Sunday in August – Fête des Bruyères; 15 August – Fête d'Armor.

HOTELS

Le Goyen, sur le port (98.70.08.88). Magnificent fish. Some of the best young chefs, have come here to learn from Adolphe Bosser. Known also for gorgeous home-grown potatoes. Superb wines. Rooms modernised. Rooms D–G. Meals D–G. Shut Monday out of season; mid-November–mid-December; mid-January–early February.

Roi Gradlon, sur la plage (98.70.04.51). Best of the beach-side hotels. Rooms C–D, modern. Meals A–E. Shut Monday low-season; mid-January–1 March.

RESTAURANT

Glacier, 1 rue 14 Juillet (98.70.18.73). Cheap and good value; fish menus. Meals A–C. Shut 1 October–1 April.

AURAY and STE ANNE D'AURAY
[MORBIHAN]

I find Auray one of the most delightful places in Brittany – a true old Breton port in attractive seascape and landscape setting, and still fairly lively.

It stands on the banks of the river Loch where it widens into the river Auray and flows into the Gulf of Morbihan, which is almost enclosed and strewn with rocky islands.

The hillside promenade lined with trees looks across a pretty bridge to the old St Goustain quarter, which is delightful, with atmosphere and character. Narrow streets and alleys are lined with truly attractive 15th-century houses which look as if they are nudging each other down the slopes. One quay is named after Benjamin Franklin. During the War of Independence he came to France to get French help. Winds stopped his vessel getting into Nantes, so he landed here at Auray and stayed in a house 150 metres from the square (marked with a plaque).

On marshy ground just north of Auray in 1364 was fought the decisive battle in the Breton War of Succession, which became virtually a war between England and France. Charles de Blois, backed for the vacant dukedom by the French and by the hero Bertrand du Guesclin, was fighting his cousin Jean de Montfort, who was backed by Olivier de Clisson and the English. De Clisson lost an eye. Charles de Blois, refusing du Guesclin's military advice, lost the battle and his life. De Montfort became Duke Jean IV and restored Brittany, which had come out of the war ruined.

Du Guesclin was captured by the English and later ransomed for 100,000 livres. Three years later he was captured again by the Black Prince, son of Edward III of England, and again ransomed. It seems that he was popular at the English court and lived very well there while his ransoms were being raised.

On the site of the battle, de Montfort had built a chapel and church which were made later into a monastery. The funeral chapel later held the bones of the Chouans who were executed in 1795 in the Champ des Martyrs nearby. The Chouans were Breton and Vendéen Royalists who revolted against the Revolution. The movement was strong here in the Morbihan and one of the leaders was Cadoudal, the twenty-two-year-old son of a farmer. He was captured and imprisoned at Brest, but escaped. Royalist émigrés landed at Quiberon (*see* page 214) and joined the Chouans, but they were hopelessly divided and defeated. Those captured were executed at what was later called the Field of the Martyrs. At least three hundred and fifty were shot. Cadoudal got away and continued the struggle with such zeal that Napoleon offered him a pardon and the rank of general. He refused. In 1804 he had a mad scheme to kidnap Napoleon. He was caught and executed and his body given to students for dissection, but the surgeon kept the skeleton and wired it together again. It was finally buried in a tomb at the gates of Auray. Alas, in 1968, when it was a home for deaf-and-dumb women, a fire damaged the old monastery terribly.

You can take gastronomic trips on a restaurant boat round the Gulf of Morbihan (also from Vannes, Port Navalo, Locmariaquer, Île aux Moines – Vedettes Vertes, Gare Maritime, Vannes 97.63.79.99).

Six km north-east of Auray is Ste-Anne-d'Auray, place of Brittany's biggest annual pilgrimage. Ste Anne is said to have appeared in 1623 to a ploughman and asked him to rebuild in his fields a chapel which had once been dedicated to her. In 1625 the ploughman dug up an old statue of her at the spot she had indicated. A church was built there. Last century a Renaissance-style basilica replaced it. The old statue was burned in 1796 but parts of the face were included in the base of a modern statue.

From 7 March there are pardons (parish pilgrimages), mostly on Wednesday and Sunday, but they reach a great climax with the great Pardon of Ste Anne on 25–6 July.

When I was younger, many who came to this festival combined it with a visit to the 1914-18 War memorial commemorating the deaths of 250,000 Breton soldiers and sailors. It was raised by public subscription all over Brittany.

TOURIST INFORMATION place République, Auray (97.24.09.75)

MARKET Friday, 2nd and 4th Mondays in the month – Auray

HOTELS
[Auray]

Le Branhoc, 1½km by route du Bono (97.56.41.55). Modern but quiet with garden. Separate restaurant (*see* Chaudron). ROOMS C–D. Open all year.

Le Loch et Restaurant La Sterne, quartier Petite Forêt (97.56.48.33). Modern, among greenery; lovely position overlooking the Loch river. Good cooking of fresh ingredients from the market. ROOMS D–E. MEALS B–E. Shut Monday except in July, August.

RESTAURANTS
[Auray]

Abbaye, 19 place St Sauveur, St Goustan (97.24.10.85). 17th-century house in the old town; super old furniture. Traditional Breton cooking. Cheap. Good value. MEALS A–E. Shut Sunday evenings, Monday.

Chaudron, at Hotel Le Branhoc (*see* above) (97.56.39.74). Rustic décor; good fish; wide range of menus. MEALS A–E. Shut Saturday lunch, Wednesday.

HOTELS
[Ste-Anne–d'Auray]

Croix Blanche, 28 rue de Vannes (97.57.64.44). Large traditional hotel. Rooms vary. Long choice of menus. ROOMS B–E. MEALS A–E. Shut Sunday evening, Monday in winter; January.

Auberge, 52 rue de Vannes (97.57.61.55). ROOMS A, simple. MEALS A–F. Shut Tuesday evening, Wednesday; 2–20 October; 10–28 February.

BAIS
[ILLE-ET-VILAINE]

Village north of La Guerche (*see* page 141) with a well-known Gothic church. Its doorway and porch are marvellous to lovers of ancient churches, sculptured in a fantasy of heads of the dead, salamanders, with a bust of Duc François I and the triumph of Aphrodite. I suppose that the sculptor could have explained it but to me it is a beautiful but muddled dream.

HOTEL

Lion d'Or, place Église (43.37.90.05). Typical cheap auberge rurale. ROOMS A–B. MEALS A. Shut Sunday evening.

BANGOR
[MORBIHAN]
(*see* Belle-Île, page 76)

BATZ, ÎLE DE
[FINISTÈRE-NORD]

Pronounced 'Ba' and you pass it in the Brittany Ferry from Plymouth as you come into Roscoff. A Welsh monk, St Pol, founded a monastery here in the 6th century. It is a tiny isle of fields surrounded by stone walls and narrow paths leading to the sea – a peaceful place still. A few of the men still go fishing but mostly they work the fields as market gardens.

Between the reefs are beaches of fine sand. There are relics of St Pol in the church, built in 1873, and a ruined chapel which he built to the east of the isle. Here a pardon is held on the Sunday nearest to 26 July. On the highest point of the isle at 23 metres is built a lighthouse of 44 metres. Nearby is Trou du Serpent, the rock where St Pol took off his bishop's regalia and used his stole to throw into the sea a serpent which had been ravaging the island. The Celtic saints were very good at seeing-off serpents and dragons. He is now called St Pol-Aurélian. The stole is said to be in the church but spoil-sport experts claim that it is of oriental cloth of the 8th century and he died in the 6th century.

You reach Batz by boat from Roscoff (twenty minutes). The current between them is very strong. The island has an important sea-rescue station.

BATZ-SUR-MER
[LOIRE-ATLANTIQUE]

Only 7km west of La Baule, this little seaside town and fishing port was here centuries before the resort. Once it formed an island with Le Croisic. What is now the Marais Salants (salt marshes) between Batz and Guérande was a sea-covered bay when Julius Caesar's galleys, under the command of Brutus, defeated the becalmed sailing boats of the Veneti tribe by hooking them with grappling irons and landing men aboard. Caesar had all the men of the tribe killed and the women and children sold into slavery.

Now Batz stands on the lovely rocky Côte Sauvage and is backed by the Marais. The rocky coast is broken by three sandy beaches, Valentin, La Gouelle and St Michel. The last is protected by a breakwater along which stands Pierre-Longue menhir, which proves that people have lived here a long time.

The 15th- to 16th-century church has a belfry 60 metres high with a pinnacle which has been a landmark for ships and a look-out post ever since it was built in 1667. You can go up it from 15 June to 15 September for fine views to sea as far as the Loire and Belle-Île, and over the salt marshes with their criss-crossed pattern of salt-pans. The church has some good statues and a window showing its consecration in 1488. This coast is very attractive from all along this stretch to Le Croisic, and the pathway Sentier des Douaniers from plage St Michel along the clifftop has lovely views of sea and coast.

Musée des Marais Salants (museum of the salt marshes) tells the story of the Paludière (salt-marsh workers) in the 18th to 19th centuries (open daily June–end September and school holidays, with audio-visual aids, October–May in afternoons of Saturday, Sunday).

FESTIVAL Second Sunday in August – Pardon de St Guénolé.

RESTAURANT

Atlantide, 59 boulevard de la Mer (40.23.92.20). By the port. Classic cooking with excellent seafood. MEALS D–E. Shut 31 October–end March.

BAUD
[MORBIHAN]

A town on N24 north-east of Lorient in beautiful countryside in the valleys of the little Tarun and Evel rivers, just before they reach the river Blavet. Several attractive roads meet and the Camor forest is just south. Baud is known mostly for a statue 2km west to the left of the Hennebont road. It stands above a large granite fountain on a pedestal near a farm which was once Château de Quinipily. It is called the Vénus de Quinipily. But there is argument about whether it *is* Venus, left behind by the Romans, or the Egyptian goddess Isis. It is a semi-naked figure about 2 metres high and is believed to have been dug up in Montagnede Castennec to the north. Anyway, it caused the church and local priests a lot of trouble.

Called 'Groac'h en Couard' (the witch of Couard) by the locals, the idol was worshipped with pagan rites in the Middle Ages by women seeking easy childbirth and girls seeking a husband. The priests got so worried about this sacrilegious worship that they kept throwing it with ceremony into the Blavet river. But the villagers kept fishing it out. It became so battered that it was recarved by order of the lord of the manor, Pierre de Lannion, in the 18th century. It is crude work, and it certainly does not look like Venus, goddess of beauty.

MARKET Saturday

HOTEL

Relais de la Forêt, 19 rue Mairie (97.51.01.77). Pleasant one-star hotel; good fish grilled over wood. ROOMS A–D. MEALS A–E. Shut Thursday low-season.

LA BAULE
[LOIRE-ATLANTIQUE]

La Baule is a remarkable seaside resort, with a seductive atmosphere. Built from scratch in the 1880s after 400 hectares of maritime pines were planted to settle the dunes, it became one of the most fashionable resorts in Europe. Even in this age of long haul jet travel, it has remained fashionable, fairly elegant and has kept its snob appeal while at the same time becoming a much-loved family resort.

Its bay is beautiful, it has 8km of clean sands, probably the best beach in north France, and nearby are attractive old fishing ports: Batz-sur-Mer, Pouliguen, Le Croisic, as well as the charming medieval walled town of Guérande. But much of its success is due to the enterprise of the local people. La Baule organises a series of high standard sporting events, including tennis, golf, show-jumping, racing and regattas. It has fine sailing schools and its pleasure-boat harbour predated by years the modern marinas. Its entertainment standards are high, its casino flourishes and it has cabaret nightclubs as well as discos.

La Baule-les-Pins, with expensive apartments, has been growing since the 1930s. The huge pine forest which backs on to La Baule, Forêt d'Escoublac, is very nice for walks and picnics.

La Baule can be expensive. It has some very good, expensive hotels and restaurants. But it remains cheaper than Deauville or Cannes. There are still many small family hotels.

TOURIST INFORMATION 8 place Victoria (40.24.34.44)
FESTIVALS Mid-July – Regattas; International show-jumping. Early August – Golf Grand Prix. Second fortnight in August – Grand Pardon et Semaine Bretonne. End August–early September – International Bridge Festival

HOTELS

Hermitage, 5 esplanade François-André (40.60.37.00). One of the great old 'palace' seaside hotels of France, with bedrooms splendidly modernised. In beautiful grounds facing the sea. Immaculate service. Called 'a Palace of Excellence'. It has several restaurants including one on the beach in July–August. The great restaurant is almost overpowering. Less charming, just as luxurious, with more ambitious, less classical cooking is 'Les Evens', which is now fashionable, with the 'best' people expecting the best. It opens on to the terrace by the swimming pool. ROOMS cost well over 1000–2000F. MEALS F–G. Open mid-April–mid-October.

Castel Marie-Louise, 1 ave Andrieux (40.60.20.60). Superb hotel, elegantly and tastefully furnished. In a park among flower gardens, with heated seawater pool and twenty-seven clay tennis courts 400 metres away. One of the best seaside hotels in France. Being quiet, it tends to attract the older rich or famous. Faces the sea. Relais et Chateaux hotel. Flag-carrier for superb old ultra-classic French cooking (Michelin star). ROOMS 1000F plus. MEALS G. Open all year.
La Palmeraie, 7 allée des Cormorans (40.60.24.41). Down-to-earth. Very charming Logis surrounded by flowers and palms, with vine-covered terrace. Rooms all renovated, many with balconies, some small. Meals cheap, choice limited. Must book. ROOMS D–E. MEALS C. Open 1 April–1 October.
Clemenceau, 42 ave Georges Clemenceau (40.60.21.33). Nice quiet cheap little family-run hotel near station. Good family cooking. ROOMS B–C. MEALS A–B. Shut Monday low-season.

RESTAURANTS

Espadon, 2 ave Plage (40.60.05.63). Great favourite with visitors and young locals. Magnificent 5th-floor position. Not luxurious but with that view over the beach and sea nobody looks at the décor. Good, fairly simple cooking, especially of shellfish. MEALS C (lunch in season), E–G. Shut Monday (in winter), Sunday evening; 2–31 January.
Ankou, 38 ave de l'Étoile (40.60.22.47). Little restaurant popular for true classic cooking. MEALS E–G. Shut Wednesday low-season; February (check – annual closing changes).
Henri, 161 ave de Maréchal-de-Lattre-de-Tassigny (40.60.23.65). Regular customers among locals for good classical cooking; lots of choice of menus. Also good *carte*. MEALS A–F. Open all year.

BÉCHEREL
[ILLE-ET-VILAINE]

On D20, to left off D137 Rennes-Dinan road, this charming village is built on a hill 176 metres high, with views towards

Dinan, Dol and Combourg. One kilometre west is Château de Caradeuc, one of the finest châteaux in France outside the Paris area and the Loire. It has been called, inevitably, Le Versailles Breton, mostly because of its splendid park.

Built in classical style, with a magnificent Court d'Honneur, it still belongs to the family of la Chalotais, great defenders of the liberty of Brittany.

The château was built by Anne-Nicolas de Caradeuc, Counsellor of the Brittany Parliament and was the birthplace in 1701 of Louis-René de Caradeuc de la Chalotais, procurator general of the king to the Brittany Parliament. A famous magistrate, he was one of those who opposed the Order of the Jesuits and persuaded the Brittany Parliament to vote for the dissolution of the Order in Brittany. La Chalotais wrote a report on the order in 1762 which was a huge success. Voltaire called it 'the only work of philosophy that has ever come from the bar'.

Duc d'Aiguillon, the Governor of Brittany, ordered parliament to reverse its decision. The counsellors refused. Louis XV summoned them to Versailles and sent three into exile. On returning to Rennes the counsellors resigned. It had become a matter of Brittany's liberty against Paris dictatorship.

In 1764 La Chalotais was arrested by Aiguillon, imprisoned in the Bull stronghold on Morlaix Bay, then banished from Brittany without trial. Eight years later the new King, Louis XVI, reinstated him and made him a marquis.

You can visit the park, which is absolutely delightful in the true French style, with ornamental ponds, wide paths, statues and monuments, designed to fit into wooded hills, with magnificent views over the Rance valley (open daily 1 April–end October; afternoons the rest of the year).

BEG-MEIL
[S. Finistère]

I have known this delightful little port and seaside resort for more than forty years and have watched sadly as its increasing discovery and popularity have flooded it with cars. But that is mainly along its huge sand beach in mid-summer, especially at weekends. Go outside the French school holidays and it returns to its old dreamier days when you meet only a few horse-riders in the dunes, the fine sands of the beach swallow the few dozen or less people sitting or walking, and the busiest spot is the little port called the Cale, still with fishing boats among the pleasure yachts. Mind you, you then miss the great festival of Bénédiction de la Mer (Blessing of the Sea) in early August. I saw that once. The whole village walked in procession from the church to the quay, many women in costume with *coiffes* and men carrying banners. There the priest got in a little motor-boat which sailed around and between the other boats, blessing them as he passed. Afterwards there was a fête with crêpes and lots of cider, dancing in Breton style to the *cornemuses* (Breton bagpipes) and in more modern style to jazzier instruments.

There is a small sandy beach by the port but the great beach backed by dunes faces the Atlantic. In front of this used to be a superb Grand Hotel, long since turned into apartments. But the little Logis de France where I used to stay, Le Thalamot, is still the same, friendly, cosy, with family cooking.

The *beg* of Beg-Meil means beak or headland. You can take boat trips in season from Beg-Meil to Concarneau (page 109). It is a good centre for walking, driving or cycling, for the area is rich in sweet chestnuts, cherries, apples, mimosa and even palms.

TOURIST INFORMATION (15 June–10 September–
98.94.97.47)

HOTEL

Thalamot (98.94.97.38). Run now by the grandchildren of the couple who were my first hosts. Four rooms added. Delightful atmosphere. French guests return annually. ROOMS C–E. MEALS B–F. Shut early October–mid-April.

BELLE-ÎLE
[MORBIHAN]

Brittany's largest island, out in the Atlantic 15km south of Quiberon, is indeed beautiful in a variety of ways. Into its area of

20km long by 10km across at its widest point it packs splendid and remarkably varied scenery – steep cliffs attacked by Atlantic waves, jagged rocks, caves where the sea rushes in, little coves of gold sand warm with sunshine and protected from winds, shady dells inland, pine-covered stretches with glimpses of the sea between the trees, and a lively harbour shared by pleasure boats, ferries from Quiberon and fishing boats.

It is strange how you can be blown by winds in one place, protected completely in another. The bathing beaches are mostly on the east coast. The beautiful sand beach at Port Donnant on the west coast is seductive – but too risky for bathing. The isle is called Belle-Île-en-Mer in Brittany because there is a Belle-Île-en-Terre on the Côtes-du-Nord.

Boats go from Port Maria on the Quiberon peninsula (information from Cie Morbihannaise et Nantaise de Navigation at Le Palais, Belle-Île (97.31.80.01). The journey takes forty-five minutes, with four boats a day in winter rising to twelve midsummer. There are summer excursions from several ports, especially Concarneau. The boats arrive at Le Palais, the chief town and port.

The island has for long attracted writers, poets, philosophers and actors and actresses. Sarah Bernhardt had a house there but the occupying Germans knocked it down in World War II to make a gun fortress. Invaders were drawn to the isle, too. The Romans took it and called it Vindilis. The first Welsh settlers called one settlement Bangor and the village has kept the name. It has a church built in 1074. The Saxons and Normans invaded annually for years. In 1006, after the Normans had settled and become Christians, it was given to the Abbey of Redon. The English attacked it on and off for five hundred years. They held the island for three weeks in 1572, so the French king sold it to the powerful Marechal de Retz, who greatly strengthened the fortifications. Around 1650 it was sold to the remarkable and notorious Fouquet, Louis XIV's Minister of Finance. He further strengthened the fortifications, adding two hundred cannons. He also had his own private navy there. His defences were not against the English. They were an insurance policy in case he was caught by the King defrauding the crown and the French nation. He had the title 'Marquis de

Belle-Île' added to his other titles. He must have had his hand very deep in the till, for he was mass-bribing people to help him succeed Mazarin as Chief Minister and he hired the greatest experts in the land to build his Château de Vaux-le-Vicomte – Le Vau as architect, Le Brun as decorator, Le Nôtre as gardener.

At the opening of the château, young King Louis XIV was so outraged by the extravagance of the château and the lavishness of entertainment that he left the party early, had d'Artagnan and his Musketeers arrest Fouquet at Nantes, confiscated the château, had Fouquet imprisoned for life and later took Le Brun and Le Nôtre to work on his new château at Versailles.

After the Dutch had attacked Belle-Île, Louis ordered Vauban, the greatest military architect, to make the citadelle at Le Palais impregnable. It is still much as Vauban built it. But the English took the isle again in 1761 and held it for two years until the Treaty of Paris, under which the English exchanged it for Nova Scotia. French-Canadian settlers from Nova Scotia were resettled on Belle-Île and some of the oldest families pride themselves on their Canadian blood. The museum in a 17th-century building contains interesting historical souvenirs and documents.

Much is made in French guides about the luxurious mansion which Sarah Bernhardt, the great actress, made from an old fortress above a creek near the northern lighthouse of Pointe des Poulins, but she was not very popular locally. The local children annoyed her. She lived theatrically. Her household included a boa-constrictor and a wildcat, she threatened taunting local children with a pistol and she would go out at six in the morning with a small negro servant and two mastiffs to shoot duck. The strongpoint with which the Germans replaced her house is called Fort Sarah Bernhardt.

A sandy isthmus joins the coast up there with Poulains Point lighthouse. There is a superb panoramic view over the bay of Quiberon and the mainland coast of Brittany. Grand Phare, the big lighthouse near the south coast, 3km from Bangor, was built on a rock in 1835. It is 84 metres above sea level and its beam can be seen from 120km out at sea – one of the most powerful in Europe. If the keeper is not too busy, you can visit it. There are tremendous views from its balcony over neighbouring tiny islands and to the coast around Lorient. Near Grand Phare is the very attractive little Port du Goulphar in a narrow inlet flanked by cliffs, like a miniature fjord. There is a superb modern hotel here, Castel Clara.

Port Donnant, up the west coast, has tall cliffs sheltering its fine sandy beach. Northwards from here is Côte Sauvage, with fantastically shaped and fearsome rocks. A cave is called Apothecary's Grotto because the cormorants which used to nest on the ledges were said to look like bottles on a chemist's shelf. Across the isle from it is the jolly little port of Sauzon on a river estuary. Yachtsmen use it. There's a nice walk to Pointe du Cardinal for good views. Le Palais has a beach, plage de Ramonette, but there is a better one 4km round the bay, plage de Bordardoué. Or go further south for 3km past Port Yorck, from which there are excellent views, to Les Grands Sables, a huge sand beach with safe swimming. The Dutch Admiral Van Tromp tried to land here in 1696 and there are some remains of the defences put up afterwards to discourage him from coming back. Further south, 500 metres from the cove of Port-Maria, is Locmaria, with two pictures in its church attributed to the Spanish painter Murillo.

HOTELS
[Le Palais]
Bretagne, quai Mace (97.31.80.14). Facing port; traditional hotel. Sea view from restaurant. ROOMS A–C. MEALS A–C. Open all year.

[Port-Goulphar]
Castel Clara (97.31.84.21). Gorgeous position above green cliffs. Elegant rooms. Relais et Châteaux hotel. Many rooms with balconies with sea views. Lovely views from dining-room. Regional, traditional cooking. ROOMS G. MEALS D (lunch), F. Open mid-March–mid-October.

[Sauzon]
Du Phare (97.31.60.36). Simple Logis; good value. ROOMS A–B. MEALS A–D. Shut October–31 March.

RESTAURANT
[Sauzon]

Le Contre Quai (97.31.60.60). In a fisherman's cottage facing the port. Straightforward cooking; very good fish. MEALS C (lunch), F. Shut mid-September–mid-June.

BELLE-ISLE-EN-TERRE
[CÔTES-DU-NORD]

Old town in attractive countryside where two rivers meet – the Léguer and the Guic. Between Morlaix and Guingamp on N12. Centre for shooting, fishing and excursions. At the Fête de Locmaria, on the third Sunday of July, a championship is held for the ancient traditional sport of Breton wrestling. Wrestlers wear short cloth breeches and blouses, exchange three loud kisses, then grab each other by the neck, trip each other and generally struggle in silence.

There are good views from Locmaria church, 1km west on D33. It contains a 16th-century rood screen. Superb views from the hill Menez-Bré, 9km north-east, with a steep 1km road at the end.

TOURIST INFORMATION Mairie (July and August mornings only 96.43.30.38)

HOTEL
Relais de l'Argoat (96.43.00.34). Simple. ROOMS B–C. MEALS A–E. Shut Sunday evenings, Monday; February.

BÉLON
[S. FINISTÈRE]

The Bélon, where the oysters come from. On the south bank of the Bélon river 17km south-east of Pont-Aven, it is a major oyster farming area. The oyster beds on the north bank can be seen at low tide.

BÉNODET
[S. Finistère]

Even if you hate crowds, you could easily be seduced by Bénodet. The resort has enormous charm. Its three sand beaches face south and the estuary of the Odet attracts so many yachts that the sea seems to be permanently *en fête* from early spring to autumn. Bénodet has many campsites (some say too many) but they are fairly unobtrusive and merely mean that there are more people on the sands and drinking in the cafés and bars at night. Many of the campers are booked by British companies such as Canvas Holidays who provide tents and equipment on site.

Its hotels are mostly old villas converted and family-run, very often with gardens. There is a lot of greenery for such a popular resort. The building of the toll bridge, 610 metres long, over the Odet river opened up the resort. Driving round or taking the little ferry seemed to take up quite a lot of precious holiday time. It has always been a busy yachting centre but the building of the Port de Plaisance has made life much easier for yachtsmen and its popularity grows. The casino is still thriving and there are several discos in summer.

Bénodet is a good centre for boat trips. The Odet is a beautiful river with wooded banks and the trips up and down it by Vedettes de l'Odet are a delight (phone 98.57.00.58 for information). The boats run from April to October and go from Bénodet to Quimper (one and a half hours one way) and on to Loctudy (an extra half an hour). There are restaurant boats with lunch or dinner cruisings. Boats go also to the isles of Glénan (*see* page 137). This takes one and three quarter hours but a hydrofoil does it in twenty-five minutes.

The little village of Letty just 2km east of Bénodet is a great place to learn to sail. It is on the edge of La Mer Blanche, the White Sea, a big expanse of water cut off from the main sea by a long dune with a passageway into the sea at one end. The sailing school here is much respected.

There are marvellous views over the Odet estuary and the sea to the lighthouse, the banks of the Odet and the Cornouaille Bridge. Over that bridge is Ste Marine, a delightful old fishing village grown popular now that you don't need to take a ferry. A stretch of sand beach runs for 6km to the little resort of Île-Tudy.

> TOURIST INFORMATION 51 ave de la Plage
> (98.57.00.14)
> FESTIVALS From June to September – numerous folklore festivals in or around the resort. Also 21 June – St Jean Bonfire; 14 July – July Festival; 14 August – Night of the Odet river; 3 September – Bénodet Pardon

HOTELS

Kastel-Moor et Ker Moor, ave de la Plage (98.57.05.01 and 98.57.04.48). Owned by the same people. Comfortable if uninspired rooms. Restaurant at Ker Moor. Heated pool, tennis, gardens. ROOMS E–F. MEALS C–G. Both open Easter–1 November.

Ancre de Marine, 5 ave de l'Odet (98.57.05.29). Nice little friendly hotel overlooking the port is one of the oldest in Bénodet. ROOMS C–E. MEALS B–E. Shut Monday (except July, August); 31 October–mid-March.

Gwel-Kaër, 3 ave de la Plage (98.57.04.38). Pleasant traditional seaside hotel; well furnished. Some rooms have balconies with sea views. Panoramic view from dining-room. ROOMS D–F. MEALS C–E. Shut Sunday evening, Monday in winter; mid-December–end January.

Minaret, on estuary corniche (98.57.03.13). Old Moroccan house with minaret and fine Moorish garden. Superb estuary views. Known for fish. ROOMS E. MEALS A–E. Shut Tuesday in April, May; 30 September–end March.

RESTAURANTS

Ferme du Letty, at Letty 2km south-east. (98.57.01.27). I knew it originally as a crêperie in an old farmhouse where I took my children. Now a restaurant known for freshest fish, starred by Michelin, ignored by Gault-Millau and disliked heartily by my favourite French restaurant critic, Marc Champérard. I'm English and neutral! MEALS E–F. Shut Tuesday low-season; 5–12 October; part February.

NEARBY HOTELS

Jeanne d'Arc, at Ste Marine, 52 rue de la Plage (98.56.32.70). They all agree about René Fargette's cooking and Michelin gives him a star, too. Local fish from this fishing port cooked the Breton way; most other dishes cooked the way of René's home country, Burgundy. Traditional and excellent. Nine ROOMS B–C. MEALS D–G. Shut Monday evening, Tuesday (except July, August); 1 October–end March.

Domaine de Kereven, at Clohars-Fouesnant (2½km north-east by D34) (98.57.02.46). Old family manor in big estate. Very comfortable; well run. ROOMS E. MEALS B (dinner only; for residents only May–September). Shut 1 October –end March.

BINIC
[CÔTES-DU-NORD]

A charming little resort in a break in the cliffs with a harbour and two beaches. Coastal fishing boats jostle pleasure yachts in the port where in winter the great cod fishing schooners used to anchor on their return from Newfoundland. You can see the beach and the port from Penthièvre jetty. The port is in the wide bay of St Brieuc to the north of St Brieuc itself, and has a tidal harbour. The main coastal road along this Côte d'Armor runs just behind it. It is increasingly popular with yachtsmen who want more atmosphere than the bigger modern marinas give. Its little museum has souvenirs of the adventurous Newfoundland fishing days but it also contains local traditional costumes and a collection of old postcards.

4km away, before you reach Trégomeur, is Zoo du Moulin de Richard, with animals such as llamas, gnus, wild goats, emus and boar running free and an island where chimpanzees, gorillas, baboons and rare birds live (open daily July–September; each afternoon in May, June; afternoons of Wednesday, Saturday, Sunday in March, April).

MARKET Thursday

HOTELS

Printania, quai Jean Bart (96.73.61.16). Simple, family-run hotel in port which specialises in fresh fish, especially shellfish. ROOMS A–B. MEALS A–D. Shut Friday low-season; January, February.

Le Galion, 4 ave Foch (96.73.61.30). One-star Logis. Good cooking. ROOMS A–C. MEALS A–F.

BLAIN
[LOIRE-ATLANTIQUE]

The Nantes-Brest canal separates this thriving market town among orchards 32km north-west of Nantes from the great old castle, Château de la Groulaie. Even the castle ruins are imposing and worth seeing, although the main remaining building is occupied by a school. The 16th-century Tour du Pont-Levis (drawbridge tower) with its conical roof overlooks now-dry moats. Beyond the outbuildings and school playground are the 18th-century King's Apartments (*Logis du Roi*). The Renaissance façade with tall dormer windows, brick patterned chimneys and impressive gargoyles is quite charming. The Constable's Tower (*Tour du Connétable*) to the right is as severe as the other is delightful. It was named after Olivier de Clisson, Constable of France (*see* Auray, page 66 and Josselin, page 156). He built the tower in 1380 on a fort founded in 1104. The de Rohan family took it over and Henri de Rohan, first Duc de Rohan, was born there in 1579. He was a great Protestant leader and son-in-law of the Duc de Sully, Henri IV's chief minister, whose financial reforms were responsible for restoring the French economy after the Wars of Religion. Rohan was a friend of Henri IV and took over the Protestant leadership after Henri was murdered. After Richelieu had taken Protestant La Rochelle in 1628 a price was put on Rohan's head and he fled to Venice. Richelieu had the fortifications of Blain demolished. He often demolished châteaux simply because he did not like anyone to have a better château than the one he had built in his new town Richelieu.

The Rohans owned the château until 1802. Their family

motto was '*Roi ne puis, Prince ne daigne, Rohan suis*' (I cannot be king, do not deign to be a prince. I am a Rohan).

The canal is used for pleasure boating. Just north is the forest of Gâvre with 4410 hectares of oak, beech and pine.

TOURIST INFORMATION place Jean-Guilhard (40.87.15.11)

HOTEL

Port, 6 quai Surcouf (40.79.01.22). Logis de France. ROOMS A–C. MEALS B–E. Shut Sunday evening, Monday; last half February.

BONO
[MORBIHAN]

Village on the Bono river estuary where it flows into Rade d'Auray in the Gulf of Morbihan. It is 5km south of Auray on the D101 and from the new roadbridge there is a lovely view over the village, the Bono river, the port and the old suspension bridge. The white tiles you will see piled up are used for collecting oysters. Tiny oysters measuring about a third of a millimetre float with the current until they reach these lime-washed tiles and attach themselves to them. After about eight months they are taken off the tiles and placed in beds. After two or three years, when they are the right size, they are taken to nurseries for a year for maturing. After another year, they go through a purification centre to wash out sand and other impurities.

Bono church has modern stained-glass windows.

BOURBRIAC
[CÔTES-DU-NORD]

South of Guingamp in almost flat country, this small town has a church with a towering belfry 66 metres high. Churches have stood here since the 11th century, with bits of each remaining.

The west tower was started in 1535. The porch and lower floor are in Flamboyant style, the rest of the tower is Renaissance, and the spire was added in 1867. The granite tomb of St Briac inside is invoked as a cure for epilepsy.

The church is surrounded by gardens.

BRÉHAT, ÎLE DE
[CÔTES-DU-NORD]

A delightful calm little island off the north coast from Paimpol, it has become rather popular in high summer, but even at that time it is a refuge from motor cars, which are banned. You walk, use a bike, or hitch a lift on a tractor.

Its rocks are pinkish and look colourful against the changing moods and colours of the sea. The island has a mild winter climate and mimosa, oleander, myrtle and figs grow in the open. Rain is scarce.

The island's fishermen were fishing the Newfoundland banks before Columbus 'discovered' America and locals say that one of their sea-captains, Coatanlen, told Columbus about the New World eight years before he sailed to it, and showed him the course used by the fishermen.

The island is really two isles joined by a narrow tongue of land and a bridge built in the 18th century. It is only 3½km long and half as wide. Most of its coast is of granite rock and it is surrounded by eighty-six islets and reefs.

You reach it by boat from la Pointe de l'Arcouest in ten minutes (all the year) or from St-Quay-Portrieux in July, August (1½ hours). For timetables phone Vedettes de Bréhat – 96.55.86.99. Boats normally land at Port-Clos, a ten-minute walk from Le Bourg, the main village grouped round a small square shaded by plane trees, with a town hall and a 12th-century church, altered in the 18th century. The church has an unusual wall-belfry in pink granite.

There are villas and gardens scattered round the isle, joined by a labyrinth of paths running from the one road which runs north from Port Clos to within 500 metres of the Phare du Paon lighthouse at the north. The occupying Germans dynamited this in World War II.

Across the island is the Chapel of St Michel, on a rock, serving as a landmark for boats. There are views over the coast and island, especially the bay of the Corderie lying between the two halves of the island. Ships used this bay as a port long ago.

The northern part of the isle is wilder, with fields surrounded by stone walls, moors and a wild coastline of cliffs, creeks and tiny bays.

Two beaches in the south, Petit et Grand Guerzido, are basically shingle but have some sand. On the southern point near Port Clos is a wood with views to Île Béniguet.

There are thirty-three bedrooms on the island and a campsite for a hundred tents.

If the weather is suitable you can have a fascinating boat trip round the island showing you the variety of the coastline, the changing colours of the sea and the ferocity of the waves, breaking on the beautiful northern rocks.

The north has been compared to Ireland's Isle of Aran. Some local families believe that they are descended from the English who occupied the island in the 15th and 16th centuries.

HOTELS
Bellevue et Terrasse, Port Clos (96.20.00.05). Right on the port, facing mainland; modernised. Famous for shellfish. Book ahead. ROOMS C–E. MEALS A–G. Shut 15 November–about 20 April.
Vieille Auberge, Bourg (96.20.00.24). ROOMS demi-pension only around 280–300F. MEALS B–G. Open spring holiday–November.

BREST
[*See* major towns, page 39]

BRIEC-DE-L'ODET
[S. Finistère]

Charming little town on the bank of the Odet river NE of Quimper. Nice quiet spot with trout fishing.

HOTEL
Midi, 10 rue Gén-de-Gaulle (98.57.90.10). Friendly Logis. Regional cooking. Rooms A–B. Meals A–E. Shut Sunday evening, Monday except July, August; 10–26 September; part February.

BRIGNOGAN-PLAGES
[N. Finistère]

Little resort on the north coast, west of Roscoff in Pontusval bay. Loyal French visitors return yearly and people of Brest escape there. It has a huge beach and other little beaches with names like du Petit Nice and all with fine white sand. They are divided by impressive rocks, and are good hideaways.

Eastward along the coast are sand dunes. Walk along the coast westward through country speckled with granite blocks and just after Chardons Bleus beach you reach Pontusval Point. Halfway there is Men Marz, a fine menhir eight metres high, topped by a cross.

Eastward along the coast past Lividic beach and round the bay called Grève de Goulven you find a 15th- to 16th-century church with a really beautiful Renaissance bell-tower, crowned with a pointed steeple. The inside of the church is beautiful, too.

Tourist Information Brignogan Syndicat d'Initiative, rue Gén-de-Gaulle, July–15 September (98.83.41.08)

HOTELS
Castel Régis, plage du Garo (98.83.40.22). Lovely position on a near-island of rocks lashed by the sea, yet in green setting with rooms in bungalows around the park. Swimming pool. Equipped

as a holiday hotel (tennis, mini-golf, sauna). Good restaurant leaning towards classic-style cooking. ROOMS D–F. MEALS C–E. Open mid-March–1 October. Restaurant shut Wednesday lunch.
Ar Reder Mor, 36 rue Gén-de-Gaulle (98.83.40.09). Simple, good value Logis. ROOMS B–D. MEALS B–C. Shut 1 November–1 May.

BROUALAN
[ILLE-ET-VILAINE]

Hamlet south-east of Dol-de-Bretagne with a 15th-century hilltop chapel. It was built by a lady of the nearby Château de Landal after a vow. The château, beside a charming lake, was built in the Middle Ages and partly rebuilt in the 19th century. It has a residence with four towers, all with conical roofs, two of which were built in the 15th century.

BRUZ
[ILLE-ET-VILAINE]

Country town well planned. The beautiful church of rose-veined schist has a square tower with a pointed spire, and pleasantly decorated stained-glass windows.

It is south-west of Rennes very near to the Vilaine river. Over a river bridge about 1km west is the elegant 17th-century Château de Blossac at the end of a fine avenue and surrounded by lakes and gardens. Down the river is Le Böel with a riverside promenade walk where the Vilaine runs between hills. On the far bank is an old mill.

RESTAURANTS
La Rabine, 3 route de Redon (99.52.60.52). Good value; best among a rather disappointing lot in Bruz. Traditional dishes. MEALS A–D. Shut Monday.

Auberge Moulin du Boël, at Boël (99.42.27.00). Good value. MEALS B–E. Shut Sunday evening; 14–28 February.

CALLAC-DE-BRETAGNE
[CÔTES-DU-NORD]

Lovely area of 'wild Brittany' 29km south-west of Guincamp with innumerable rivers and streams (Hyères, Aulne, Guic, Blavet). In a lake surrounded by forest and in the river Hyères which goes through the town are canoeing, sailing and fishing – 200km of trout fishing rivers around here. A stud farm for horses has a bronze statue of a stallion, 'Naous', at the gate. Breeding place, too, for Breton spaniels. At a melancholy spot on the Bulat-Pestivien road by the Burthulet chapel, local legend says that the Devil died of cold.

HOTEL
Garnier, facing station (96.45.50.09). Very simple; food good value. ROOMS A–B. MEALS A–D. Shut Monday; mid-September–mid-October.

CAMARET-SUR-MER
[S. FINISTÈRE]

This little port at the end of the wild Crozon peninsula is full of life and colour. It is the most important langoustine port in France, and you can watch the boats landing them on the quayside. But it is a happy little beach resort, too, with three well-sheltered sand and shingle beaches. It is protected by a natural breakwater of large pebbles called Sillon de Camaret.

The port is on the western end of the peninsula called La Presque-île de Crozon, with the Rade de Brest on the north side, the Bay of Douarnenez to the south, and Crozon itself in the centre. The resort of Morgat is south of Crozon. It is a popular sailing centre.

On the sillon is built a 17th-century chapel called Chapelle Notre-Dame-de-Rocamadour. It was restored after a fire in 1910. It seems strange to find a chapel in Finistère named after a shrine in Lot in the south-west of France. But Rocamadour was a very important shrine for pilgrims from all over France and outside it, and it seems that a lot of the pilgrims from northern countries landed at Camaret on their way to it. An important pardon based on the chapel is held on the first Sunday of September.

At the point of the sillon is a fort called Château Vauban, built by Sébastien Le Prestre de Vauban, the military engineer who revolutionized siege warfare in the 17th century. It has a look-out over the port, the approaches to Brest and Pointe des Espagnols to the north. It is now a small historic and maritime museum.

To the south-west (3½km) is the remarkable Pointe de Penhir, where a memorial to the Bretons of the Free French Forces operating from Britain in World War II stands on the cliff 150 metres from the road. From the platform at the end of the point you can look straight down to the sea 70 metres below. The setting and the panorama are magnificent. There are paths to other views if you have a head for heights, don't mind scrambling over rocks and are wearing non-slip shoes.

The Crozon peninsula used to be a sort of advance defence post for Brest. So it was attacked often by the English, Spaniards and Dutch. Five years after Vauban fortified it in 1689, an Anglo-Dutch fleet tried to land an invading force but Vauban had done his job well, as usual. Hidden batteries played havoc with the enemy ships, and the first landing force was decimated. Dragoons attacked them after the guns had scattered them, then local militia laid into them with pitchforks and scythes. 1200 Anglo-Dutch were killed, 450 taken prisoner and the French lost only forty-five wounded. Most of Vauban's fortifications gave way to Hitler's 'Atlantic Wall'.

In Camaret Bay in 1801, an American engineer who had settled in France, Robert Fulton, carried out a submarine experiment for the French government. He had built a small vessel which, with a crew of five, could travel at two knots under water propelled by jointed oars, and could remain submerged for six hours. The idea was to fix a bomb containing 100 lb of explosive to a ship's hull, and explode it with a time mechanism after the 'sub' had got away. A British frigate kindly dropped anchor in the bay and Fulton saw his chance. But before his 'sub' reached it, the frigate had upped-anchor and sailed away. The first practical sub did not operate until the end of the 19th century.

TOURIST INFORMATION Quai Toudouze (98.27.93.60)
FESTIVALS Fourth Sunday in July – Fête. First Sunday in September – Pardon

HOTELS

France (98.27.93.06). Modern, in old Breton style; on harbour quay. Delicious fish. Lobster from *viviers*. Bedrooms pleasantly furnished; some in annexe. Interesting paintings and tapestries. ROOMS D–F. MEALS C–F. Shut Friday low-season; 11 November–1 April.
Styvel (98.27.92.74). Cheap. ROOMS B–D. MEALS B–D. Shut 1 October–31 March.

CANCALE
[ILLE-ET-VILAINE]

The only time I was the worse for food rather than wine was in the little port of Cancale, east of St Malo. I could not drive away. Lobsters, clams, mussels, most fish are so plentiful that they almost nudge out the visitors from Cancale, but, above all – oysters. Bred at sea, farmed in pounds (*parcs*) down on the muddy sands, they are sold in tens of thousands to wholesalers; in boxes to retailers; in dozens to travellers from stalls on the quayside and in fiercely competitive restaurants which line the quay.

Let's face it – Cancale is not a pretty place but it *is* interesting and satisfying. And more Muscadet and Gros Plant wine must be consumed there than anywhere in France, for just about everyone drinks a bottle or more with their oysters.

I arrived innocently once to find the oyster festival at its peak. Two restaurateurs recognised me. Mountains of shellfish appeared and there was no way of avoiding a single oyster, hillock of moules marinière or stuffed clam. Luckily I was driving a motor-caravan. I waved goodbye but round a corner I drove into a field, pulled the curtains and went to bed. Next morning I made coffee and escaped.

Louis XIV had Cancale oysters sent to him at Versailles twice a week by special convoy. In Napoleon's day forty-eight million oysters were eaten in one season.

In the 1920s a mysterious disease destroyed the Cancale native spat, so now the tiny oysters are brought from Auray and fed in Cancale on the rich plankton of the bay.

The oyster boats (*Challand*) go out at exceptionally low tides to the oyster parcs to tend them. The oysters are kept two or three miles out from Cancale for two years or so. Then they are brought to the parcs you can see from the quayside for cleaning – mostly of the mud in which they live out at sea. A machine is used for this now. A conveyor belt carries the oysters through a jet of clean water.

Oysters are said to be an aid to convalescence, a cure for depression, for anaemia and pregnancy disorders. They are also, of course, said to be aphrodisiacs. Casanova must have thought so, for he ate fifty each evening to keep up his strength. If he opened them himself, I bet his hands were cut to ribbons.

It is said that Claude Debussy wrote his orchestral sketches *La Mer* after sailing over from St Lunaire for an oyster lunch in Cancale and being caught in a storm on the return journey.

The old port La Houle is alongside the oyster-cleaning beds and from its jetty, La Fenêtre, at low tide you can see the far-away oyster beds or at high tide get a good view of the bay. There is another good view from Pointe de Hock, between the beds and the beach. From the Point you can take the walk, Sentier des Douaniers (the Custom Officers' path), above the beach.

There's a wonderful view from Pointe du Grouin, 4½km to the north of Cancale, right over the Bay of Mont-St-Michel. The wild rocky headland looks down at the sea from a height of 40 metres. At low tide you can take a path to a cliffside cave, 10 metres high and 30 metres deep. The island opposite, l'Île des

Landes, is a seabird and wildlife sanctuary, which must be somewhat vexing to the Cancale fishermen.

There are very good views from Hotel La Pointe du Grouin (*see* Hotels).

Between Cancale and Pointe de Grouin is a tiny hidden beach called Port-Mer with a nice bar-restaurant for eating fish.

TOURIST INFORMATION Syndicat d'Initiative, rue du Port (99.89.63.72)

MARKET Daily

HOTELS

Pointe de Grouin, at Pointe de Grouin (99.89.60.55). Panoramic views from the dining-room. Yves Simon cooks very well. ROOMS C–E. MEALS C–F. Open 30 March–30 September.

Phare, at the port (99.89.60.24). All local fish and good fish soup in generous portions. Eight bedrooms. ROOMS D–E. MEALS A–F. Shut Thursdays except midsummer; 30 November–1 February.

Continental, at the port (99.89.60.16). Try their lobster *à l'Armoricaine*. Rooms vary. Overlooks harbour. ROOMS E–G. MEALS C–E. Shut Monday; also Tuesday lunch except midsummer; mid-November–mid-December; end February–mid-March.

RESTAURANTS

De Bricourt, 1 rue Duguesclin (99.89.64.76). One of the best restaurants in Brittany; two deserved Michelin stars. Former engineering chemist Olivier Roellinger is a superb chef. He cooks so delicately and arranges food so attractively that you could mistake it for nouvelle cuisine but for portions. He scours markets and countryside for the best produce, so dishes change almost daily. Excellent *cotriade* (Breton fish soup-stew). Heavenly desserts. Pretty garden with pond and rare ducks. 18th-century house. Now has six bedrooms, too. M. Roellinger was trained at the Savoy in London and is now adviser to the Meridien in Boston. ROOMS G. MEALS B (weekdays); F–G. Shut 2 Jan–15 March. Restaurant shut Tuesday, Wednesday; 15 December–15 March.

Armada, quai Thomas (99.89.60.02). Another on the quayside with fine view and superb fish. ROOMS B–E. Shut Sunday evening, Monday except July–August; evenings in mid-winter.

CARANTEC
[N. Finistère]

Between the two estuaries of the Penzé and Morlaix rivers is a long wooded peninsula with Carantec at the end of it – an attractive family resort of little white houses with two long sandy beaches and various small sandy bays littered with rocks. Oysters are farmed here.

Islands and reefs dot the sea. An isle which you can reach on foot at low tide is Callot, an excellent place for fishing. The Chapel of Notre-Dame built on it was founded in the 16th century as a celebration by locals for a victory over Danish pirates. It was rebuilt in the 17th and 19th centuries. The statue of the Virgin draws big crowds to the pardons at Whitsun and on the first Sunday after 15 August. Carantec's church is modern. Pardons are held there on the third Sunday in July. From Pen-Lan Point 1½km south of Carantec, are long coastal views. But you must walk for about fifteen minutes on a track to reach it. Good walking area and excellent sailing in the sheltered bay.

TOURIST INFORMATION rue A. Louppe, April –15 September (98.67.00.43)

MARKET Thursday June–September; first Thursday in the month low-season

HOTELS

Pors Pol, plage Pors Pol (98.67.00.52). Family-run for families. Nice garden overlooking the beach. Excellent value cheap menus. Demi-pension only high-season. ROOMS B–D. MEALS A–E. Open spring holidays and mid-May–mid-September.

Falaise, plage Keleur (98.67.00.53). Big mansion overlooking beach with good views over Morlaix Bay. Cooking praised. ROOMS B–D. MEALS B–E. Open spring holidays and early-May–mid-September.

CARHAIX-PLOUGUER
[N. Finistère]

A pretty inland town near the cool valley of the Hyères, with good fishing on the Nantes–Brest canal.

In Roman days, Carhaix was an important centre. Now it is a dairy town for the cattle-farming area around it. There are one or two fine old buildings, notably the Renaissance Maison du Sénéchal, which houses the tourist office.

On the tympanum of the church tower doorway is a statue of St Trémeur, the saint who revenged the killing of his mother by his father Cornorre, the original Bluebeard (*see* Quimperlé, page 224).

The statue most revered in Carhaix is in the main square. It is of the soldier-scholar La Tour d'Auvergne (1743–1800). In fact he was born in Carhaix as Théophile Malo Corret. His widowed mother was determined that he should be a soldier and his own main interest was the Breton language. The only way of getting on well in the French Army was to be an aristocrat. The aristocratic officers wore blue-and-red uniforms and were called 'Reds' and the bourgeois officers wore blue and were called 'Blues'. They were unlikely to rise above lieutenant. As the son of a lawyer he was very bourgeois, even if he had been brought up in one wing of Château de Kergoat at St Hernin, a few miles south-west of Carhaix. Through research he discovered that an ancestor, Adèle Corret, had been the mistress of Duc Henri de Bouillon, Prince de la Tour d'Auvergne. So he cheekily asked the current Duc Godefoy de Bouillon if he could use the name. The Duc must have had a strong sense of humour, for he told Corret that he could not only use the name but carry the family arms, but with a bar denoting bastardy. So he became La Tour d'Auvergne-Corret. D'Artagnan of the Three Musketeers had done much the same to advance himself. But it did Corret very little good, for he was forty before he got any promotion (to second-class captain) and his only fighting, until he distinguished himself against the English in Minorca when he was thirty-seven, was in a duel in which he was badly wounded. He studied languages and worked on a book on Celtic origins and language.

When the Revolution came he was in Brittany on convalescent leave. Most officers, bourgeois or not, were against the Revolution. They had, after all, taken an oath to serve the King. Rather than take an oath to the new Constitution, his colonel and other officers in his regiment emigrated. He stayed and was rewarded with command of the 80th Grenadiers. To show his egalitarian stance, he fought on foot with his soldiers against the Austrians in the Alps when his rank entitled him to fight on horseback. This gesture got him a good Press in Paris, and he was offered the rank of colonel in another regiment, but refused.

He fought the Spaniards until he was fifty then got permission to retire to Carhaix to complete his work, *Origines Gauloises*, on Celtic origins. He went overland from Bayonne to Bordeaux, then picked up a ship to sail to Brest. He was shipwrecked off Camaret, picked up by an English frigate and taken as a prisoner-of-war to Bodmin in Cornwall, where he was paroled and allowed to wander the streets wearing French uniform and sword. He spent his time in Cornwall making notes about the similarities with Welsh and Breton speakers, researching in public libraries, and he started a French-Celtic dictionary. Then he was exchanged for an English officer of similar rank. At fifty-four, to help an old friend's son to get out of the army he volunteered to exchange with him and returned to the Rhine Army as an ordinary soldier for a year. The boy he replaced was the last of a family of twenty-two. All the others had died in Napoleon's campaigns of 'glory'.

Two years later Tour d'Auvergne rejoined as a Captain First Class, fought in the Swiss Campaign, and retired yet again. Then at fifty-seven, he wrote to Napoleon volunteering as an ordinary soldier to replace another young man in the army. Napoleon sent him a sabre of honour and appointed him a seat in the Legislative Council but he refused. He was sent to the Front to fight the Austrians as a morale booster to Napoleon's rather downcast army. He was killed in Bavaria. The French Army went into official mourning. His great work on Celtic origins includes quotations in Catalan, Frisian, Icelandic and Persian.

In 1889 his remains were re-interred in the Panthéon. The

exploits of La Tour d'Auvergne are told in bas relief round the base of the statue in Carhaix. Each year on the last Sunday in June, the town holds a fête to celebrate his extraordinary deeds.

Another man not so welcome around Carhaix in his day and uncelebrated now was Guy de la Fontanelle. A Breton educated in Paris, he joined the Catholic League, the army set up by fanatical Catholics to fight Protestants but which turned into an organisation of thugs who plundered and terrorised the country. They ran riot in 1589 in the hill-country around Carhaix, turning it into a wilderness, then captured Île Tristan off Dournenez and used it as a headquarters to plunder and sack the coast (*see* Dournenez, page 123). 5½km south of Carhaix is the little Port-de-Carhaix on the Nantes–Brest canal.

TOURIST INFORMATION Syndicat d'Initiative, rue Brizeux (98.93.04.42)
MARKET Saturday
FESTIVALS *see above*

HOTEL

Gradlon, 12 boul. République (98.93.15.22). Modern but vaguely Breton style. Rooms comfortably functional. Meals praised. ROOMS D. MEALS A–D. Restaurant shut Friday night, Saturday lunch low-season.

RESTAURANT

Auberge de Poher, at Port-de-Carhaix (98.99.51.18). Pretty; Breton dishes; large portions. Good value cheapest menu. MEALS A–E. Shut Monday; February.

CARNAC
[MORBIHAN]

Our great-grandfathers went to Carnac to marvel at Alignements du Ménec – the lines of stones 1km long and 100 metres wide with 1009 menhirs, with one as tall as four metres and Alignements de Kermario, more than 1km long.

Most people go these days for the bathing at Carnac Plage,

over 2km long and one of the finest on the south coast of Brittany. But they, too, marvel at the mystery of the stones, for even the greatest experts on prehistory have never discovered who put them there and why. Of course, religious rites are suspected, but the astronomical accuracy of the placing of the stones has led to a more modern theory that they were giant observatories linked to the movements of stars and planets, giving the priests knowledge of dates for sowing seed and harvesting. Gustave Flaubert, who said last century that there was more nonsense written about the site than there were stones standing on it, poked fun at the theorists by putting up several theories of his own, from marking graves of warriors to marking the spot to build huts and to the super theory that they were giant tent-pegs or supports put up by Caesar's Roman Legions to stop their tents blowing away! His certain conclusion was that they are large stones!

It is also certain that there are more than 4000 of them, some weighing up to 350 tons, and that they have been placed with great precision. Their impressiveness is their sheer numbers, and they can look sinister in shadowy moonlight or dusk mist.

There are two types – single stones (menhirs) and dolmens, with two uprights and a horizontal stone laid across them. Dolmens were almost certainly burial chambers, covered with mounds of earth. Archaeologists believe that they were erected at much the same time as those at Stonehenge – 3500–1800 BC. The local legend of the stones is very Celtic. St Cornelius (Cornély in French), the patron saint of horned cattle and of Carnac, was an early pope, martyred around AD 250. Fleeing from the pagan armies attacking Rome, he came to Gaul and to Carnac in a chariot drawn by oxen. At Carnac he saw the pagan army still chasing him. So he cursed them and they turned to stone, still in the columns in which they were marching.

The Alignements du Ménec begin with a semi-circle of seventy stones partly surrounding Carnac village. These and the Alignements de Kermario are to the north of the village. Other lines of menhirs and tumuli (barrows) lie beyond. On the north edge of the village is the vast tumulus of St Michel, 120 metres by 12 metres, with a great chamber and connecting galleries leading off to smaller chambers. On top is a chapel (St Michel), a calvary and a *table d'orientation* with views over the stones, the coast and isles beyond. (Tumulus guided tours, Easter–September.)

Most of the finds from the tumulus are in the most interesting Musée de préhistoire J. Miln-Le Rouzic in the village centre (shut Tuesday except July and August). Miln was a rich Scottish archaeologist who made most of the finds locally and Le Rouzic was his assistant who took over when he died. Especially interesting are polished axes made of rare stones, necklaces and pendants made of callais (a blue stone like turquoise) and vases with gold-leaf ornaments. Miln had his headquarters in Carnac at the Hôtel des Voyageurs from 1873 until 1880. He died in 1881.

The charming little church of St Cornély has a relief of the saint grinning between two oxen. One of the main festivals in Brittany is the Pardon of St Cornély on the second Sunday of September. It used to be a big cattle fair.

Carnac Plage is a mere 3km away and has such a splendid beach of fine sand that I am surprised that it did not become a popular resort earlier. It is very modern and still expanding. There have been hotels here for years but not on the present scale, nor so many apartments. There's a yachting harbour now, too, and good small yacht sailing, protected by the long Quiberon peninsula.

You can hear the Gregorian Chant at the Benedictine nuns' abbey of St Michel de Kergonan, 3km away (approach 2km on right by D781 towards Lorient) and at the Benedictine monks' abbey of St Anne-de-Kergonan 3½km away – D781, then D768 towards Auray).

TOURIST INFORMATION 74 ave Druides (end March–end September – 97.52.13.52)

FESTIVALS Third Sunday in August – Fête des Menhirs; second Sunday in September – St Cornély Pardon.

HOTELS

Diana, 21 boul. Plage (97.52.05.38). Luxuriously furnished, even to the beach chairs; expensive. Opposite beach; garden; nice terrace. Rooms vary a little. ROOMS F–G. MEALS F. Open spring holidays and end April–early October.

Lann Roz, 39 ave de la Poste (97.52.10.48). Delightful restaurant with fifteen rooms in attractive garden. Real regional cooking of local products; especially good fish. Rooms in a setting of greenery. ROOMS E. MEALS C–F. Shut 3 January–3 February.
Marine, Carnac village, 4 place la Chapelle (97.52.07.33). Traditional hotel with medium prices. ROOMS C–F. MEALS C–F. Restaurant shut 1 January–1 February.

CHAMPEAUX
[ILLE-ET-VILAINE]

9km north-west of Vitré. True Breton hamlet with typical village square – old houses, a *mairie*, and old church standing around a well. The 14th- to 15th-century collegiate church has Renaissance canopied stalls and two good stained-glass windows, especially the Renaissance Calvary. Tombs of the Espinay family who built the church include an elegant one in white stone and polychrome marble, with two naked figures of Guy d'Espinay and his wife. The Espinay Château (14th to 15th centuries) is to the south.

The well at Champeaux

CHÂTEAUBRIANT
[LOIRE-ATLANTIQUE]

The castle of this town on the edge of Brittany and Anjou, 55km from Rennes, 70km from Nantes, was the scene of an appalling revenge in the 16th century.

Françoise de Foix was married at the age of eleven to Jean de Laval, Count of Châteaubriant. As she grew older, she grew in beauty, spirit and culture and he grew very jealous. He started to build for her a Renaissance addition to the feudal castle. But he kept her in the castle away from the world.

François I, the king who spent much of his life hunting game and women, heard of her beauty and asked to see her. Laval took no notice. When François insisted, Laval went to court without her. She was, he explained, a weak-minded recluse. And he told her not to follow him unless she received a certain signal. His valet sold the secret to the king. One day Laval saw his wife getting out of her carriage, received royally by François. Laval was so angry that he fled back to his castle, leaving Françoise behind and, of course, François seduced Françoise, who had a child. As his mistress she had considerable influence at court until he was taken prisoner in Madrid. On his return she was pushed out of the royal bed by the Duchess of Étampes, who nastily persuaded the king to make Françoise return all the jewellery which he had given her. The rejected Françoise got her revenge by having the jewels melted down and returned in the form of a bullion. But she had to leave court with her child and return to Châteaubriant. Laval took a terrible revenge. He shut her and her seven-year-old daughter in a room totally hung with black. The child soon died. Françoise lasted ten years. Then, it is said, he ran a sword through her. All this time he had been continuing to rebuild the castle. You can see the result – a lovely building with dormer windows. Part of it is the public library.

The feudal part of it had been partly dismantled by the French fighting the Bretons in the 15th century. A few ramparts, a fortified gate, a powerful keep raised on a height and a recently-restored chapel remain. In this older castle another Duchess had died dramatically.

Geoffrey de Châteaubriant went with Louis IX on the 1248 Crusade. He was wounded and taken prisoner by the Saracens. His wife Sibylle thought that he was dead. Two years later he arrived home. She died of joy in his arms. It was from the Châteaubriant-Beaufort branch of the family that the writer Châteaubriand was descended. The château is illuminated June to September. (Visits to castle mid-June to mid-September except Sunday morning, Tuesday. Gardens open all year.)

A more modern tragedy is remembered by a monument on the road to Pouancé recalling 20 October 1941, when the Nazis shot twenty-seven local people in reprisal for the French Resistance's shooting of Colonel Holz, the Nantes garrison commander. They shot twenty-one people of Nantes at the same time.

The red sandstone St Jean-de-Béré church in the north-west suburb was founded by the Benedictines in the 11th century.

TOURIST INFORMATION rue de Couéré (40.81.04.53)
MARKET Wednesday

HOTEL

Ferrière, route de Nantes, 2km south on D178 (40.28.00.28). Elegant 19th-century manor; turreted, creeper-clad in gardens and three hectare park. Quiet. Terrace for summer eating. Good value. ROOMS D–E. MEALS B–E. Shut Sunday evening in winter; 24–6 December.

RESTAURANT

Poêlon d'Or, 30bis rue 11 Novembre (40.81.43.33). Excellent classical cooking; welcoming atmosphere. MEALS B (weekdays), C–E. Shut Saturday evening, Sunday evening low-season; 25–31 December, part February.

CHÂTEAUGIRON
[ILLE-ET-VILAINE]

A very nice little town 16km south-east of Rennes on D463. It is built on slopes rising to the castle which has a great separate keep. Built in the 15th century, the castle was what history books call 'much disputed' and was knocked around and rebuilt regularly from the 13th to 18th centuries. In 1592 the odious Duc de Mercoeur, the Catholic League leader, captured it and hanged the whole garrison, making his name as hated around this countryside as it was in so much of Brittany.

MARKET Thursday

HOTEL

Cheval Blanc et Château (99.37.40.27). A fine old-style hotel in the main street (get a back room). Wide range of menu prices. Good value. ROOMS A–C. MEALS A–D. Shut Sunday evening low-season.

RESTAURANT

Aubergade (99.37.41.35). Very good restaurant with meals for most pockets. Some critics find some dishes over-complicated, but you can take your choice. Nothing complicated about excellent lamb noisettes. MEALS A (weekdays), B–F. Shut Sunday evening, Monday.

CHÂTEAULIN
[S. FINISTÈRE]

Very pleasant little town famous for salmon fishing, on a bend of the canalised river Aulne, surrounded by wooded hills. The tide does not quite reach it but stops a little lower downstream at Port Launay, where small sea-going boats tie up to the quay. Châteaulin has two lines of shady quays and locks with small waterfall overflows which the spawning salmon try to leap. Fishing is done mostly 10–15 metres below the lock (fly or spinner). Early months of the year are most popular.

There are some very attractive riverside walks and drives around here; also attractive roads north-west and especially westward to the Ménez Hom regional park and Crozon peninsula (*see* page 116).

South-west towards Douarnenez (7km) is Cast, with an attractive sculpture in front of the church of St Hubert with his squire and two basset hounds kneeling beside a tiny horse and in front of a stag bearing a cross. Hubert was an aristocrat leading a lazy life of luxury until he saw this stag with a crucifix between its horns. He was converted and in AD 708 became Bishop of Liège.

TOURIST INFORMATION quai Cosmao (April– September – 98.86.02.11) & Mairie (low-season – 98.86.10.05)

MARKET Thursday

HOTELS

Ducs de Lin, 1½km on Ancienne route de Quimper (98.86.04.20). On a hill above the Aulne river which runs alongside the grounds. Salmon from the river are grilled over charcoal in a granite fireplace and served with *beurre blanc*. Superb! Louis Le Meur himself does the grilling of meat and fish and he is coming up to seventy – not much younger than me. Try too anything in puff pastry (*feuilletés*) whether for a starter or pâtisserie dessert. Terrace for fine river views. Six pleasant rooms (book ahead). ROOMS E. MEALS C–F. Shut Monday lunch in summer; Sunday evening, Monday rest of year; 1–15 March; 25 September–9 October.

Bon Accueil, Port Launay, 2km north-east by D770 (98.86.15.77). More riverside views; excellent simple cooking at reasonable prices. You can park your boat alongside! 59 rooms here. ROOMS A–D. MEALS A–E. Shut Sunday evening, Monday in winter; January.

CHÂTEAUNEUF-DU-FAOU
[S. FINISTÈRE]

If war should ever again threaten Finistère, look at dawn from Châteauneuf-du-Faou to the Montagnes Noires. If up there on the crests of the hills you see thousands of *fantassins* (foot soldiers) and knights in order of battle, then reach for your arms or flee. It is, they say, the army of King Arthur come to defend his land, and they have said so for more than a thousand years.

CHÂTEAUNEUF-DU-FAOU

Do not wonder that you should see King Arthur here, for La Cornouaille lies over those hills. This is called Les Monts de Cornouaille and the name was given to it by the Celts who fled here from Cornwall and the Anglo-Saxon invaders of Britain. And the story of King Arthur's knights, round table, holy grail (Saint-Graal in French) and all, has been part of Breton folklore at least since the 6th century. (The knight with the pure heart is called Perceval.)

The town is a calm, restful place on the slopes of a hill above the Aulne river where it is canalised as part of the Nantes–Brest canal, and, as at Châteaulin, the salmon come up the river to spawn and the fishermen come to catch them. There are pike and various white fish, too, and the hillside streams that feed the river are still rich in trout. It is a place where Celtic traditions in myth, dance and song, are strong. In mid-August it holds a well-known festival of dance and it has a colourful pardon on the last Sunday in August, starting with a candle-lit procession from a chapel. In the parish church the baptismal font was decorated in 1919 with episodes from Christ's life by Paul Sérusier (1865–1927), who had been at Pont-Aven with Gauguin and, when Gauguin left Pont-Aven, came here to live and die, saying that it was impossible for the true artist to paint anywhere but in Brittany.

In the same church is a memorial to forty-three men of the town shot by the Nazis.

TOURIST INFORMATION rue Mairie (98.81.83.90)
FESTIVALS *see above*

HOTELS

Gai Logis, route de Quimper (98.81.73.87). Logis de France. Good value. Never translate French directly – gai means jolly, joli means pretty. ROOMS A–C. MEALS A–E. Shut Monday in winter.

CHÂTELAUDREN
[CÔTES-DU-NORD]

Just north of the Guingamp–St Brieuc road N12, this village is a commercial centre for the Goelo area. It is built beside a little lake at the head of the valley of the Leff, a river famed for trout. The resort of Binic (*see* page 82) is 13km north-east. Perched on a hillside is Notre-Dame-du-Tertre, a 14th-to 15th-century chapel. Ninety-six painted panels which decorate the nave are very rare. They show scenes from the Bible.

CLÉDEN-POHER
[FINISTÈRE]

10km from Carhaix-Plouguer, this village lies between the Aulne river and the Nantes–Brest canal where they are *not* one and the same waterway. I have happy memories of camping with our children in a windmill site by the Aulne and walking, bathing and fishing along the river banks.

It has a renowned 15th- to 16th-century church in a parish close – the typical old Breton grouping of tiny cemetery, church, calvary and charnel house (ossuary) in a small village square. The church has interesting altar pieces, statues, carved panels and modern stained glass. The ossuary has been made into a chapel. The calvary has many figures which include horsemen.

COMBOURG
[ILLE-ET-VILAINE]

I have great affection for Combourg. Its haunted castle where Châteaubriand lived; little lake; old streets with small shops; and remarkably cheap restaurants and its delightful Hotel du Château have the beguiling atmosphere of a small Breton town. Yet, being at the hub of six locally important roads and near a good Castel campsite, it can be quite a lively place in mid-summer.

Combourg is 24km south-east of Dinan and 17km south of Dol-de-Bretagne, but the best approach to see the lake and castle in their setting is along the Rennes road.

The feudal castle with machicolated towers and witches' hat turrets looks sinister in its huge park surrounded by trees. Below it in the square is a statue of Châteaubriand, looking glumly thoughtful. I don't suppose it was such a dull place when the boisterously warlike du Guesclin owned it. But Châteaubriand's father was a man of moods – violent, then silent (*see* St Malo, page 36). He bought the castle in 1761. His son describes in his great work *Memoires d'Outre-Tombe* how the sinister gloom affected him as a schoolboy. His mother was an invalid, his sister Lucile was his only companion, and months would pass without a visitor. His father would pace up and down after supper saying nothing, then at precisely ten o'clock send the family to bed. He made his family sleep as far from each other as possible in the eerie château. So young Châteaubriand spent much of his time in the Tour du Chat, a tower supposedly haunted by a previous owned who had lost a leg in the Battle of Malplaquet. He and his cat walked up and down at night, the wooden leg clomping, the cat miaowing. Later, a skeleton of a cat was found under some stairs. Since then, it is said, the disconsolate leg haunts alone, looking for the cat!

Châteaubriand admits that those nights in the castle led to melancholy, and melancholy hangs over his writing. To an Englishman brought up on Fielding, Smollett, Swift, Dickens and Mark Twain, he seems to have affected French literature with introspective melancholy from Flaubert, Victor Hugo and Balzac to Françoise Sagan. No wonder Châteaubriand later loved wide-open seascapes so much and chose to be buried on an isle off St Malo (*see* page 35). Of the château's four corner towers Tour de More (11th century) and Tour de Croise are attractive. There is a small museum in Châteaubriand's room. (Château de Combourg open 1 March–30 November except Tuesday.)

I have found no melancholy in over thirty years of visiting the Hotel du Château in the square, either when sitting in its lovely garden drinking Muscadet or in its dining-room eating lobster in Bourgueil sauce, *pré-salé* lamb in cider or steak with an old-style Châteaubriand sauce.

Château de Lanrigan, 5km east, is like a Loire château, built in granite with a lovely Renaissance façade and flanking turrets. An elegant staircase joins the octagonal tower to the building. You can see it from the outside Wednesday, Thursday and Friday from 1 July to 31 August.

TOURIST INFORMATION Maison de la Lanterne (June–15 September – 99.73.13.93)

MARKET Monday

HOTELS

Château, pl. Châteaubriand (99.73.00.38). '*De belle allure*' as the French say. Comfortable, excellently run, with lovely garden (*see above*). Rooms of character in main hotel or more luxurious in a nice stone annexe in the garden. ROOMS B–E. MEALS B–F. Shut 20 December–6 January. Restaurant shut Monday lunch; Monday and Sunday evening low-season.

Lac, pl. Châteaubriand (99.73.05.65). Opposite Château, nearest substitute if Château is full. Views of lake and castle. Cooking less ambitious. Cheap menus are good value. ROOMS B–D. MEALS A–F. Shut Sunday evening and Friday low-season; November.

France, 18 rue Prince (99.73.00.01). Near castle entrance. Simple rooms; cheaper menus very good value. Excellent fish. Super wine list. ROOMS A–B. MEALS A–F. Shut Monday; February.

COMMANA
[N. FINISTÈRE]

In an isolated spot at the foothills of the Arrée mountains, on D764, 20km west of Huelgoat. It is a good example of the old Breton village with an enclos paroissial (parish close) which are a feature of old Breton life and art. All the church buildings, from church to cemetery, are in one square and often proudly ornamented. The 16th-century church in Commana has three interesting altars and a fine font ornamented with five statues representing Faith, Hope, Charity, Justice and Temperance.

CONCARNEAU
[S. Finistère]

Concarneau may be a tourist cliché but it is also a place of dramatic interest and a really genuine working fishing port. To avoid it because of its popularity would be stupid. The streets of the superb Ville Close, the medieval walled town, may now be lined with souvenir stalls and tourist bars and restaurants, but once you have crossed the bridge from the mainland and walked under the arch into the entrance courtyard, you do not even have to half-close your eyes to imagine yourself back in the Middle Ages when this was a formidable fortress against pirate raids and invasions. I have been there at least twenty times and I am still impressed.

The medieval fortress is surrounded by the modern fishing port, protected in the Baie de la Fôret, and across the point is the seaside resort around Les Plages des Sables Blancs. Concarneau has thriving canning factories for tunny and sardines and, these days, vegetables too.

Ville Close is totally enclosed by the thick granite walls built in the 14th century. Vauban, the military strategist, made the town even stronger in the 17th century for Louis XIV. During

Concarneau

the Breton Wars of Succession, the English, who were backing Jean de Montfort as Duke, mainly to prevent the French nominee Charles de Blois from getting the job, occupied Concarneau and held on to it for thirty years. It took the great du Guesclin three separate sieges to get out the small English garrison.

Go up the steps to the left as you enter and you are on the wide sentry walk round the walls. Through loopholes you have glimpses of the fishing fleet and harbour. You can see also the Moulin à Poudre (the old gunpowder tower). There are more rampart walks at the far end of the island. The main street is rue Vauban where former houses have been given shop windows and have become shops, restaurants and bars with tables outside. On the second from last weekend in August the Fête des Filets Bleus (the Festival of the Blue Nets) is held here. It has grown from a religious festival of blessing the fishing boats to become one of the liveliest celebrations in Brittany. I remember when the nets the fishermen hung out all around town on that day *were* blue. Now they are mostly brown and I suspect that some of the blue ones which do appear are kept for the occasion. Anyway, they still sell you tiny blue nets to pin on your dress or shirt, the proceeds going to fishermen's charities. A lot of the girls who sell them – young and older – wear Breton costume. And it's a great party.

In the old arsenal and barracks as you enter Ville Close is Musée de la Pêche (fishing museum). Exhibits, including ships models and early tins for canning fish, trace Concarneau's fishing history. There are forty aquaria of live fish and tortoises (open all year).

Another exhibition (Exposition d'Oeuvres en Coquillages) is of scenes, people and flowers made from shells. There is a superb landscape scene of the Ville Close, with waves made of mussels washing its walls (open June to end September).

In the port outside is a marinarium belonging to the Maritime College of France, including aquaria and audio-visual explanations (open to the public Easter and mid-June to mid-September).

It is really worth getting up early to see the big fish market at work. To this day row after row of boxes literally gleaming and sparkling with wet fish are sold at the gallop and shifted just as fast by porters. At almost any time there is something interesting to see in the fish harbour.

The painter Gauguin had a punch-up in Concarneau and broke his leg badly. He and his painter friends visited Concarneau from their artists' colony in Pont-Aven nearby (*see* Pont-Aven, page 205). He took his current mistress called Anna the Javanese, who carried a tame monkey around on her shoulder. Local children threw stones at her. One artist caught a child by the ear. A brawl started. Gauguin knocked down a ships' pilot who fetched his crew of fifteen to beat up the artist. He was laid up for months. Anna looted his studio, sold his possessions and went off.

Originally it was the Americans who made this area an artists' haven. It was discovered by a group of American artists headed by Robert Wylie in 1866 when they visited a then well-known American painter called Alexander Harrison, who was working in Concarneau. They stayed at Hôtel des Voyageurs in the main square opposite the entrance to Ville Close. And they despised the scenery at Pont-Aven as being 'ready-made for female English water-colourists'. Then they set up a Pont-Aven colony using the same hotels and studio used later by Gauguin and his friends. The American painters in Concarneau and in Pont-Aven formed baseball teams to play each other!

There are various boat trips from Concarneau in season including Concarneau–Beg-Meil across the bay, from June to September, by launch *Jeanne-Yvonne* (apply tourist office, Concarneau – 98.97.01.44); Concarneau–Bénodet four hours (July, August, *Le Glenn* – 98.97.10.31); Concarneau–Glénan Isles (15 June–15 August, *Le Glenn* – 98.97.01.44). Hydrojet – Concarneau–Glénan Isles (July–September, 98.50.72.12).

TOURIST INFORMATION quai d'Aiguillon (98.97.01.44)
MARKET Monday, Friday
FESTIVALS Third Sunday in August – Fête des Filets Bleus (*see above*)

HOTELS

Océan, plage Sables Blancs (98.50.53.50). Concarneau badly needed a new beach hotel. Opened by the popular Henaff family from the Baie, Forêt-Fouesnant. Panoramic restaurant;

duplex rooms for families; heated pool; demi-pension midsummer. ROOMS E–G. MEALS D–F. Open all year.

Le Galion, 15 rue St-Guénolé, Ville Close (98.97.30.16). In the old walled town, heavy with Breton atmosphere; extremely attractive and alluring with very good cooking but I am not the only British travel writer to have noticed the mean portions – nouvelle cuisine style, which don't go with Breton tradition. Five rooms. ROOMS F. MEALS D–G. Shut Sunday evening, Monday except summer; 9–25 January.

Belle Étoile, Le Cabellou-plage, 5½km south-east (98.97.05.73). Luxury hotel which changed hands recently. Rooms pricey. Cooking very good. ROOMS G. MEALS E–G. Shut January, February; restaurant shut Tuesday low-season.

RESTAURANTS

Douanne, 71 ave A-Le Lay (98.97.30.27). All-action, sometimes noisy and chaotic bistro; my old favourite. Has gone upmarket apart from good cheap weekday lunch. Fish direct from market almost alongside. MEALS A (lunch), D–F. Shut Sunday low-season; mid-November–mid-December.

Coquille, 1 rue du Moros (98.97.08.52). In new harbour among the ships; terrace for viewing the scene; beams and oil lamps within. The best fish cooked in the old simple style. MEALS D–G. Shut Monday; Sunday evening except July, August; mid–end May; 3–17 January.

CONLEAU
[MORBIHAN]

Small port at the mouth of the Vincin river on the Gulf of Morbihan, 3km south of Vannes. It is joined by a causeway to Île de Conleau. Boats leave from Conleau for the isle of Arz, 3km long, with several megalithic monuments. Good views of the Golfe de Morbihan from here.

HOTEL

Le Roof (97.63.47.47). Popular; modern; good views from many bedrooms. Named for the eccentric, multi-coloured roof of previous fin-de-siècle hotel. Very good food. ROOMS D–E. MEALS B–G. Shut mid-January–mid-February.

LE CONQUET
[N. FINISTÈRE]

Little fishing port for lobsters, crawfish and crabs in a wild-looking but beautiful position 24km west of Brest. A beach almost enclosed by great rocks. On the other side of the Kermorven Peninsula is La Plage des Blancs Sablons. Superb sight at night of the lighthouses of Ouessant (Ushant), Jument, Pierres Noires, Vieille, Ar Men and Île de Sein flashing successively at sea and along the coast. Boats sail to Ouessant.

HOTEL
Pointe Sainte-Barbe (98.89.00.26). Holiday hotel in lovely situation facing the sea. Good food. Quiet hideout. Rooms vary. ROOMS B–E. MEALS A–G. Shut 2 January–early February.

CORSEUL
[CÔTES-DU-NORD]

North-west of Dinan on the D794 to Plancoët, this was the capital of the powerful Cunosolite tribe of Celts which took over all the area called Armorica. They were mentioned by Julius Caesar. Archaeological digs have brought to light many vestiges of the Gallo-Norman period. The most important is 1½km towards Dinan, a ruined octagonal tower of Roman stonework, Temple de Haut-Bécheral, usually called the Temple of Mars. The remains do not look like a temple.

LE CROISIC
[Loire-Atlantique]

On a point west of La Baule by the very attractive D45 road along the coast past Pouliguen and Batz-sur-Mer, Le Croisic is everybody's idea of a Breton fishing port, even though crowded with visitors in midsummer. I still find it fascinating and delightful after more than fifty years. Sardines used to be the great catch in my youth but these days oysters, shellfish and prawns are the main landings. Not many visitors see the great morning sales from the balcony of the good new market, for the great season is winter and sales are 3 a.m.–7 a.m. There is a second market at 3 p.m. and there is nearly always a certain amount of fish being sold.

The port is divided into several basins by three islets and the quays are flanked by charming 17th-century houses. It is a very protected port, for it overlooks the Grand Trait lagoon which separates it from the Marais Salants (salt marshes). This was the sea where Caesar's Roman galleys defeated the becalmed Veneti tribe's sailing boats (*see* Batz-sur-Mer, page 70).

Now it is a haven for sailing boats on the lagoon and bigger pleasure yachts from the sea. I can sit for hours outside a café eating oysters and prawns and drinking good, cold Muscadet-sur-lie, watching the people and the boats. The marina holds two hundred and forty boats.

Across the little town is the Atlantic coast, with Port-Lin beach and the three beaches of Batz-sur-Mer only about 1km away. The best views of the salt marshes are from Mont Esprit. This is a pile of old ships' ballast turned into a hill and drive.

Croisic is a very old port. Its chapel is in Flamboyant Gothic style of the early 16th-century, and its town hall 17th-century (it includes a little naval museum).

In 1759 Lord Hawke's Royal Navy Squadron defeated the French fleet, and many French ships ran aground here. Previously in 1692 an Anglo-Dutch fleet under Admiral Russel defeated the French under Tourville at the Battle of Le Hougue off La Manche in Normandy. The French were on their way to land an invading force in Britain to put James II on the English throne. At the north-east edge of Le Croisic is a memorial at the foot of Mont Lénigo to the Croisic pilot Hervé Rielle who after the defeat led twenty French ships to safety through a dangerous channel.

Croisic's Côte d'Amour aquarium has indeed some queer fish, including pink lobsters from the Canaries, giant deep-sea spiders, coral fish of many colours and Polynesian shellfish (closed Tuesday in winter).

TOURIST INFORMATION place Gare (40.23.00.70)

HOTELS

Vikings, Port-Lin (40.62.90.03). Most comfortable hotel; by the sea; no restaurant. Stay here, eat around in many nice restaurants. ROOMS E–G. Open all year.

Océan, Port-Lin (40.62.90.03) Same owners as Vikings; rooms more modest; excellent very expensive restaurant. ROOMS E–F. MEALS F–G.

RESTAURANTS

Bretagne, quai de petit-Chambre, Port (40.23.00.51). The place to eat fish. Huge restaurant, huge choice of menus. Fish lovers come for miles to eat here. MEALS B–G. Shut Wednesday (except July, August); 12 November–17 December; 5 January–28 February.

Pornic, 4 quai du Port-Ciguet (40.23.18.56). Bistro in an old house at the port; fishing décor. Superb fish cooked simply. MEALS E–F. Shut Monday evening except July, August; mid-November–mid-March.

LE CROUESTY
[MORBIHAN]

Big pleasure boat marina holding 1100 boats beside a modern residential area south-east of Port Navalo at the entrance to the Golfe de Morbihan. It is in a little bay opening into the big Baie de Quiberon. The marina is called Arzon-Le Crouesty (97.41.23.33). (*See also* Arzon and Port Navalo). Pleasant quayside walks to see the boats.

CROZON
[S. Finistère]

Town at the centre of Presqu'île de Crozon (Crozon Peninsula). It overlooks Baie de Dournenez, is virtually attached to the resort of Morgat (*see* page 185) and is a good centre for some very attractive coastal drives.

Take D355 north-west past a military camp, turn left at St Fiacre almost into Camaret (*see* page 89), then right on D355. You pass Chapelle de Notre-Dame-de-Rocamadour (Camaret, *see* page 90) and along the road are great views of the Atlantic up to Pointe des Espagnols, from where you can see the town and harbour of Brest, and the ships going through the passage below you to reach it. It was called 'Spaniards' Point' because here a Spanish force set up a base in 1593 to try to capture Brest. They were thrown out by the Marshal d'Aumont's forces, helped by 1800 English troops sent by Queen Elizabeth who knew, no doubt, that if the Spaniards had Brest it would be a perfect base for setting up another Armada to invade England. In the battle, Sir Martin Frobisher, the English sailor-explorer and companion of Drake, who had been knighted for gallantry against the Armada, was wounded so badly that he died shortly after in Plymouth.

The road continues with attractive sea views past Roscanvel to St Fiacre. Roscanvel's church, rebuilt in 1956, has some splendid and unusual modern, dark stained-glass windows by Labouret with dark-blue predominating, and a coloured terracotta Stations of the Cross by Claude Gruer. They are both worth seeing. Le Fret, across the next point, is a charming small port used now for boat services from Brest (forty-five minutes – coach connections with Crozon, Morgat, Camaret). D55 is still attractive until it hits D155 back to Crozon.

In Crozon the church has a remarkable altar piece of 1602 with 400 carved and painted wooden figures, all very expressive. They show the martyrdom of 10,000 Christian soldiers in Armenia under the Emperor Hadrian.

Tourist Information place l'Église (98.27.21.65)
Market Fourth Wednesday of the month

HOTELS

Moderne, 61 rue Alsace-Lorraine (98.27.00.10). Rooms comfortable but vary. ROOMS B–E. MEALS A–D. Shut Monday; October.
Hostellerie de la Mer, at Le Fret (98.27.61.90). Peaceful, attractive, on port. Restaurant has old Breton furniture. ROOMS C. MEALS B–F.

DAOULAS
[N. FINISTÈRE]

Lively and picturesque little town in one of many deep creeks of the Brest roads in the estuary of the Daoulas river. Plougastel-Daoulas is 10km west. It has a classic enclos parossial (parish close) with an old sincere and vital calvary of 1604 in the cemetery, and an abbey church. Of the abbey itself the 12th-century cloisters have a side and the roof missing, but are a remarkable example of Breton Romanesque architecture. They have thirty-two arches supported by small columns.

DINAN
[CÔTES-DU-NORD]

Dinan is one of the most enchanting places in France to me, and although I still love to go there, I take a smug delight in remembering it before it had quite so many visitors. It is not only a wonderful old medieval town with delightful old houses and streets, surrounded by 13th- to 15th-century ramparts and guarded by a castle, but all this is in a spectacularly attractive setting 75 metres above a charming stretch of the lovely Rance river with a nice little port. It is a beautifully kept little town, too, with trees and flower gardens, and you can eat very well at reasonable prices.

Most visitors come in from the Dinard road (D766). Be prepared to walk or you just won't see Dinan. A lot of roads are cobbled and slope but anyway you will take lots of rests just to

The waterfront at Dinan

look and admire. Park if you can by Tour St Julien then walk round the Promenade des Grands Fossés, a superb avenue which follows the north ramparts, with gardens between the trees and walls. Rue de l'École, passing behind the former Franciscan Monastery, now a college, leads to the old town. Here are lovely old streets and squares such as place des Merciers with old triangular-gabled houses with wooden porches. The 15th-century Tour de l'Horloge (clock tower) contains a clock given by Duchess Anne.

In place St Sauveur is St Sauveur's basilica, partly 12th-century, a mixture of Romanesque and Flamboyant styles. The heart of the French hero du Guesclin is here in a cenotaph. He asked to be buried in Dinan when he died at the siege of Châteauneuf du Radon in 1380. The funeral convoy set off for Brittany. At Le Puy they had to embalm him and left his insides buried in the Church of St Laurence. The embalming didn't work, so at Monteferrand they boiled him and buried the flesh. At le Mans an officer of the King brought an order to take the body to St Denis in Paris, where the kings of France were buried. The skeleton was sent. The heart went on to Dinan!

On what was the cemetery is Jardin Anglais, a terraced

garden with fine views down the river Rance, the port, the Pont Gothique, a bridge which had to be rebuilt after World War II, and the viaduct. The viaduct is 250 metres long and 40 metres high and carries the N176 road from Dol-de-Bretagne, linking with roads to St Malo and Rennes.

From the garden you can take Promenade de la Duchesse Anne beside the ramparts as far as the entrance to the garden of the château, where she often stayed. You can visit the 14th-century Coëtquen Tower, the keep and the gallery between them (shut Monday and mornings in winter). The highest part is called the dungeon of Duchesse Anne (14th century) consisting of two linked towers and a parapet walk. It houses a rather disappointing museum, though the reconstruction of an old room is quite interesting. Beside Tour de l'Horloge a strange duel took place in 1359. The Duke of Lancaster was besieging Dinan, which was defended by Bertrand du Guesclin and his brother Olivier. When he was getting the worst of the battle, du Guesclin asked for a forty day truce. If the town were not-relieved by then, he would surrender it. Lancaster agreed. The brother Olivier wandered from the town into the country unarmed. Against the terms of the truce and laws of chivalry, a cad called Sir Thomas Canterbury arrested him and demanded a thousand florins in ransom. Bertrand du Guesclin, outraged, challenged him to single combat. Lancaster, the English commander, acted as referee.

Du Guesclin won. Lancaster made Canterbury return Olivier and pay a thousand florins to him. He then withdrew the English forces. Canterbury was then thrown out of the English army, though whether for unchivalrous conduct or losing to a Frenchman we are not told.

A Dinan girl, Tiphaine Raguerel, attractive and scholarly, was so impressed that she married the rough, ugly but brave soldier du Guesclin, and the marriage lasted.

The tourist office is in a charming 16th-century mansion, Hôtel Kératry.

Across the viaduct from Dinan at Lanvallay and around are superb views of Dinan, its walls and towers and also of Dinard (*see* Major Towns, page 52).

Boat trips on the Rance are controlled partly by tides. From mid-April to the end of September boats go to Dinard to visit the tidal power plant (returning by coach) from quai de la Rance – Dinan's port (96.39.18.04). Rance estuary trips go to and from St Malo (Vedettes Blanches – 99.56.63.23). Gastronomic boat-restaurant trips of discovery on the Rance operate 1 June–15 September from quai de la Rance (99.46.44.44) and non-restaurant trips between the same dates (Vedettes Reine d'Armor, rue du Quai – 96.39.94.72).

TOURIST INFORMATION 6 rue l'Horloge (96.39.75.40)

MARKET Thursday, Saturday

HOTELS

D'Avaugour, 1 pl. du Champ Clos (96.39.07.49). Georges Quinton is part of the folklore of Dinan. In an old house in a superb position with a garden seemingly suspended above ramparts and castle lawns, he makes imaginative dishes from fresh market produce. Good cheap bar-lunch. Summer restaurant in garden tower. Very comfortable rooms. ROOMS E–F. MEALS C–E. Restaurant shut Monday in winter.

Marguerite, 29 pl. du Guesclin (96.39.47.65). Nice friendly Logis in good position with balconies overlooking main square. Old style comfort (some noise in front rooms). Good value cheap menus. ROOMS B–E. MEALS A–E. Shut Sunday evening, Monday in winter; December.

RESTAURANTS

Terrasses, at Port (96.39.09.60). Most attractive riverside position with terrace enclosed in colder weather. Locals fill it off-season. Super fish. MEALS B–F. Shut Tuesday; mid–end November.

Merveilles des Mers, at port (96.39.86.54). Superb fish. MEALS C–G. Shut Tuesday.

Mère Pourcel, 3 pl. Merciers (96.39.03.80). Another Dinan institution. In 15th-century Breton house (historic monument) with a remarkable centrepiece staircase. Strictly traditional cuisine, too – good! MEALS A (lunch), D–F. Shut Sunday evening, Monday; January, February.

Caravelle, 14 pl. Duclos (96.39.00.11). Dinan's posh eating place. Simple décor, excellent cuisine, puzzling price structure. Carte prices very high. MEALS C (set meal, lunch only), E (weekdays),

G. Shut Wednesday (low-season); 10 October–early November.

DINARD
[*See* Major Towns, page 52]

DOL-DE-BRETAGNE
[ILLE-ET-VILAINE]

St Samson, the saint from Wales who could tell a dragon to eat its own tail and drop dead, founded Dol in AD 548 on a cliff which in those days overlooked a vast forest which stretched past Mont-St-Michel and some say as far as Jersey.

In the 8th century a massive tidal wave put vast areas of land under the sea, leaving Mont-St-Michel as an island. The waters surrounded Dol, too. When the waters retreated the forests had turned to marshlands. Dol was 8km from the coast and called capital of the marshes. Nominoë was crowned there as first Duke of an independent Brittany in 848. It was the Breton frontier town with the dukedom of Normandy, and successfully resisted William the Conqueror in 1057, though Henry II of England took it in 1164.

It is a sleepier town these days, with some lovely old houses and a feeling that it is unbothered by the present world, except perhaps in midsummer when holiday campers from the coast come to shop, eat and drink. At least it is no longer 'a long street without a glass window' as the cynically critical British agriculture traveller Arthur Young wrote in 1788.

Grand-Rue des Stuarts, the main street, has some very interesting houses. Maison des Plaids in bonded granite was built in the 12th century and is one of the oldest houses standing in France. Its round arched windows are original. Maison de la Guillotière (15th-century) houses a single museum of wooden statues of Breton saints.

The cathedral of St Samson has an English character to its

Norman-Gothic style. It was built by King John of England in the 13th century. After he had burned down the previous cathedral he had an attack of remorse and had a new one built – at the expense of the English taxpayer, of course. It has three towers, one uncompleted. The sanctuary to the north was obviously intended for defence; its crenellated parapet has arrow slits. Inside, the eighty carved choir stalls from the 14th century are delightful. The tomb of Bishop Thomas James (1405–29), though mutilated, still has beautiful friezes, including fantastic animals. One of the first Italian Renaissance monuments in Brittany, it was designed by the Florentine Justo brothers who founded a renowned school in Tours.

Just beyond the cathedral is a pedestrian-only Promenade des Douves (moats) with a very fine view across the fertile drained marshes to the remarkable 65-metre-high granite rock Mont Dol, 3km north. This strange mound has been described as having 'an eerie atmosphere', which is not surprising, for here are holy wells, ruined chapels, grottos from Roman pagan altars, Druid sanctuaries and the sanctuaries of Christians. It was a refuge for several saints, including St Malo, St Samson and St Maglorius and is in the Bayeux tapestry. Its 12th-century Chapelle de l'Espérance is still a centre for pilgrimage. Excavations here have revealed the remains of prehistoric mammoth elephants and rhinoceroses and Stone Age tools and weapons.

1½km south rises the Pierre du Champ-Dolent, a menhir nine metres high, fabled to mark the spot of an ancient battle ended by the falling of the stone from Heaven.

Château des Ormes, 8km south, a former palace of the bishops of Dol, is in a pleasant setting outside Epiniac but looks rather severe. It has a lovely Flamboyant door (15th century). Two pavilions (16th to 18th centuries) are joined by the plain main building.

Château de Landal, 12km south-east, built in the Middle Ages, rebuilt in the 19th century, is a striking feudal castle beside a lake, and approached by a nice walk under trees. Surrounded by trees, it stands among lovely lawns. You can visit the courtyard.

Tourist Information 3 Grande-Rue des Stuarts
(June–September – 99.48.15.37)
Market Saturday

HOTELS

Logis de la Bresche Arthur, 36 boul. Deminiac (99.48.01.44). Excellent classical cooking by friendly Christian Faveau. Fish often served in traditional Breton way *aux algues* (with seaweed – cooked like spinach – nice taste). Home-smoked fish, fresh shellfish from an underground tank; hot goats' cheese from Beaufort monastery. Outstanding value meals. ROOMS D–E. MEALS A–E.

Bretagne, 17 pl. Châteaubriand (99.48.02.03). Good value cheap menus of traditional dishes. In the same family since 1922. ROOMS A–C. MEALS A–C. Shut October. Restaurant shut Saturday in winter.

RESTAURANT

Roches-Douves, 80 route de Dinan (99.48.10.40). Young chef much praised by modern light cuisine enthusiasts. MEALS C–F. Shut Sunday evening, Monday.

DOUARNENEZ and TRÉBOUL
[S. FINISTÈRE]

The very heart of old Celtic Brittany, with its legends, history and its bond with the sea, Douarnenez was already old when the Romans came to Gaul. Legend says that Mark, King of Cornouaille had his palace here. So it is the setting for the story of Mark's betrothed Iseult and his nephew Tristan, immortalised by Wagner in his opera. Mark sent Tristan to Ireland to bring back Iseult for the royal wedding. With Iseult was sent a philtre to make her love Mark for ever. Tristan and Iseult drank it in error on the ship and passion was almost instant. The story has various endings. In some Tristan marries her and lives in his Brittany castle. In others Mark kills Tristan but Iseult follows him to the grave. You can see Tristan's isle looking particularly attractive from Plage des Dames. It was a sinister isle later in Breton history.

Douarnenez is on the southern side of the Bay of Douarnenez on the east side of Port-Rhu estuary. Across this a bridge has been built to Tréboul and they are now joined as one town. But they have very different life-styles. Tréboul is a very pleasant beach resort with a marina and sailing school. Across the town of Douarnenez from the estuary are two ports – Nouveau Port and Port du Rosmeur – and from here sails one of the last big fishing fleets of Brittany, fishing off Ireland, south-west England and the west coast of Africa. In season they fish for tunny, too. And there is a canning industry, including sardines. There is always something to see on the harbourfront. The commercial port, Port Rhu, is on the estuary.

Douarnenez is a great centre of Breton folklore, with several festivals.

It was very heavily fortified until the late 16th century. Then La Fontanelle, posing as a Catholic league fighter but really running a terrorist army, looting, pillaging and destroying its way round Brittany, found things getting a bit hot for him, so he captured Douarnenez and the isle of Tristan, dismantled Douarnenez's fortifications and used them to turn the island into a great fortress, from which he continued his raids and cruelties. He would attack even a small peasants' house, kill the family, loot it and burn it down. When Henri IV became king and finally defeated the Catholic League, La Fontanelle decided in 1598 to make peace. For some reason Henri, who was trying to keep the peace between his old Protestant and his new Catholic supporters, let him keep the isle of Tristan so long as he kept the peace. He was caught conspiring against the crown four years later and condemned to death.

In Douarnenez Bay near the town is the mythical town of Is (or Ys) said to be buried beneath the sea and sands. It happened in the time of King Gradlon in the 6th century (*see* Quimper, page 218). It was capital of Cornouaille, a town so beautiful that when the people of Lutitia wanted a name for their new city they called it 'Like Is' or 'Par Is' – Paris.

Is was protected from the sea by locks to which the King himself had the only key. His beautiful daughter Dahut, who was very fond of men, bedded a very attractive young stranger without realising that it was the Devil in disguise. To test her love he asked her to open the sea gate. She stole the key while the King was asleep, opened the gate and the city was flooded. The

DOUARNENEZ and TRÉBOUL

King fled on his horse with his daughter on his back but the waves chased him and a voice from heaven told him he could only escape by pushing the devil off his back. So he pushed Dahut into the waves. King Gradlon set up a new capital at Quimper. Dahut turned into a beautiful mermaid known as Marie-Morgane and she lures sailors to the bottom of the sea. She will go on doing so until the Good Friday when Mass is celebrated in one of the churches of the drowned city. The story has been retold by several poets, and Debussy's piano prelude *La Cathédrale Engloutie* portrays the church bells of Is ringing under the waves.

Plage des Sables Blancs at Tréboul is a splendid beach and between this and plage St Jean is a sea water treatment centre with a big swimming pool. The marina is at the river mouth opposite Tristan island. Tréboul is a very active sailing centre.

TOURIST INFORMATION 2 rue Dr Mével (98.92.13.35)

MARKET Monday, Friday, Saturday

FESTIVALS Third Sunday in July – Fête des Mouettes (seagulls) with procession of floats and Breton costumes; beginning of August – Fest-Noz (*Fête de Nuit*), song and dance festival; Second Sunday in August – *Voile et Folklore* – Breton dancing. Various fêtes and pardons through summer.

HOTELS

Auberge de Kervéoc'h, route de Kervéoc'h, 5km SE on D765 (98.92.07.58). Old farmhouse converted into quiet country hotel, hidden in trees. Cooking is very good now. Old furnishings. You are expected to take dinner if you book a room. No hardship! ROOMS D–E. MEALS B–E. Open Easter–mid-October; French November holidays; Christmas.

Clos de Vallombreuse, 7 rue E. d'Orves, Douarnenez (98.92.63.64). Quiet, comfortable hotel in lively town. ROOMS F. MEALS C–F. Restaurant shut December–April; also Monday.

Auberge Fouesnantaise, rue Roches-Blanches, Tréboul (98.74.03.33). Simple auberge with five rooms. ROOMS C. MEALS A–E. Shut mid-September–Easter.

RESTAURANT

Feu Sainte-Elme, 17 rue du Grand-Port (98.92.37.05). Simple restaurant in an old house with superb fish; reasonable prices. MEALS B–E. Shut Sunday evening; Wednesday.

ERQUY
[CÔTES-DU-NORD]

A busy little scallop-fishing port which has seven beaches and several lovely sea views nearby. I am surprised that it has not grown into a bigger resort. The beaches are wide and clean as the tide goes out, and sheltered by high cliffs in a little bay which is almost enclosed. Caroual beach is the best for fine sand but smaller, rockier coves are more private. Around the harbour are lots of cafés selling very fresh fish. Pine trees keep out the wind. Two kilometres round the bay is the tiny fishing village of Tu-es-Roc, then Cap d'Erquy. The road ends just before it, so you must walk to the point. From there are splendid sea views and pleasant heath walks.

TOURIST INFORMATION boul. Mer (96.72.30.12)

HOTELS

Brigantin, square de l'Hôtel-de-Ville (96.72.32.14). Very pleasant hotel. Still being improved. Old Breton furniture in bistro-type restaurant. Big choice of menus. ROOMS C–F. MEALS A–G. Open all year.

Beauséjour, rue de la Corniche (96.72.30.39). Simple cheap auberge. ROOMS B–D. MEALS A–D. Shut Friday evening, Saturday out of season; first week March; Christmas.

RESTAURANT

Escurial, boul. de la Mer (96.72.31.56). Not much to look at but outstanding fish at reasonable prices. MEALS A–F. Shut Sunday evening, Monday; one week late June; 5–18 January; 3–18 October.

ÉTABLES-SUR-MER
[Côtes-du-Nord]

Small resort on a nice stretch of coast between St Quay-Portrieux and St Brieuc. Two sheltered sand beaches are separated by a point. Chapelle de l'Espérance just north, built in 1850 on a clifftop, has attractive blue-toned windows, a fine tableau and a tapestry by Toffoli. Étables has a curious old church. Good fishing.

TOURIST INFORMATION 9 rue République
(96.70.65.41)
MARKET Tuesday

HOTEL
Colombière, at Notre-Dame de l'Espérance (96.70.61.64). Shady garden overlooking sea. ROOMS E–F. MEALS E–F. Shut Sunday evening, Monday except summer; 1–16 October.

LE FAOU
[S. FINISTÈRE]

In the Faou estuary, near to Cranou forest, a delightful town with old houses and Renaissance church spire mirrored in the harbour at high tide.

The main street is lined on one side with lovely old granite houses with overhanging upper storeys and slate-covered façades. In the wide main square is a 16th-century covered market and a hotel called Vieille Renommée which really is famous but is now in a modern building. The 16th-century church stands on a terrace overlooking the river. The coast roads are splendid, especially Corniche de Térénez round the bay. The Térénez bridge over the Aulne estuary is attractive. Its central span is 272 metres long.

TOURIST INFORMATION Syndicat d'Initiative, 10 rue
Gén-de-Gaulle (15 June–15 September – 98.81.06.85)
MARKET Saturday

HOTELS

Vieille Renommée, 11 place la Mairie (98.81.90.31). Comfortable; large restaurant; popular. ROOMS B–D. MEALS B–E. Shut November. Restaurant shut Sunday evening, Monday except July, August.

Relais de la Place, place la Mairie (98.81.91.19). Excellent regional lower-priced menu. ROOMS A–C. MEALS A–E. Shut Saturday except July–September; 23 September–mid-October.

LA FAOUËT
[MORBIHAN]

Large village in attractive wild scenery between the little Ellé and Inam rivers which flow down from the Montagnes Noires (Black Mountains). It is on D769 Carhaix-Lorient road and is the centre for seeing three attractive and interesting chapels. Even more attractive to me is La Faouët's own great covered market hall (16th century). Its three naves are supported by granite columns and there is splendid woodwork holding up the vast slate roof. In Grand Place is a statue to Corentin Carré, France's youngest soldier of the 1914–18 War. He enlisted aged fifteen in 1915 and was killed in aerial combat in 1918. His rank was adjutant (warrant officer).

The chapels owe a lot to their beautiful and unusual positions. Ste Barbe, 2½km north-east of Faouët is in an unusual and quite beautiful site on a road hillside 100 metres above a ravine near Grand Pont. A local story tells us why it was built in this curious spot. In the 15th century the Sire of Toulbodou was hunting in this valley of the Ellé when a terrible storm dislodged a great rock, threatening to kill him. He prayed to Ste Barbe and the falling rock stood still. So next day he started to build a chapel to Ste Barbe. In Flamboyant Gothic it has room for only an apse and a single aisle, decorated with Renaissance stained glass, carved panels and statues. A monumental Renaissance stairway leads to the little oratory of St Michael, near to which is a little bell-tower where pilgrims toll the bell to bring down blessings from heaven. It is a wonderful scene. Pardons are held on the last Sunday in June and 4 December. (Chapel open mid-May–end September daily; Wednesday, Saturday, Sunday rest of year.) There is a steep descent to Grand Pont.

Continue along the attractive D132 and after 5km turn right and right again to the chapel of St Nicolas, which stands isolated in a lovely setting of pines. It is Gothic in style with a carved Renaissance rood-screen showing rather comically the story of St Nicolas in nine panels.

Back on D132, turn left up D109 with good views over Étang du Bel, a large lagoon. After 6km the road leads to Abbaye de Langonnet, rebuilt in the 17th to 18th centuries. It still has a 13th-century chapter-house. Its position in a lovely wooded valley of the Ellé is delightful. It contains a museum of African missions.

The Chapelle St Fiacre, 3km south of Le Faouët, is known for its *clocher-pignon* (steeple placed directly on the roof) and beautifully carved and coloured figures on its rood-screen from 1480. The figures expressing cardinal sins are crudely funny. Laziness is represented by a Breton peasant playing bagpipes and a bombast, which sounds like hard work to me! It is said that St Fiacre and the beautiful chapel at Kernascléden (*see* page 161) were built at the same time by the same builders, who were transported by angels from one to another. They must have worked harder on Kernascléden, which was ready for consecration nearly thirty years earlier.

FOLGOËT
[N. Finistère]

At the magnificent basilica of Notre-Dame is held one of the great pardons of Brittany. It lasts three days around the first Sunday in September. There are lesser pardons, too, every Sunday in May and on 15 August. And on the fourth Sunday in July is the Pardon of St Christopher, when motor cars and their drivers are blessed.

The legend behind the church and the pardon comes from the 14th century. A simple man named Salaun who could speak only four words: ('Oh blessed Virgin Mary'), lived and died in the woods. He was called 'the fool of the woods' or in Breton 'ar foll coat', from which the name Folgoët came.

From his grave a lily grew and its golden pistils formed the words 'Ave Maria'. News of the miracle spread, the War of Breton succession was on and one of the claimants to the throne, Jean de Montfort, swore that if he won he would build a great chapel there to the Virgin. He won at Auray, became Duke, and had the building started, with the altar to stand over the spring where the simpleton used to drink. Montfort's son finished the bassilica in 1423.

To save it during the Revolution, twelve farmers bought it. It was returned to the church at the Restoration and has been repaired since.

The church stands on a vast esplanade and is square. One of the two towers is unfinished. The north tower has a stone spire with four pinnacle turrets. A large stained-glass window in the apse lights the panelled choir and nave. The 15th-century roodloft, in Kersanton stone, is regarded as a great masterpiece of Breton art. The waters of the spring under the altar lead to a fountain outside, where pilgrims come to drink.

Beside the church is a little 15th-century manor, Le Doyenne, forming a nice group with the church and the old Auberge des Pèlerins (pilgrims' inn).

FESTIVALS First Sunday in September – Pardon of Notre-Dame

LA FORÊT-FOUESNANT
[S. FINISTÈRE]

I used to hide away in this little village at the head of La Forêt Bay when the only other visitors were a few knowledgeable Britons staying with the Henaff family at the Baie Hotel and playing golf opposite, and a few richer Britons and Americans who had discovered the 18th-century Manoir du Stang, 1½km north – the first old manor or château I saw converted into an hotel after World War II. The Manor is still a real hideout, in lovely gardens with lakes. It has been the Hubert family home for 200 years.

Then the Port-la-Forêt was built across the estuary with a huge yacht harbour, but although that means that the little beach is more crowded and that you may have to book for dinner on weekends at the little hotels, it is still no lively resort, and I still like it.

It is only 12km from Bénodet, and 10km from Concarneau. Mild climate allows mimosa and fuchsias to flourish. There is a small enclos paroissial with 16th-century calvary and church.

Port-la-Forêt takes nearly six hundred boats (mostly permanent moorings but some provision for visitors). It is a port for boat trips to the Glénan Isles (15 June–15 September – 98.94.97.94), and up the Odet river (same times, phone number).

TOURIST INFORMATION 2 rue du Port (98.56.94.09)

HOTELS

Baie (98.56.97.35). Friendly, family-run Logis with good cooking; wide choice of menus. English spoken. ROOMS B–E. MEALS A–E. Shut 1 November–1 March.

Espérance, place l'Église (98.56.96.58). Another Logis, with gardens, terrace. Rooms vary considerably. ROOMS B–E. MEALS A–F. Shut end September–Easter; restaurant shut Wednesday.

Manoir du Stang, 1½km north by D783, then private road (98.56.97.37). Delightful and quiet; rose-garden, lawns, tennis, fishing in lakes, terrace. Own farm produce. ROOMS G. MEALS F. Shut end September–early May except for groups.

RESTAURANT

Auberge St-Laurent, 2km route Concarneau by coast road (98.56.98.07). Good restaurant in old Breton cottage; near sea, garden, log fires; lobster from *vivier*. Cheap wines. MEALS A–D. Open Easter–end September.

FOUESNANT
[S. Finistère]

Surrounded by apple and cherry orchards in the greenest part of Brittany, a mile from the sea, it is an important little town to the Bretons because it has a good bus service linking the district with its railway station and Quimper, including the airport.

Facing south, it is a charming place and is only 2½km from Cap-Coz, 15km from Quimper, 13km from Concarneau, 8km from Bénodet and Beg-Meil, so it is an excellent little holiday centre. La Forêt-Fouesnant is 3½km north-east.

Fouesnant cider is probably the best in Brittany, and the Apple Festival (Fête des Pommiers) on the third Sunday in July is a very happy event indeed. Here and at the Pardon of Ste Anne on the following Sunday you can see the beautiful Breton costumes and *coiffes* worn by the girls of all ages. The 12th-century church, partly rebuilt in the 17th century, and the 17th-century calvary with a fine carving of a peasant woman in a *coiffe* are both well worth seeing.

The Pardon of Ste Anne is held at a chapel in a pretty setting 1.7km north.

Fouesnant faces the Glénan Isles (*see* page 137). Cap-Coz, which juts into the Baie de la Forêt, has splendid views of the coast and the passing sailing boats. It has a superb long beach and nice coastal walks.

Tourist Information 5 rue Armor (98.56.00.63)
Festivals *see above*

HOTELS

Armorique, 33 rue de Cornouaille (98.56.00.19). Delightful old Breton inn with super dining-room, flowery courtyard, modern bedrooms in garden annexe. Bourgeois cuisine, old Breton dishes. Good cider, shellfish. Rooms B–E. Meals A–E. Shut Monday low-season; 1 October–20 March.

Arvor, pl. l'Église (98.56.00.35). Old house, pleasant rooms, low prices. Rooms A–C. Meals A–E. Shut Thursday (October–April); November. Restaurant shut evenings in winter.

Celtique, at Cap-Coz, ave de la Pointe (98.56.01.79). Attractive classic hotel on edge of the beach among dunes. Rooms B–D. Meals A–D. Check closing dates.

FOUGÈRES
[Ille-et-Vilaine]

An attractive historic town built in an enclosed ravine in the winding valley of the Nançon river, it has a lot to see and pleasant walks in the surrounding country. Once the centre for sailcloth, with its sails flapping on every French boat, it graduated through carpet slippers to leather shoes, and still makes something like a million pairs of women's shoes each year, with a big annual trade fair; also a centre for cattle, which provide much of the leather, and an agricultural centre.

On the very borders of Brittany and Normandy, Fougères was for centuries a very important frontier fortress town. Its barons were powerful in the Middle Ages. When the weak Duke of Brittany, Conan IV, submitted to Henry II of England in the 12th century, the Baron de Fougères, Raoul II, roused the Bretons to rebel. Although Henry took Fougères castle and knocked much of it down, Raoul immediately rebuilt it. Some of his work, including the Cadran (sundial) Tower, still remains.

Fougères

The castle was taken at various times by the French – Louis IX, du Guesclin, the Breton-turned-French marshal, and the Duc de Mercoeur of the Catholic League, who made it his headquarters in the Wars of Religion. The English took it, of course; so did the Chouans, the peasants who revolted against injustices of the Revolution and became linked with a return of the monarchy.

You have only to climb the parapets to see how powerful the castle was. Duchess Anne of Brittany called it 'the key to my royal treasure'.

The original surrounding walls, which were once protected by a loop of the river Nançon, have thirteen towers and enclose two hectares. The spectacular 14th-century tower called La Mélusine was built by the Lusignan family, descendants of the great Guy de Lusignan, the Crusader who became King of Jerusalem and then of Cyprus. The tower's walls are 3½ metres thick, 13 metres in diameter and it rises 30 metres above ground. It was called after a fairy of Arthurian legend from which this strange family claimed descent. She is still said to haunt Fougères.

The large inner courtyard of the castle is used sometimes as an open-air theatre. The castle is illuminated from 1 June to 15 September, and in summer an exhibition of shoemaking is held there. It is a breathtaking walk from river to castle (open 1 March to 31 October).

Fougères was heavily bombed in 1944 but most of the old quarter survived, and it is very rewarding to wander round the old streets. Because of the town's history, many writers came to gather background and material, including Châteaubriand, Victor Hugo and de Balzac. Hugo introduced the town into *Quatre-Vingt-Treize* (*Ninety-three*), his story of the Chouans and his last great prose novel. He stayed in Fougères with Juliette Drouet, his mistress who was from there, and he loved the town. Balzac based his great novel *Les Chouans* on the town.

The Chouans' revolt in Brittany and the Vendée (*see* History, page 22) sprang partly from a movement started by a Fougères man, the Marquis de la Rouerie. A wild youth led to a warrant for his arrest. He would have gone to the Bastille. So he fled to Switzerland. Then he joined a Trappist monastery – a trick used by those wanted by the law right up to Nazis fleeing after World War II.

From there he fled to America where the War of Independence was being fought and became a general in the American army. He returned to France on the eve of the Revolution, refused to emigrate and planned a Breton maquis-style resistance movement. He got together hidden stores of arms and provisions and recruited a secret army, but he was betrayed and he had to flee. He died in hiding, worn out, in January 1793. The following month the Revolutionary Assembly in Paris declared a mass levy (a sort of poll tax) and brought in conscription. The peasants of Brittany and the Vendée revolted. Ironically, the Royalists – aristocrats and bourgeoisie – joined them. The Breton peasants had been in favour of the Revolution. It was the excesses of the leaders they objected to. The revolt went on with a few breaks until 1804.

Many of the picturesque houses are in Place du Marchix, which painters have long loved. They include two fine 16th-century houses (Nos. 13 and 15). You can see the backs of them from rue des Tanneurs, which leads to a river bridge. There are more old houses in Rue du Nançon.

St Sulpice church, with an elegant slate bell-tower, is next to the château. It contains interesting 18th-century paintings, fine stone Flamboyant altar pieces and a statue of the Virgin suckling the infant Christ, called *Notre-Dame-des-Marais*, which is traditionally miraculous and once drew many pilgrims. Across the river in place des Arbres are terraced gardens made from old ramparts.

Fougère State Forest 3km north-east has some very pleasant walks and also some dolmens and a line of megalithic stones.

TOURIST INFORMATION place A.-Briand (99.94.12.20)
MARKETS Saturday – general, Friday morning – cattle
FESTIVALS end January – Assemblée de la Bozière
(music of Haute-Bretagne); July – Festival du Livre
Vivant, based on Victor Hugo's works; end March –
Commercial Fair

HOTELS

Voyageurs, 10 place Gambetta (99.99.08.20). Behind an old façade is a modern hotel. Restaurant is separately run. (99.99.14.17). Good, regional, cheap weekday menu. Popular locally. ROOMS B–C. MEALS A–E. Hotel shut 23 December–3 January. Restaurant shut Sunday evening, Saturday except July, August; 17–31 August.

Mainotel, 4km SE by N12 at Beaucé (99.99.81.55). Modern, air-conditioned. ROOMS C–E. MEALS A–E. Restaurant shut Sunday evening.

Commerce, place Grand Marché (99.94.40.40). Simple Logis de France. Meals good value. ROOMS B–E. MEALS A–C.

CAP FRÉHEL
[CÔTES-DU-NORD]

One of the best views in Brittany from this 70-metre-high cliff west of St Cast, and it looks beautiful at sunset. In clear weather you can see from Grouin Point and the Cotentin Peninsula to the Isle of Bréhat on the left. Local people claim to have seen the Channel Isles. From the sea the cape's vertical face of red, grey and black, with seas breaking on the reefs below, is most impressive.

You can visit the lighthouse (Easter to mid-September) and the view from the top tower is even better than from the Cape itself, with Jersey visible on a good day. The light carries 110km on clear nights.

The rocks which you can see from the extreme end of the point (Rochers de la Fauconnière) are covered with seagulls and cormorants. A steep path from the Restaurant Fauconnière takes you to a platform where you can see the rocks, but only take it if you don't mind heights. There is a lovely walk from Sables-d'Or-les-Pins along the cliffs to Cap Fréhel, with several fine viewing points. Sailing school at Plage du Vieux Bourg.

HOTEL

Plage et Fréhel, at Plage du Vieux Bourg, 5km along coast south towards Sables-d'Or (96.41.40.04). Logis de France. ROOMS B–D. MEALS A–E. Shut Tuesday except peak season; 15 November–late March; 5–25 October.

LA GACILLY
[MORBIHAN]

Town 16km north of Redon where they manufacture cosmetics. An attractive, well-kept town, it has artisans' workshops lining the narrow streets – woodworkers, basket makers, weavers, jewellers, leatherworkers. French tourists come to watch.

HOTEL
France (Annexe Hotel Square) (99.08.11.15). Old-fashioned Logis, simple traditional cooking. ROOMS A–D. MEALS A–C. Shut 24 December–2 January. Restaurant shut Sunday evening in winter.

GRAND-FOUGERAY
[ILLE-ET-VILAINE]

A little town with the ruins of a castle which du Guesclin captured by a trick in the War of Breton Succession. He heard that firewood was to be delivered to the castle. He and his men disguised themselves as woodcutters carrying sticks. Once inside, they brought out their weapons and slew the garrison. There is a partly Romanesque church.

GLÉNAN, ÎLES DE
[S. FINISTÈRE]

Almost surrounded by reefs, this little group of nine isles lies off Concarneau. They can be reached by boat from Bénodet, Beg-

Meil, Concarneau, Forêt-Fouesnant and Loctudy. The smaller uninhabited isles are bird sanctuaries. Some are private. The boats go to St Nicolas, where there are some houses, a *vivier* for farming shellfish and an underwater swimming school. Three other isles, Penfret, Cigogne and Drenec, are used by a sailing and sea navigation school.

GROIX, ÎLE DE
[MORBIHAN]

Island off Lorient, 8km long and about 3km wide. The north and west coasts are wild, with giant rocks, cliffs, valleys and creeks which give shelter to fishing boats and yachts. The safe harbour is Port-Tudy, used by trawlers and, in summer, many pleasure boats. It once had a tunny fishing fleet. On Tudy church steeple a tuna fish replaces a cock as weather-vane. Treeless, the isle is called in Breton *Enez-Groac'h* (Witch's Island) because of ancient associations with Druids.

Pen Men to the west has a new lighthouse, Trou de Tonnerre, and caves in its cliffs. The capital, Groix, has 2,600 people.

East and south are flatter, with sandy creeks along the coast. Grands Sables is a fine beach. Locmaria Bay is picturesque and surrounded by an area rich in rare minerals, including garnet.

Trou de l'Enfer in the south has good coast views. Boats from Lorient take forty-five minutes to Port-Tudy (for times telephone 97.21.03.97 – in summer reservations needed for cars).

TOURIST INFORMATION 4 rue Gén-de-Gaulle, Tudy (97.05.81.75)

HOTEL

Ty-Mad, Port-Tudy (97.05.80.19). ROOMS B–E. MEALS A–F. Open 1 April–15 October. Two campsites and a youth hostel on the island.

GUÉRANDE
[Loire-Atlantique]

Built on a plateau 50 metres above sea level and overlooking the salt marshes (Marais Salants) north of La Baule which were a sea when the Romans defeated the Veneti tribe in a naval battle. A change of level of 16 metres caused by sand deposited by currents turned the gulf into marshes.

Guérande was there in the Middle Ages and it keeps its ramparts almost intact, so it looks from the outside like a medieval town. Despite more modern buildings outside the ramparts, I always feel that I should approach it across those infertile salt marshes riding a horse.

The present ramparts were built in the 15th century and you can still walk round them. Flanked by eight towers, they have four fortified gateways. In the 18th century, the Duc d'Aiguillon, Governor of Brittany, had most of the moats filled in and replaced by the present circular promenade, which you can drive round. Parts of the moat are filled with water. The St Michel gate, once the Governor's house, has a museum of old furniture, old salt-workers' costumes on lifesize dummies, and a plan of how the salt-pans work (open Easter to 30 September).

The granite church of St Aubin has an outside pulpit, used for preaching to lepers.

The salt-pans are fed by a channel at Le Croisic through which the sea pours. On the mud flats exposed at low tide, oysters and mussels are raised. Some of the salt-pans have been abandoned because of competition from the salt mines of East Europe and those of southern France favoured by hotter sunshine. The drying and refining of the salt is now done in a modern plant at Batz.

The chessboard of salt-pans is formed between low banks of clay. The seawater is let in at high tide through *étiers* (canals) and is trapped in a series of reservoirs with the water getting shallower down to two inches. The salt crystallises as the water evaporates. It is scraped up by rakes and spades, dried on platforms, then stored in sheds.

Guérande grew very rich on salt until the Revolution. It is easy for us to forget just what salt meant to people before canning was invented around 1804 and refrigeration later. Without salt, people could starve in winter. And rulers took full advantage with iniquitous salt taxes. In France the tax (*gabelle*) caused mass discontent and even uprisings, especially in Louis XIV's reign. Salt smuggling was a national curse leading to gang warfare. Under a relic of old privileges Guérande and area could produce salt and send it all over the Province tax free. There was a huge smuggling trade across the Loire between Brittany and Anjou. Guérande really prospered.

The sands moved wildly before pines were planted to hold them. In 1527 they were blown so fiercely in a violent gale along La Grande Côte between Le Croisic and Pointe de Penchâteau that they buried the village of Escoublac.

Guérande needed the ramparts which were built by Jean de Montfort. In the war with Charles de Blois which made Montfort Duke of Brittany, Guérande had supported him, so Charles' forces under Louis of Spain took the city and massacred 8,000 inhabitants. You had to be very careful which supporters' club you joined in those days. It was before the great altar of Guérande's St Aubin church in 1365 that the King of France and de Montfort signed the treaty giving him the Dukedom.

In the Wars of Religion, Guérande, alone in the Nantes diocese, backed Henri IV and the Protestants, and played an important role. At Château Careil, the fortified castle 6km south on D92, the Prince of Condé, the Protestant leader, hid from the Catholic League forces of the Duc de Guise. The castle is still inhabited. Built in the 14th century, it was altered in the 15th to 16th centuries and has one delightful Renaissance wing and another ornamented at roof level with armorial decorations. Candlelight visits are arranged at night from 15 June to 30 August.

The Parc Régional de Brière starts south-east of Guérande, stretching to St Nazaire. It covers 40,000 hectares of which nearly forty per cent is marsh, with drainage canals built up between the 15th and 20th centuries. Using blins, flat-bottomed boats propelled by a pole, the Briérons lived for centuries by cutting peat, gathering reeds for thatching, trapping eels, catching pike, tench and roach and hunting wildfowl. They kept sheep and cattle which they moved from pasture to pasture in their blins. Even those who now work in St Nazaire factories continue these pastimes. The canals are ablaze with yellow iris from mid-May to mid-June and water lilies follow until late July. You can often arrange with boatmen to be poled around.

TOURIST INFORMATION (Guérande) 5 place Marhallé (40.24.96.71)

MARKET Saturday

FESTIVALS June – Music Festival; July–August – folklore fêtes; August – International Music Academy

HOTEL

Remparts, 14 boul. du Nord (40.24.90.69). Only eight bedrooms but good and peaceful. Very good restaurant. Excellent fish, very fresh. Wide range of menus. ROOMS D–E. MEALS C–F. Restaurant shut evenings in winter; also 20 December–4 January.

RESTAURANTS

Collégiale, 63 faubourg Bizienne (40.24.97.29). In a beautiful 17th-century house; ludicrously expensive. Moves in winter (1 October–31 March) to Paris (Collégiale Olivia Valère, 40 rue du Colisée, near Champs Elysées). MEALS G. Shut winter; lunch Tuesday, Wednesday; lunch all July, August.

Manoir Le Cardinal, 2.5km N near Mirou (40.24.72.56). Charming restaurant. Excellent, good value lunch menu, otherwise expensive but good. MEALS D (lunch), F–G. Shut Monday, Tuesday except July, August; fifteen days before Easter.

Fleur de Sel, 9 rue Juiverie (40.24.79.39). Excellent value. Cheap lunch not served in July, August. MEALS C. Shut Wednesday; Sunday evening out of season; 10–20 February; 10–25 October.

LA GUERCHE-DE-BRETAGNE
[ILLE-ET-VILAINE]

This little town between Châteaubriant and Vitré was once just a manorial estate owned by du Guesclin. It has old arcaded houses in and around Place de la Mairie, an interesting Romanesque

Church at La Guerche-de-Bretagne

church and is renowned for its cider. The church has a range of styles from the 12th-century chancel to the 15th- to 16th-century nave and the modern north aisle and belfry. The stalls have interesting carvings and there are 15th-century stained-glass windows. It is all very pleasant. So is the surrounding countryside, either for walking or gentle car touring.

Take D463 towards Rennes, then D48 past Étang de Marcillé and on your right you pass La Roch-aux-Fées (Fairies' Rock), one of the best of Brittany's megaliths. It is like a little longhouse built in purple schist, and if you want to know before you plunge into matrimony whether it is going to work out well, the fairies who built it will tell you. The man walks round the rock in a clockwise direction, the woman anti-clockwise. They count the stones. If their numbers are the same, the marriage will be ideal. If the difference is no more than two, it might work out. If the numbers vary by more than two, find yourself another partner.

At Le Theil take D94 through a little forest to Les Lacs des

Mottes, artificial lakes where you can fish on Thursdays and Sundays.

There is a bigger lake reached by a footpath in the Forêt de la Guerche, south of La Guerche and of Rannée, and a long lake Étang de Carcraon north along D95 which takes you through Bais (*see* page 68) to Louvigné-de-Bais, where the arcaded church has magnificent 16th-century stained glass.

La Guerche has pleasant cheap hotels and is a good touring centre, with Rennes only 40km away, Châteaubriant 30km, and, beautiful Vitré a mere 22km.

Tourist Information place Gén-de-Gaulle
(99.96.21.51)
Market Tuesday

HOTELS

Calèche, 16 ave Général-Leclerc (99.96.20.36). Quiet Logis, nice atmosphere. Good value. Rooms A–C. Meals A–D. Shut Friday, Sunday evening; 1–15 October; Christmas.

Dupont d'Anjou, 11 faubourg d'Anjou (99.49.23.10). Good fish; boiled salt beef off season. Very cheap. Excellent value. Rooms A. Meals A–B. Shut Sunday evening.

LAC DE GUERLÉDAN
[Côtes-du-Nord]

Man-made as a winding reservoir by damming the Blavet river, Lake Guerlédan is outstandingly attractive, a delightful place for sailing or fishing, and has lovely walks around it. 14km long, it has the lively little town of Mur-de-Bretagne (*see* page 189) at one end. At the other end it runs alongside the Forest of Quénécan (mostly of pine and heath) to the nice little village of Gouarec at the meeting of the Nantes-Brest canal and the river Blavet. It has an old hunting lodge of the Rohan family. In places the lake is overlooked by wild rocky hills. There are many campsites on the shores or nearby and one- and two-star hotels. There is water-skiing and canoeing as well as sailing, and many local festivals in summer. The Nantes-Brest canal runs to the lake, with beautiful tree-shaded towpath walks.

Footpaths follow the shore in many places. Roads are often set back with lake views.

South from Mur-de-Bretagne follow D35, then D31 to St Aignan, a village with a charming little church and a 1km side road to the lake dam, an ugly thing. The road continues through the forest, with another side road to the bay at Sordan (Anse de Sordan). From here you can take boat trips round the lake (mid-June to mid-September). Back on the forest road you reach the delightful village of Les Forges-des-Salles. Take the little D15A road south for 2km then walk for 2km along a path to the right to reach Étang des Salles, a little lake, and the partly ruined Les Salles château, original home of the Rohan family. Go back to Les Forges (named for the furnaces where iron ore was smelted over charcoal until coal replaced it last century). Continue north over the Blavet river to an avenue on the right between walls which takes you to the ruins of the 12th-century Abbey of Bon Repos in a lovely woodland setting near an old creeper-clad bridge.

Take D44 up the Gorges of the river Daoulas. The river runs through a narrow, twisting valley with steep sides to join the Blavet. From N164bis south of the gorges going eastward you get fine views over Lake Guerlédan and even better views if you take the right turn to Keriven and the little road alongside

Bon Repos, le vieux pont

the lake (D111). It rejoins N164bis and a few kilometres further on the D63 through the picturesque deep Gorges de Poulancre reaches the village of St Gilles-Vieux-Marché, a delightful place famous for its flowers. Good fishing on its lagoon.

Mur-de-Bretagne is 4½km south.

TOURIST INFORMATION (*see* Mur-de-Bretagne page oo)

HOTELS
(*See* also Mur-de-Bretagne).

Blavet, at Gouarec (96.24.90.03). Very pleasant Logis overlooking the river. Comfortable rooms. Wide range of meals. ROOMS B–F. MEALS A–G. Shut Sunday evening, Monday except July, August; 18–25 December; February.

Hostellerie de l'Abbaye at St Geven (Bon Repos) (96.24.98.38). Restored farm of the abbey. Five charming rooms; flowery terrace. ROOMS C–D. MEALS A–D. Shut Wednesday; 8 January–2 February; 5–30 October.

La Vallée, Le Bourg, at St Gilles-Vieux-Marché (96.28.53.32). Logis. Cheap menus. ROOMS B–E. MEALS A–C. Shut Saturday low-season; September.

Touristes (96.28.53.30). Popular locally for cheap, good value meals. ROOMS A–B. MEALS A–C. Shut Saturday in winter.

GUILVINEC ET LECHIAGAT
[S. FINISTÉRE]

Guilvinec, along the coast of the Penmarch Peninsula south-west of Pont-l'Abbé, is a very active fishing port where a lot of the fish is still canned immediately it arrives, especially tunny and sardines. A lot of langoustines landed, too. Watching the boats come in is one of the great tourist sights.

It forms a well-sheltered harbour with Lechiagat, where a lot of pleasure boats are moored in summer. Not at all pretty but I find these two ports more interesting than the small ex-fishing ports which make pretty pictures.

TOURIST INFORMATION 24 rue J-Stephan (98.58.10.79)

FESTIVALS Last Sunday in July – Pardon; 15 August – Fête de la Mer

HOTELS
Port, at Lechiagat (98.58.10.10). France-Accueil hotel. Boat trips and deep-sea fishing organised. ROOMS B–C. MEALS B–E. Shut 24 December–5 January.
Centre, rue Penmarch (98.58.10.44). Regional cheap menu is popular. ROOMS B–C. MEALS A–F. Shut Monday in winter; February.

LE GUILDO
[CÔTES-DU-NORD]
(*See* St Cast, page 238).

GUIMILIAU
[N. FINISTÈRE]

Little village 6km south-west of St Thégonnec is famed for its enclos paroissial. Whether from religious fervour, as some writers assume, or village pride, around 1580 to 1640 the people

Guimilau parish close

of this village built a parish close of remarkable Renaissance magnificence. The calvary must be the most ornate in Brittany. A large cross with a thorny column bears the statues of the Virgin, St John, St Peter and the local lad St Yves. Crowds of figures on the platform tell the story of the Passion and of the servant-girl Catell-Gollet (Catherine the Lost) who concealed her love-affair at Confession only to find that her lover had turned into Satan himself, who clawed her down to hell fire. How that must have frightened wayward peasant girls when the priest thundered the story from the pulpit! It appears on several calvaries. Among the carvings of the Disciples and Christ's family is a woman in 16th-century court dress, said to be Mary, Queen of Scots, who was executed in 1587, about the time of the carving of the Calvary.

The church was rebuilt in Flamboyant style, in the early 17th century. It has a beautiful south porch and inside a truly magnificent, ornate baptistry carved in wood. There are many more fine carvings.

3km west on country roads is an attractive parish close at Lampaul-Guimiliau with a superb arch and remarkably good wood carving in the church. But the calvary here is very sober.

HOTEL

Enclos at Lampaul-Guimilau (98.68.77.08). Two-star Logis. Popular locally. ROOMS C–D. MEALS A–D. Open all year.

LE GUIMORAIS
[CÔTES-DU-NORD]

Quiet, simple seaside resort to west of Pointe de Grouin and Cancale. Its fine beach stretches from Pointe de Meinga round the bay to the harbour of Rothéneuf. The road round this coast is very attractive. Over an inlet from Guimorais is Le Lupin, a château built by a rich shipowner from St Malo in the 17th century.

GUINGAMP
[CÔTES-DU-NORD]

This lovely old feudal town with old houses in winding streets used to be just a farming market town but it is expanding fast with new industries. It is still a very pleasant town, astride the river Trieux and in the place du Centre, gorgeous medieval houses look towards the beautiful Renaissance Fontaine de la Pompe which has three basins ornamented with the heads of rams, nymphs, dolphins and winged horses. Perhaps the sculptor had not forgotten that a fertility god was worshipped here in Pagan times.

The castle and ramparts are in ruins – one of the castles pulled down by Richelieu. Being between the Armor (the coast country) and the Argoat (the inland hills and woods) and at the meeting place of many important roads, its castle was fought over for centuries. The English besieged it several times in the War of Succession. In 1489 Vicomte Rohan took the town for the French King Charles VIII, who became first husband of Anne, Duchess of Brittany, and in the Wars of Religion it was a fortress of the Catholic League.

Guingamp is still known best for its spectacular Pardon at the Basilica of Notre-Dame de Bon-Secours. This takes place on the first weekend in July and is one of the greatest festivals in Brittany.

The church was built in the 14th century, but two centuries later a tower collapsed, wrecking the right side of the nave. The town held a competition for rebuilding plans and all the architects except one suggested a traditional Gothic design like the left side of the church. But one young fellow named Le Moal submitted a new-fangled Renaissance plan and the people of Guingamp accepted it. So the church is Gothic on one side and Renaissance on the other.

The statue of Notre-Dame-de-Bon-Secours, the Black Virgin, is in a side chapel. Black Virgins are believed to have miraculous powers and this one draws thousands of pilgrims, especially during the Pardon. On Saturday evening she is carried through the streets clothed in silk, followed by a huge procession carrying candles. Then three bonfires are lit by the bishop presiding. A writer on Brittany last century said that the procession was followed by an orgy, with many young girls having plenty to confess at Mass next day. I have not, alas, been to this pardon but I am told that the feasting and dancing after the procession are still fairly lively. So is the other festival of Breton dance in mid-August. On both occasions you can see some lovely old Breton costumes. Markets are lively, too.

The 17th-century town hall is very impressive. The river is known for canoeing, including competitions.

TOURIST INFORMATION 2 place Vally, April – September (96.43.73.89)

MARKET Saturday

FESTIVALS *see above*, plus Commercial Fair in July

HOTELS

Relais du Roy, place Centre (96.43.76.62). In a 16th-century inn where Louis XIII appreciated the cooking. So they called it the King's Relais. He also appreciated the local duchesses. Fine old building furnished with taste and comfort, impeccable service. Excellent traditional cooking. Small, so book. ROOMS E–G. MEALS C–F. Shut Sundays except July, August; 26 August–4 September; 22 December–6 January.

Armor, 44 boul. Clemenceau (96.43.76.16). No restaurant. Good value rooms. ROOMS C–D. Open all year.

RESTAURANT

Chaumière, 42 rue de la Trinité (96.43.72.47). Well run; traditional cooking. MEALS A–E. Shut Sunday evening, Monday; February holidays; 19 July-10 August.

HÉDÉ
[ILLE-ET-VILAINE]

A charming village on a hill with castle ruins and hanging gardens to houses, set between a pool and the Ille-Rance canal. It is only 14km from Combourg and 20km from Rennes, so it is an excellent place for a short stay. The countryside to the east, dotted with small lakes, canals, windmills and woods, is little known and delightful. The canal 1½km north-east has eleven locks raising the level 27 metres. There are nice walks along the old towpath.

Les Iffs, 7km west, has a fine Flamboyant village church with an elegant modern spire. There are nine lovely 16th-century stained-glass windows and a font carved with a hare playing a musical instrument. The unusual 15th-century high altar was discovered beneath a later wooden altar piece.

Less than 1km north of Les Iffs, along a lovely avenue, is Château de Montmuran, a rather severe 12th-century castle dominating the countryside. From the original château remain the two massive towers with conical tops. A more recent building (17th to 18th centuries) joins them to the 14th-century fortified entrance with a drawbridge. Du Guesclin was knighted here in 1354 and later his second marriage to a member of the Montmuran family took place here.

MARKET Monday

HOTEL

Vieux Moulin, on N137 (99.45.45.70). Very attractive old mill, on main road but not noisy. Garden. Good value meals. ROOMS B–D. MEALS A–E. Shut Sunday evening, Monday; 23 December–31 January.

RESTAURANT

Vieille Auberge, N137 (99.45.46.25). Hidden behind poplars with nice terrace for fine days. Good straightforward cooking. MEALS C–D. Shut Sunday evening, Monday; mid-January–mid-February; 28 August–5 September.

HENNEBONT
[MORBIHAN]

Rather near to Lorient, so this medieval town on the steep banks of the Blavet river caught too many stray bombs and fierce bombardments in World War II. The Germans used it as a dormitory for their naval and gun crews, to make them safer from the RAF's night bombers attacking the important submarine base at Lorient. Much of its medieval splendour was destroyed.

What is left of the 15th-century ramparts has gardens running along the walls. There are lovely views over the river Blavet. The 16th-century church Notre-Dame-de-Paradis, in the large place du Maréchal-Foch, has a huge belfry topped by a 65-metre-high steeple.

If the RAF and the American guns destroyed much of old Hennebont, in 1341 the English saved it. In the War of Succession the French imprisoned Jean de Montfort in the Louvre and his wife, Jeanne de Laval, was besieged by the French and their nominee for the Duchy, Charles de Blois. She held out until the French breached the walls, then made a deal that she would leave the town if reinforcements did not arrive within three days. Two days later an English fleet sailed up the Blavet and saved the town.

Horse-lovers love Hennebont. Its stud has no fewer than 140 stallions (draughthorses, Breton post horses and some bloodstock) which are sent out to breeding studs over much of Brittany (guided visits all day mid-July to mid-September; afternoons only mid-September to end of February. Shut Sunday).

Two big main roads bypass Hennebont, so its traffic problems have been relieved. The little D23 road north is pretty and leads to very pleasant side roads as far as Pontivy.

TOURIST INFORMATION Syndicat d'Initiative, place Maréchal-Foch (97.36.24.52)

MARKET Thursday

FESTIVALS Last Sunday in September – Fête de Voeu (Festival of Vows)

HOTELS

Château de Locguénolé, Kerrignac, by D781 (97.76.29.04). Very comfortable, very good cooking and very, very expensive. In a lovely park setting by the river, with river views and a swimming pool, it is luxuriously furnished with antiques and fin-de-siècle tapestries. Also charming bedrooms in an old cottage two minutes away. Good fishing; 9km from the sea. The great chef

Michel Gaudin has gone to the Mas de Chastelas at Saint-Tropez but his young successor has hung on to two Michelin stars. ROOMS F–G. MEALS F–G. Shut January. Restaurant shut Monday in winter.

Centre, 44 rue Maréchal-Joffre (97.36.21.44). Down-to-earth. Pleasant welcome; good value. ROOMS A–C. MEALS A–E. Shut Sunday evening.

Auberge de Toul-Douar, old route de Lorient (97.36.24.04). Two-star Logis. ROOMS B–D. MEALS A–E. Shut Sunday evening, Tuesday lunch; 5–27 February; 1–8 November.

ÎLES DE HOUAT ET HOEDIC
[MORBIHAN]

Two isles 15km off the Morbihan coast, reached by boats from Quiberon (1 hour and 1½ hours – Cie Morbihannaise de Navigation, 97.50.06.90 in Quiberon) *Houat* means 'the duck', *Hoedic* 'the duckling'.

Houat, north-east of Belle-Île, controls the entrance to the Gulf of Morbihan, so was inevitably occupied three times by the English in the 17th to 18th centuries. 5km long by 1.3km wide, it has several beaches, most hidden in little creeks. The best beach faces the isle of Hoedic at the entrance to an ancient port destroyed by a tempest in 1951. The new port used by shell-fishermen is on the north coast. Oyster farms were set up in 1972 to repopulate the coast.

Houat is fertile and flowery. Its little town is a delightful scene of white houses decked with flowers in winding roads and alleys. St Gildas came here from England around AD 499 and returned to die in AD 570.

The story of Gildas is one of the great typical stories of Brittany – history woven into legend. He came from Cornwall and set up an oratory on Houat, then went to the mainland to settle by the Blavet river. Here he arranged for Waroch, Count of Vannes, a marriage between Triphine, Waroch's daughter, and Comorre, Count of Cornouaille, without knowing that Comorre was a brutal Bluebeard who killed his wives when they became pregnant because it had been predicted that his son would cause his death. Triphine fled when she discovered that she was to have a baby but he found her hiding in a wood and cut her head off. Waroch told Gildas. The infuriated priest went to Comorre's castle, prayed and threw a handful of dust at it. It fell down, killing Comorre. Then Gildas put Triphine's head back on her shoulders and she came back to life. The grateful Waroch gave him the monastery at Rhus. Triphine's son became a saint, too. Gildas died on Houat but the locals put his body in a boat and pushed it out to sea, and it landed miraculously at Rhus where it still lies. Until the 1880s, property on the isle was communal and the priest virtually ruled.

Hoedic is rockier, more barren, but it has little beaches, good sea views and three tiny ports. It lives mostly by tourism.

HOTELS

Îles (97.30.68.02). 7 ROOMS B. MEALS A–D. Open April–September.

Sirène (97.30.68.05). Lovely fish, shellfish 'guaranteed fresh'. Sailing, windsurfing centre; superb beach. 'Helicopter pad'! ROOMS E–F. MEALS B–E.

HUELGOAT
[N. FINISTÈRE]

Huelgoat is in a beautiful spot – the very essence of Argoat, the old, once-wooded centre of Brittany which to this day most beach-loungers of Bénodet never explore. On the edge of the Monts d'Arrée, an area of savage grandeur, it is in a fantastic landscape of rocks, hollows, streams, waterfalls in the middle of thick, hilly woods up to 175 metres high. It is a pleasant place to visit, a delightful place in which to stay, and a little heaven for anglers – trout in the river, carp and perch in the lake.

The woods are of beech, oak, Norway spruce and pine, scattered with great stones of granite and sandstone.

From the lake, a path along the right bank of the river leads to Chaos du Moulin, a picturesque pile of round granite rocks in a green setting. From here, within 100 metres, are the extraordinary Grotto du Diable (Devil's grotto), reached by climbing down an iron ladder, with a looped path to a stream below; Roche Tremblante (Trembling Rock), a 100-ton block you can cause to sway on its base; and an enormous pile of rocks called Ménage de la Vierge (Virgin's Kitchen) because they are supposed to be shaped like cooking pots. There are fine walks along allée Violette, and along the canal and into the woods by Promenade du Fer à Cheval. There are car parks on D769A east of the town, from which you can pick up woodland walks. A good walk is from Ménage de la Vierge along Sentier des Amoureux (Lovers' Walk), then left to Grotte d'Arthus (Artus Cave) and on to the very pretty La Mare aux Sangliers (Boars' Pool) where two waterfalls crossed by a bridge cascade into a pool. Further on is Artus Camp (Graeco-Roman).

The pool and canal were dug in the 18th century to supply silver and lead mines. These were already known to the Romans, and were worked by a German company from the 14th century to 1914. The canal now serves a hydro-electric plant. Alas, there is also a housing development beside the lake. Nice for the owners!

The town, with an old fountain in its central square, has a 16th-century church with a pleasant statue of St Yves, the Breton lawyer, refusing a rich man's bribe to take a poor man's petition.

Years ago we hired a horse-drawn caravan (a *roulotte*) to wander the green wooded paths from Locmaria-Berrien-Gare 7km south-east. You still can in season (Cheval Bretagne, Locmaria-Berrien 29218).

TOURIST INFORMATION place Mairie (spring holidays;
June–September–98.99.72.32)
MARKETS second and fourth Thursday each month;
stalls in main street most days
FESTIVAL Pardon first Sunday in August

HOTELS

An Triskell, route Pleyben (98.99.71.85). Ordinary little useful hotel without restaurant. ROOMS B–C. Shut 15 November–15 December.

Truite at Locmaria-Berrien station, 7km south-east by D764 (98.99.73.05). May Madame Le Guillon continue forever cooking her traditional meals. She is in her eighties and some modernist has taken away her Michelin star, but Brittany is still proud of her. Wines you can no longer get elsewhere at such reasonable prices. Seven simple rooms. ROOMS A–C. MEALS C–G. Shut Sunday evening, Monday (except July, August); 2 January–1 March.

RESTAURANT
Ty Douz, rue Gén-de-Gaulle (98.99.74.78). Good value restaurant with lakeside terraces. Old-style, simple dishes; trout from lake. Five menus A–D. Shut Friday (except 1 July–30 September); January.

ÎLE-TUDY
[S. FINISTÈRE]

Despite its name, it is a narrow spit of land which half blocks the Pont l'Abbé estuary west of Bénodet, and is reached by a causeway road. It can also be reached by boat from Loctudy (passengers and bikes only).

It has a pretty little fishing port which has recently become a small resort, but mostly for day visitors. Its shingly beach is a treasure trove of seashells.

TOURIST INFORMATION Tourist Office (98.56.43.11)

HOTELS
Euromer, 6 ave Teven (98.56.39.27). Mainly for families, with all family rooms except two; also studios with kitchenette. No restaurant. ROOMS B–G. Open 1 April–30 September.

Moderne, 9 place Cale (98.56.43.34). Not modern and a Logis. Lively, friendly, still used by fishermen. ROOMS C. MEALS A–C. Hotel shut winter (1 October–30 March). Restaurant shut Saturday (low-season); 15 October–15 November.

JOSSELIN
[Morbihan]

Josselin is a magic little town. When children first see the pepperpot towers of its formidable castle mirrored in the waters of the river Oust, they believe that their fairy tales have come true.

The first time I saw it I had taken a boat from La Roche-Bernard up the Vilaine river to Redon, then cut across to Josselin through Malestroit by the river Oust. To see the great walls and towers above me on the river's edge, looking sinister and threatening, was awesome. I felt that a shower of arrows would descend on me from the ramparts alongside the towers.

It is a magnificent castle with a pretty town beside it, and if the number of tourists filling the town in summer has multiplied greatly since my first visit, that is the price Josselin pays for

Château de Josselin

having such a splendid and historically interesting château. Most of them leave by early evening, so stay overnight.

From outside the castle, with four pepperpot towers, is warlike. The inside is much more delicate and friendly. It has stood there for nearly a thousand years. The fortress itself was built by Guthenoc de Porhort about the year 1000. His son Josselin finished it and built the town named after him.

The castle has been severely damaged and repaired immediately several times. Henry II of England, who attacked all the Breton lords who refused to accept the overlordship of his son Geoffrey, besieged Josselin in 1168, finally took it and destroyed most of the castle and the town. The castle was rebuilt within seven years and survived the Hundred Years War. It figures in one of the most remarkable stories of Josselin's history known as Le Combat des Trentes (the Battle of the Thirties). In the middle of the 14th century during the Breton War of Succession, the castle was owned and defended by Jean de Beaumanoir who supported the French-backed Charles de Blois. The camp of the English-backed Jean de Montfort, commanded by an Englishman Richard Bembrough, was nearby at Ploërmel.

The two commanders got so tired of skirmishes and killings that they agreed to settle for a combat of thirty knights from each side, fighting with sword, dagger, battle-axe and pike, at Mi-Voie, 5km from Josselin. A stone pyramid marks the spot. On 27 March 1351 they met. The Montfort team was of four Bretons, six Germans and twenty English. They fought hand-to-hand all day. Though Beaumanoir was wounded, the French of Josselin won. Bembrough and eight others were killed, the rest of Montfort's men taken prisoner. From 1370 it was acquired by Olivier de Clisson when he married de Beaumanoir's widow, Marguerite de Rohan. He built the present tremendous walls towards the end of the 14th century. Clisson (1336–1407) was successful, thuggish and arrogant. His motto was 'I do as I please'. He fought with the English and Jean de Montfort against Charles de Blois, du Guesclin and the French in the War of Succession because his father had been falsely accused of betraying France and beheaded. His infuriated mother nailed her husband's head to the ramparts of Nantes and made her children swear to avenge him. With four hundred men she took six French châteaux and butchered their garrisons. Then she took to sea and sank every French ship she met.

By the Hundred Years War Olivier was fighting with the French and his brutality got him the name of Butcher of the English. In 1380 when du Guesclin was killed, de Clisson succeeded him as Constable of France, in command of all the French armies. But he was unpopular, and when Charles VI went mad de Clisson had to flee to Josselin, and greatly strengthened the castle, giving it nine towers. When Clisson died in 1407 at Josselin, it passed to the very powerful Rohan family.

In 1488 Vicomte Jean II de Rohan supported France against Duke François II of Brittany, so François had Josselin's defences dismantled. When Duchess Anne became Queen of France shortly after, she forgave de Rohan and the castle's fortifications were rebuilt. At the same time Jean de Rohan added the magnificent living quarters which contrast with the fortress, with superb and rare sculptures in hard granite. The Flamboyant Gothic façade of the inner Court of Honour is superb. The monogram 'A' topped by a crown appears frequently in the lavish decorations – de Rohan's tribute to Anne.

In the Wars of Religion, Henri de Rohan, a great soldier, was one of the leaders of the Protestants and had to flee for a while from Richelieu after the Protestants were beaten at La Rochelle. Richelieu knocked down five of Josselin's nine towers, saying to Rohan later: 'I have just thrown a fine ball among your skittles.'

In the 17th and 18th centuries the château was almost abandoned and it was used as a prison during the Revolution. On the return of the monarchy last century the Rohans got it back and made a good job of restoring it. It contains some fine portraits and porcelain and interesting old Court clothes. The grand dining-room is decorated with the coats of arms of all Rohans and related families; also a statue of Olivier de Clisson on a horse. It is still a private home, but is open in the afternoons April, May, June and 1–8 September, mornings also in July–August.

In the stables is a super collection of 500 old dolls – Musée des Poupées (open 1 May to 30 September except Monday; rest of year afternoons of Wednesday, Saturday, Sunday).

You can see the castle excellently from the Ste Croix bridge over the Oust.

The church of Notre-Dame-du-Roncier (rose-bush) was founded in the 11th century but rebuilt and remodelled several times since, with a transept spire erected in 1949. The legend of its name is that a peasant cutting down brambles found a statue of the Virgin in a bramble bush. He took his prize home, but discovered it the next day returned to the bush. Each time he took it home it went back to the bush until a chapel was built on the spot.

A pardon is held around the fountain behind the church (second Sunday in September). It has been called since 1728 Pardon des Aboyeuses (Barker's Pardon) because that year three children were cured of that form of epilepsy. The other legend is that the Virgin appeared in Josselin as a beggar seeking alms, but the women set their dogs on her. So each woman's voice was changed to a dog-like bark at Whitsun and on Pardon day until they had kissed holy relics.

TOURIST INFORMATION Syndicat, place Congrégation (June–September–97.22.36.43) and Mairie (low-season 97.22.24.17)
MARKET Saturday
FESTIVALS *see above*

HOTELS

Château, 1 rue Gén-de-Gaulle (97.22.20.11). Facing château, very good, so full of tourists in midsummer. River views from window tables and some rooms. Terrace overlooking river. ROOMS B–E. MEALS A–E. Shut Sunday evening, Monday 15 October–1 March; February.

Commerce et Restaurant Blot, 9 rue Glatinier (97.22.22.08). Located high above river. Used to be the locals' hideaway, now discovered by tourists. Copper-pan, garlic-string décor but superb value, with wide range of prices. Light, traditional dishes. Seven rooms C–D. MEALS A–F. Shut Wednesday; February.

Pélican (97.22.22.05). Where most locals go now, including for local weddings. Very cheap. Simple. Good shellfish. ROOMS A. MEALS A–C. Shut Saturday low-season.

France, 6 pl. Notre-Dame (97.22.23.06). Not pretty but traditional Breton auberge with traditional dishes, nicely served. Eight Rooms B. MEALS A–E. Shut Thursday; 15 January–15 February.

Relais du Porhoet at Guilliers, 16km NE by D16 (97.74.40.17). Typical Breton village inn with typical good, uncomplicated cooking. ROOMS C–D. MEALS A–E. Open all year.

JUGON-LES-LACS
[CÔTES-DU-NORD]

Little town alongside a lake of 67 hectares and a reservoir at the meeting of Rosette, Arguenon and Rieule rivers, 22km west of Dinan by N176. It is one of the places called 'Station Verte' (Green Resort) organised to give open-air holidays. It has a sailing school, riding school, big camping site, caravans for hire, hotel rooms, good fishing and bathing in the lake. Northwards are the Forests of St Aubin and Hunaudaie and on the edge of them Château de la Hunaudaie – a ruin half-hidden by brambles and ivy. Once a huge medieval castle, it is still a formidable sight, with great machicolated towers above its moat, grass in the courtyard and ruins of its 17th-century Renaissance living quarters. Built by the de Tournemine family in 1220, it was partly destroyed in the War of Succession but rebuilt and owned by the same family for at least four centuries. In the Revolution it was partly knocked down, then burned. Locals went on stealing its stone until the State rescued it in 1930 (open daily in July, August; Sunday afternoons in April, May, June, September).

TOURIST INFORMATION Hôtel de Ville (96.31.61.62)
MARKET Tuesday, Friday

HOTEL

Grande Fontaine (96.31.61.29). ROOMS A–C. MEALS B–E. Shut 15 October–15 November.

KERDRUC
[S. Finistère]

Little port on the Aven estuary south of Pont-Aven in a pretty position. Its little harbour is full in summer of yachts and fishing boats. Bar on the quay.

KERFANY-LES-PINS
[S. Finistère]

A posh name for a little resort on a point at the entrance to the river Bélon estuary, opposite Port-Manech. A beach of fine sand and rocks backed by pine trees. A crêperie, fine views over Aven estuary and super cliff walks.

KERMARIA
[Côtes-du-Nord]
(*See* St Quay-Portrieux, page 246)

KERNASCLÉDEN
[Morbihan]

As well as the remarkable church this whole area is attractive and worth exploring, especially the forest of Pont-Calleck. It lies about 40km north of Lorient, or you can reach it easily from Quimperlé by D22 and D2 to Plouay, then the pretty D178.

The church was built for the Rohan family and legend says that the same workers built it and the chapel of St Fiacre at the same time (*see* Faouët, page 129). Each day angels carried the men and their tools from one site to the other. But Kernascléden was consecrated in 1453 and St Fiacre thirty years later. A pity! I like the Breton legends, and this one had the possibilities of an angelic helicopter service.

Kernascléden church is famous for the obvious striving after perfection in every detail by its builders and sculptors. You can see it in the very slender tower, the foliage of the pinnacles, and rose carvings and delicate tracery. But the finest work is inside. The roof has stone vaulting instead of wood. The vaults and walls above the main arches are decorated with frescoes of the life of Christ, a *danse macabre* (dance of death), eight musical angels and the horrors of hell, which must have frightened the wits out of simple 15th-century peasants. I personally can get tired of looking into churches, but Brittany is certainly rich in those worth the effort of finding them.

Take the D782 road west from Kernascléden for 1½km to Kerchopine, then turn left on D110 and by taking a very steep road branching left you see Notre-Dame-de-Joie, formerly Château de Pont-Calleck, now a children's home. You can walk along one shore of the lake. At the entrance to the grounds is the very tiny chapel of Ste Anne-des-Bois.

Go back on the D110 towards Plouay and you are on the edge of Pont-Calleck forest. The road is very attractive all the way, passing through the narrow valley of the Scorff.

LAMBALLE
[CÔTES-DU-NORD]

A charming and photogenic town with a pig and cattle market and a renowned stud for horses, Lamballe was just a busy little commercial town when I first knew it in the 1950s. It has been publicised for tourism since but it is not overcrowded and still gets on with its other activities. I wonder if it was a sly comment by the local people to put the tourist information office in the 15th-century Maison du Bourreau – the Hangman's House.

Lamballe, 21km south-east of St Brieuc and 16km from the coast at Le Val-André, was the capital of the old county of Penthièvre from 1134 to 1420 and Charles IX made it a Duchy.

Mercoeur, the notorious Catholic League leader, used it as a stronghold in the Wars of Religion, and it was besieged by the

Protestant captain La Noué, nicknamed 'Bras-de-Fer' because he had a metal hook to replace an arm he had lost in battle. He was killed in the siege and Henri IV said: 'What a pity that such a little stronghold destroyed such a great man. He alone was worth an army.'

Henri's son by Gabrielle d'Estrées, César de Vendôme, became the Duke. After Henri's death, César went on fighting for Protestants' right and so annoyed Cardinal Richelieu that in 1626 he ordered the castle to be pulled down. Only the chapel remains. Richelieu would use any excuse to knock down somebody else's castle.

The eldest sons of the Dukes were called Prince de Lamballe and in 1767 one prince aged twenty had led such a dissolute life that his father tried to reform him by marrying him off to a gentle seventeen-year-old Piedmontese princess. Unreformed, the prince went on regardless and died three months later, worn out by debauchery.

Marie-Antoinette, just married to the future Louis XVI, made friends with the young widowed Princess of Lamballe, who remained loyal for twenty years, which cost her her head in the Revolution. In the massacres of September 1792, a year before the King and Queen were guillotined, a mob cut off her head and paraded it on a spike.

The church of Notre-Dame at Lamballe stands on a spur high above the valley of the Gouessant, with attractive views from its terrace. It was the chapel of the castle and the doorway, beautifully framed with twenty columns with fine capitals, is truly impressive.

There are many old streets and houses in the town below, and more old churches.

The best time to visit the stud is after mid-July, for many stallions are sent out to do their duty around Brittany from mid-February to mid-July. There are usually about 150 stallions, mostly Breton draught-horses, old-style post-horses, and thoroughbred *anglais*. They go out daily in tandem, pairs or fours. There is also a dressage school. (Stud open mid-July to mid-February afternoons.) Riding schools at Manoir des Portes Hotel (*see below*) and at stud, covered heated swimming pool, uncovered in good weather. Boating on a small lake.

TOURIST INFORMATION place Martray (spring holidays; June–September. 96.31.05.38)
MARKET (general) Thursday
FESTIVAL Second Sunday in July – Folklorique Festival 'Ajoncs d'Or' (Golden Gorse)

HOTELS

Manoir des Portes, La Poterie, 3½km by D28 (96.31.13.62). In the middle of fields and woods, with a little fishing lake, converted manor-farm of charm. Good traditional cooking. Bedrooms vary in size. Quiet. ROOMS E–F. MEALS C–F. Shut 31 January–1 March. Restaurant shut Monday (except evenings high-season).

Angleterre, 29 boul. Jobert (96.31.00.16). Old-style pavement terrace saves the looks of this old hotel. Member of France-Accueil association of independent hotels – always a good recommendation. ROOMS A–D. MEALS A–E. Restaurant shut Sunday evening, Monday lunch in winter, also 6 February–6 March.

Tour d'Argent, 2 rue Dr Lavergne (96.31.01.37). Just off main square. Old inn, and more modern annexe. Cheap weekday menu. Bedrooms vary. ROOMS A–E. MEALS A–E. Restaurant shut Saturday (except evening in July, August) and last fortnight in June.

RESTAURANT

Forge, 9 rue Paul Langevin (96.31.03.50). Simple meals; open-fire grill. Good value. MEALS A–D. Shut Tuesday evening, Wednesday; 1–15 July.

LAMPAUL-GUIMILHAU
[N. FINISTÈRE]
(*see* Landivisiau, page 167)

LANCIEUX
[CÔTES-DU-NORD]

Quiet little beach resort on north coast between Dinard and St Cast. Extensive beach of fine sand surrounded by rocks with good fishing. Beautiful views to St Cast and St Jacut fishing village.

At Ploubalay, 3km south, is a watch-tower with excellent views from its terrace 104 metres high. There's a restaurant up there.

Horse-races in August.

HOTEL
Mer, rue Plage (96.86.22.07). ROOMS A–D. MEALS A–E. Shut January, February. Restaurant shut Sunday evenings in winter.

LANDERNEAU
[N. FINISTÈRE]

Old town delightfully situated on the banks of the Elorn river in the estuary 20km east of Brest. Good touring centre. It is the port of the estuary where trout and salmon are landed. As it narrows the estuary is crossed by an attractive 16th-century bridge with houses on it. There are many old houses round the 16th-century church dedicated to St Thomas of Canterbury and more by the old bridge on the right bank of the Élorn river. It is a lively market town, too, with a market on Saturdays. Many hotels and restaurants.

At Pencran, 3½km south-east, is an interesting 15th-century church in a parish close with an old porch with statuettes showing scenes from the Bible. The statues of the apostles were beheaded in the Revolution, as if they were French aristocrats. There's another Parish Close at La Roche-Maurice, 5km north-east.

TOURIST INFORMATION Kiosk on Pont de Rohan (98.85.13.09)

MARKET Saturday; first Monday in the month

HOTELS

Clos du Pontic, rue du Pontic (98.21.50.91). Old house, quiet, uphill from port, with a modern extension behind. Excellent fish; superb desserts. Flower garden and terrace. ROOMS D–F. MEALS A–F. Restaurant shut Saturday lunch, Sunday evening, Monday.

Amandier, 55 rue de Brest (98.85.10.89). Excellent modern dishes served with festive spirit in a nice setting, though no outside view from the dining-room. Eight ROOMS C–E. MEALS E–F. Restaurant shut Sunday evening, Monday.

RESTAURANT

Mairie, 9 rue Tour-d'Auvergne (98.85.01.83). Plenty of space, used by locals and tourists. Good straightforward cooking at reasonable prices. MEALS A–E. Shut Tuesday; 1–15 July; 15 November–1 December.

LANDÉVENNEC
[S. FINISTÈRE]

Little harbour in a pretty position where the Aulne river flows into the Brest roadstead. It is on a little fertile peninsula joined to the north of the Crozon peninsula and is so sheltered that palm trees grow. The town falls steeply down to the harbour jetty on a bend in the river in a near-Mediterranean setting surrounded by woods.

A Benedictine abbey was rebuilt in 1956, and you can attend services. The ruins of the old abbey, which disappeared during the Revolution, are on a different road. (Open daily mid-July to mid-September; rest of the year Sunday afternoons). There are ruins of a 5th-century monastery founded by St Guénolé, son of a British nobleman, who was said to have converted the drunken and licentious King Gradlon to Christianity and sobriety.

HOTEL

Beau Séjour (98.27.70.65). Family run; views of river from restaurant and many bedrooms. Good fish; locals like the restaurant.

Rooms B–D. Meals A–F. Shut Monday (evenings only May–September); January.

LANDIVISIAU and LAMPAUL-GUIMILIAU
[N. Finistère]

Just south of the main N12 trunk road and 29km south of Roscoff, Landivisiau is a busy town with one of the most important cattle markets in France.

The fountain of St Thivisiau was built after the Revolution from 15th-century sculptures taken from the tombs of local lords. One shows a shivering Christ being urged by John the Baptist to enter the water. The holy spring is fed straight to a communal laundry place showing that cleanliness is next to godliness but it is little used in these days of washing machines.

4km south-east is Lampaul-Guimiliau, with the most complete enclos paroissial (parish close) in Brittany. This close in particular is worth seeing not only as part of old Brittany but for its own charm.

The Triumphal Arched gateway of 1669, topped by three crosses, is more ornate than most. The calvary is plain, in great contrast to the one at Guimiliau, 3½km east (page 147). Inside the mortuary chapel are statues of St Roch, St Sébastien and St Pol (Paul). St Pol is killing a dragon, as on the Île de Batz (page 69), with his bishop's stole tied round its neck, but it is a puny dragon here.

The church has rich decorations and furnishings. Alas its spire, 70 metres high when built in 1570, has been sawn off after it was struck by lightning last century. Among all the impressive decorations, I was most impressed by the Entombment sculpture (1676). The crucified Christ's face is in white stone, the other people are coloured in polychromes.

Tourist Information (Landivisiau) Forum de l'Hôtel-de-Ville (98.68.03.50)
Market Tuesday Cattle Fair (auction)

HOTELS

Avenue, at Landivisiau, place du Champ-de-Foire (98.68.11.67). Simple Logis. Quiet annexe in car park. Cheap meals. ROOMS A–C. MEALS A–C. Shut Saturday evening, Sunday low-season. Restaurant shut 1–24 October.

Enclos, at Lampaul-Guimiliau in country 3km on N12 (98.68.77.08). New, comfortable. ROOMS C–D. MEALS A–D.

RESTAURANT

Elorn, 10 rue Gén-de-Gaulle, Landivisiau (98.68.38.46). Traditional cooking of high quality products. Five menus. MEALS B–F. Shut Sunday evening, Monday evening; part February.

LA LANDRIAIS
[ILLE-ET-VILAINE]

Port on the left bank of the river Rance, 8km south of Dinard. Naval yards. Fine river views along promenade des Hures, the old customs officers' walk.

LANNION
[CÔTES-DU-NORD]

Something old, something new. The rose-granite town of Lannion has an 11th-century port down on the banks of the river Leguer and on a hill 3km north an advanced research centre for the French telecommunications and electronics industry.

It is a pleasant and surprisingly spacious town for one so old. The old houses in the pedestrianised streets leading to place Général Leclerc and bordering it are delightful.

To reach Brélévenez church, founded in the 12th century by the Knights Templars, you must climb 140 granite steps. The church was remodelled in the Gothic period, anyway, and is not very exciting. It has a 15th-century tower.

The Thursday market spreads from the river up the old streets and serves a big area around.

Lannion is splendidly placed for reaching a variety of northern beaches, including Trébeurden (9km), Trégastel-Plage (13km), Ploumanach (14km) and Perros–Guirac (11km).

Close by, 8km west downriver, is Le Yaudet, at the head of a little horseshoe bay with rocks and sand at low tide, backed by pines and a grass headland with views over the beach. A chapel on the headland has, above the high altar, an odd, sculptured panel of God, Mary lying on a bed with the infant Jesus and a hovering dove, presumably symbolising the Holy Ghost. A pardon is held on the third Sunday in May.

The road to Locquémeau round the coast passes a hamlet called Christ. Locquémeau village, with a pretty little 15th-century church, overlooks a little resort with a fishing harbour. A walk to Séhar Point has views eastward to Trébeurden and westward to Primel Point.

Just off D11, 10km south of Lannion, is Château de Kergrist, gardens of which are open to the public. It is a handsome house, built between the 14th and 17th centuries and interesting for the variety of styles of its façades. Its gables, pepperpot towers and superb terrace overlooking the valley certainly make it look a desirable place to live (garden visits, afternoons, daily from mid-May to 1 July. Shut Tuesday).

More formidable and warlike is the ruined castle of Tonquédec to the north-east of Kergrist, still with enough of two towers and fortifications left to see why Richelieu had it dismantled in 1622 because he thought it was too strong – a prospective centre of Breton rebellion.

At Pleumeur-Bodou, north-west of Lannion, you can see the big white dome of the important space telecommunications centre, built originally for television via Telstar in 1962, now used by the French Post Office (PTT) for TV, telephone and telegraph transmissions (visits Easter to mid-October. Shut Saturdays except June, July, August – telephone 96.48.41.49).

TOURIST INFORMATION quai d'Aiguillon, Lannion
(96.37.07.35)
MARKET Thursday
FESTIVALS Festival d'Orgues (Organs) in summer

HOTELS

Porte de France, 5 rue J.-Savidan (96.46.54.81). Sadly, no restaurant now in the place where the great Louis Le Roy was King of the Kitchen a few years back. In 17th-century house. Quiet. ROOMS C–D.

Genêts d'Or at Le Yaudet (96.35.24.17). Small, pretty; restaurant popular locally. Simple ROOMS A–C. MEALS A–D. Shut Sunday evening, Monday low-season; hotel (not restaurant) shut 8 January–mid-March.

RESTAURANT

Serpolet, 1 rue Félix-le-Dantec (96.46.50.23). Quiet restaurant with charcoal grill in old stone building. Interesting blend of modern and traditional cooking, with traditional portions. MEALS B–F. Shut Sunday evening, Monday.

LARMOR-PLAGE
[MORBIHAN]

Seaside resort and suburb for Lorient. Multi-coloured 16th-century statues in the church. On the Sunday before or after 24 June is held a blessing of the channel Coureaux between the coast and Groix island. A procession of boats passes through the channel. Warships from Brest salute the church of Notre-Dame-de-Larmor with three guns, while the priest at the church has the bells rung, blesses the ship and hoists the flag.

Pleasant curving beach opposite Port Louis.

HOTEL

Beau-Rivage, plage de Toulhars (97.65.50.11). Really fresh fish. Excellent straightforward cooking; big range of menus. Overlooking beach ('pieds dans l'eau'); quiet. ROOMS A–C. MEALS A–F. Restaurant shut Sunday evening, Monday; five weeks after last Sunday in October.

LESCONIL
[S. Finistère]

Lively fishing port on the south coast of Penmarch peninsula, south of Pont-l'Abbé. Renowned for shellfish, especially langoustines. Fine sand beaches are well sheltered between picturesque rocks, and more and more French people are discovering it for holidays. Working port, so not so picturesque as those where fishing is dying. Deep-sea fishing for visitors.

Tourist Information place Résistance (season 98.87.86.99)

HOTELS
Atlantic (98.87.81.06). Attractive garden. Rooms B–E. Meals A–E. Shut October.
Dunes (98.87.83.03). Rooms E–F. Meals A–G. Open mid-March–mid-October.

LÉZARDRIEUX
[Côtes-du-Nord]

Sleepy-looking town on a hill above the river Trieux estuary by a suspension bridge over which the road leads 5km east to Paimpol. View across to the tree-lined opposite bank of the wide Trieux is very pleasant. So is the big market square. The 18th-century church has an attractive elegant belfry. Oyster farms in the estuary.

Market Friday

HOTELS
Relais Brenner, pont Lézardrieux (96.20.11.06). Just over the bridge, high among trees with splendid estuary views from its dining-room and bedrooms. A handsome, modern, Breton-style building in a pleasant garden, beautifully furnished, very comfortable bedrooms. Exceptional regional cuisine, with superb fish. Superb service. Rooms E–G. Meals C–G. Shut Monday (low-season); January, February.

Pont (96.20.10.59). No restaurant. Charming little hotel. ROOMS B–D. Open all year.

LOCMARIAQUER
[MORBIHAN]

At the end of the long peninsula at the entrance to the Gulf of Morbihan our prehistoric ancestors left some of the most impressive megaliths in the world. Most impressive are Men-er-Hroëc'h (fairy's stone), 200 tons, with 23 steps up to its funeral chamber; Dolmen de Mané-Lud, with carvings in its chamber; and Grand Menhir, in five pieces weighing 347 tons, the biggest menhir known.

Nice little port from which boats (*Vedettes Vertes*) take you for tours of Morbihan Bay and the Auray river. A road south takes you in 1½km to Kerpenhir Point with views over Morbihan channel. The port has a 12th-century church.

TOURIST INFORMATION Syndicat d'Initiative (mid-June–early September–97.57.33.05)

HOTELS
Escale, le Port (97.57.32.51). Holiday hotel, with rooms, restaurant and terrace overlooking sea. ROOMS C–E. MEALS A–D. Open end April–mid-September.

Lautram (97.57.312.32). 50 metres from sea. ROOMS B–C. MEALS A–E. Open spring holidays–end September.

LOCMINÉ
[MORBIHAN]

A very pleasant spot inland just south of N24 between Josselin and Lorient, in picturesque hilly countryside close to small rivers rich in trout. It grew round an abbey founded in the 7th century. 16th-century houses and church. A pleasant centre for a relaxed touring holiday of the country. It is an important cattle market for a big area.

TOURIST INFORMATION 30 rue Général-de-Gaulle (in
season – 97.60.09.90)
MARKET Monday afternoons and third Thursday of the
month – cattle

HOTELS
Argoat, 34 rue De Clisson (97.60.01.02). ROOMS B–E. MEALS
A–E. Shut Saturday off-season; 24 December–24 January.

LOCQUÉMEAU
[CÔTES-DU-NORD]
(*See* Lannion, page 169)

LOCQUIREC
[N. FINISTÈRE]

Little fishing port and lively summer resort 22km west of Lannion. Long jetty. The tide goes out a long way, leaving wide sandy beaches. A stream trickles through one of them. Another, Sables Blancs, has fine sand between rocks. Beautiful corniche coast road southwards and coast road west. Sea views from Pointe de Locquirec.

TOURIST INFORMATION Tourist Office at harbour
(January–September–98.67.40.83)
MARKET Wednesday (in season)

HOTELS
Port (98.67.42.10). Very simple but all rooms with sea views.
ROOMS B–C. MEALS B–C. Shut early September–Easter.

LOCRONAN
[S. FINISTÈRE]

A 'Cotswold village' in granite on a wooded hillside, Locronan (10km east of Douarnenez) grew rich making sailcloth and the

Locronan

fine cobbled square and Renaissance houses left behind from its golden days make it one of the most photogenic villages in Brittany. In the middle of the square is the old village well with wrought-iron cage and opposite a fine Flamboyant 15th-century church (St Ronan) and attached, Pénity chapel built in 1505 to house the tomb of Ronan, an Irish missionary who converted this part of Cornouaille to Christianity. He was sculpted in a granite-like stone called kersanton. A stained-glass window tells his story.

Pilgrims came to Locronan to pay homage to St Ronan from early times, even kings, queens and Yves, who became a saint himself. *Troménies* (local name for pardons) are devoted to him. At the Petit Pardon on the second Sunday of July, the pilgrims follow the route up the Locronan mountain which the saint was said to have taken every day, barefooted and fasting, to his hermitage. There is a chapel and an outside pulpit with the statue of the saint. You will also be rewarded with a fine panorama of Douarnenez Bay.

The *Grande Troménie* takes place every sixth year (last in

1989). The pilgrims come from a wide area, going round the hill stopping at twelve places where each parish displays its saints and relics.

8km north-west on the coast at Ste-Anne-la-Palud the chapel contains a highly-venerated painted granite statue of Ste Anne dating from 1548. The pardon is one of the most picturesque (last Sunday in August) with a torchlight procession on the Saturday.

Locronan is a *ville d'art* – one of those places where artists and artisans set up shop to preserve and recall the past. It is not as phoney as most. You can see the old workshop in the square where they weave linen by hand, the Tour Carrée workshop in rue Lann shows weaving of wool, linen and silk, and St Ronan workshop also for weaving, with a shop. It is all well done and in lovely old buildings.

TOURIST INFORMATION Syndicat d'Initiative (15 June–
15 September – 98.91.70.14)
MARKET First Tuesday in the month
FESTIVALS *see above*

HOTELS

Prieuré (98.91.70.89). In town, very attractive old granite house; pretty, flowery bedrooms. Good value menus. ROOMS C–E. MEALS A–F. Shut Monday low-season; October.

Manoir de Moëllien (98.92.50.40), at Plonevez-Porzay (3km north-west by C10). When we saw the condition of this historic 17th-century house, once the home of Châteaubriand's mistress, Thérèse de Moëllien, we wondered how Marie Anne le Corré and her husband could possibly restore such a ruin. They did, lovingly, and the hotel is a superb hideout of calm and tranquillity without pretentiousness. Bedrooms in the converted stables. ROOMS E–F. MEALS A–F. Shut January, February. Restaurant shut Wednesday low-season.

Plage at Ste-Anne-la-Palud (98.92.50.12). Modern and not pretty but in a delightful spot on the beach, very comfortable, quiet, excellent cooking deserves a Michelin star. Relais et Châteaux hotel. Worth the expense. Demi-pension in midsummer. ROOMS G (from 500F in 1989). MEALS E–G. Open 24 March–10 October.

LOCTUDY
[S. Finistère]

This pretty little port has become more popular as a bathing resort and as the target for a boat trip from Bénodet, and down the Odet river from Quimper. It is only 6km south-east of Pont-l'Abbé, on the point where the sea squeezes Pont-l'Abbé estuary. But it is still a charming place, with views towards Île-Tudy and of the isle of Garo. A ferry goes to Île-Tudy but does not take cars. There are summer trips to the Glénan isles (*see* page 137). Restaurant boats with lunch or dinner aboard make trips to Quimper (April–October). For information telephone Vedettes de l'Odet in Bénodet (98.57.00.58). Its 12th-century church is always described as 'the best preserved Romanesque building in Brittany', but in fact it was refaced in the 18th century. It is elegant. The beach is bordered by villas.

3km along D2 road to Pont-l'Abbé is Manoir de Kerazan-en-Loctudy, with two wings dating from the 16th and 18th centuries, in a big park. Joseph Astor, one of the rich American Astor family, left it to l'Institut de France in 1929 to help young Breton countrywomen to learn embroidery and needlework. The furnished rooms contain pictures and drawings of Flemish, Dutch and French schools from the 15th century to the present. Those of Auguste Goy, a pupil of Ingres, show Breton life of the past (open June to mid-September).

Market Tuesday

LORIENT
[Morbihan]

In 1666 the Compagnie des Indes (the India Company) picked the fine big estuary of the Scorff and Blavet as a base for their trading expeditions to India and China and called it L'Orient (the East). The company was founded by Richelieu at Port-Louis but went bankrupt. Colbert revived it in Louis XIV's reign (1664) at Le Havre but the ships were too easily captured in the Channel by the old enemy, the English, so they moved it to this new, more easily protected port on the Atlantic coast. A big port and town developed there, especially about fifty years later when the Scottish financier, John Law, became Controller General of the French Treasury. He made it into a flourishing commercial centre with an expanding population.

This was one of the few things Law got right in France. Born in 1671, he was the son of an Edinburgh banker who was proprietor of the Lauriston estate. But young John had to flee from London in 1694 after killing a society 'gentleman' in a duel. He went to Amsterdam and studied credit banking, returning to Edinburgh as an advocate of paper money. The Scottish parliament turned down his proposals, so he and his brother set up a bank in Paris which was successful. The Regent (Duc d'Orleans) adopted Law's plan for a French national bank in 1719. Law bought himself an expensive château, lived literally like royalty, became Controller of Finance and started wildcat companies and schemes, including a company to reclaim land and settle the Mississippi valley. Inevitably the bubble burst, a lot of people lost their savings or went bankrupt; Law had to flee and died in Venice in 1729.

Lorient is a triple port – naval base, with an arsenal and shipbuilding, Brittany's most important commercial port and the third most important fishing port of France.

The Germans used it as a major submarine base from June 1940 and on 27 September 1940 the first RAF bomber raid was made. It was incidently my first night raid of the war. I was twenty. By the time the Americans freed it in August 1944 after very heavy fighting, only about fifteen per cent of the town was left standing. But the huge submarine base at Keroman harbour, the fishing harbour, had been built by the Germans (or rather by slave labour) under such thick concrete that it had withstood every aerial attack. The French took it, of course, after the war, and still use it as a submarine base.

The new city is of rather dull, typically post-war white concrete but at least the boulevards are wide. The modern church of Notre-Dame-de-Victoire, in granite and concrete, with a tall bell-tower, is highly noticeable if not very beautiful. The nave is square with a flattened cupola and the inside rather bare. But happily there are attractive touches, like the little panes of yellow and plain glass which reflect the outside light. Lower down are windows of warm coloured glass, principally red. Behind the high altar is a mural in pastel tones. The stations of the cross drawn in outline are most original.

Of old Lorient, two Louis XV pavilions at the entrance to the Arsenal survive and two 17th-century powder mills flank Tour de la Découverte. In one mill is a museum tracing the history of the India Company.

Keroman fishing port is right back to its old life and colour despite recessions in the fishing industry. Go fairly early in the morning. It was designed in 1927, especially for fishing, with two basins at right angles arranged to be accessible at all times.

The submarine base is named after Engineer-General Stosskopf who, under pretence of collaborating with the Germans in World War II, told the Allies of German submarine movements. He was found out and shot by the Germans.

Lorient has good sandy beaches and little fishing harbours within easy reach.

TOURIST INFORMATION quai de Rohan (97.21.07.84)
MARKET Wednesday, Saturday
FESTIVALS First fortnight of August – Festival Interceltique (the greatest international Celtic festival with participants from Celtic groups of many countries); September–October – Fair-Exhibition (commercial)

HOTELS

Most of the bigger hotels are large and chain-owned, aimed at business people and without restaurants.

Novotel-Lorient, zone Commerciale Kerpont-Bellevue, Lanester (97.76.02.16). Though in commercial area, one of the best chain hotels for position – woodland setting outside town, quite near beaches. Simple but comfortable rooms. Restaurant. ROOMS F. MEALS D–E. Open all year.

Terminus et Gare, 5 rue Beauvais, opposite station (97.21.14.62). The grand, attractive old station hotel has been well renovated. ROOMS B–E. MEALS A–C. Shut 15 December–15 January. Restaurant shut Friday, Saturday, Sunday.

Vivier, at Lomener, 8km south-west by D163 from Ploemeur, 9 rue Beg-er-Vir (97.82.99.60). My choice for a hideout from city traffic. Hotel with character on a rock facing the sea. Modern comfortable rooms. Cooking highly regarded locally. ROOMS C–E. MEALS B–F. Restaurant shut Sunday evening from September to June.

Astéries, at Ploemeur, 5km west of Lorient, 1 place FFL (près Église) (97.86.21.97). Modern, well decorated; fish meals excellent. ROOMS C–E. MEALS B–F. Restaurant shut Sunday evening September–June.

RESTAURANTS

Poisson d'Or, 1 rue Maître Esvelin (97.21.57.06). Attractive, elegant restaurant; really excellent fish. MEALS B–F. Shut Saturday lunch, Sunday (except July, August); part February.

Pic, 2 boul. Franchet-d'Esperey (97.21.18.29). Reliable cooking with modern tendencies, good ingredients. Warm welcome. Open until midnight. MEALS B–F. Shut Saturday lunch, Monday; 2 weeks end December; 2 weeks in June.

LOUDÉAC
[CÔTES-DU-NORD]

Agricultural town, with greatly expanding food industry, at the meeting place of roads between Rennes and Morlaix, St Brieuc and Vannes, 22km north-east of Pontivy, and on the edge of Forêt de Loudéac. Big agricultural fairs are held and important horse-races on the racecourse on the Pontivy road D700. Main meetings are at Easter and mid-September. Alas in this area they produce chicken and pork 'without sun', keeping the animals in vast hangars you can see around the countryside. Local rivers are well stocked for fishermen.

TOURIST INFORMATION place Gén-de-Gaulle (May–September–96.28.25.17)

MARKET Saturday

HOTELS

Voyageurs, 10 rue Cadélac (96.28.00.47). A nice old hotel attractively restored. Remarkable cheap menus. ROOMS B–D. MEALS A–F. Shut 20 December–10 January.

Moulin de Belle-Isle, at Belle-Isle, 5km west by D69 Hémonstoir (96.25.04.91). Very old mill owned by the Glon family since 19th century. It ceased turning in 1973 and was made into an hotel in 1984 to avoid abandonment. The wheels are turning again, too. On the banks of the river Oust – largely rebuilt in 1930 after a fire. Looks splendid in silver-grey stone. Fishing. ROOMS C–F. MEALS B–E. Shut Sunday evening, Monday lunch; part November; February.

RESTAURANT

Cheval Blanc, 6 place l'Église (96.28.00.31). In a 300-year-old house, restaurant full of character. MEALS A–F. Shut Sunday and Monday evening.

MALESTROIT
[MORBIHAN]

In an attractive area on the river Oust 35km north-east of Vannes, it is a pleasant medieval town, unhurried despite being on the main D776 road in the direction of Rennes. Many old Gothic and Renaissance houses survive. One near the old St Gilles church in place Bouffay shows a man in his nightshirt beating his wife – presumably a medieval warning to wanton wives. The church is interesting for a strange mixture of 12th- and 16th-century styles and for its internal decoration. The river is partly canalised and there are pleasant walks along it. Very attractive drive by the river south-east on D764 towards Redon. 3km west at St Marcel is the place where the Maquis fought a German division in 1944. In the *mairie* is a museum of the Resistance, including reconstruction of a street as it was in 1944, and of life in Brittany under the German occupation 1940–44.

LA MEILLERAYE-DE-BRETAGNE
[Loire-Atlantique]

19km south of Châteaubriant on D178 and divided by a little forest from Grand Réservoir de Vioreau, a good place for sailing, it grew up on a hill near the Abbey of Meilleraye, founded in 1142. The abbey itself is 2½km down D18 south-east and stands in gardens well tended by the monks who still live there, beside a great pool surrounded by trees. The abbey church of 1183 has been restored and is open during services. Opposite the entrance is an unusual 15th-century granite calvary.

The reservoir, held by a dam, has green banks. It is linked to a great network of streams and pools down to the Nantes–Brest canal and the wide Erdre river south of Nort, right down to Nantes itself.

MÉNEZ-BRÉ
[Côtes-du-Nord]

Highest point in northern Brittany (330 metres), in a lovely spot 6km east of Belle-Isle-en-Terre. You can see it soon after leaving Guingamp on the Morlaix road. There is a wide panorama of north Brittany from the Chapel to St Hervé at the summit.

St Hervé is possibly the most remarkable of Breton saints. He cures fears, irrational terrors and nervous depression, believed in ancient times to have been brought on by seeing a werewolf (*loup garou*)! So he holds a wolf on the end of a leash. But the wolf was also his guide dog, for Hervé was blind. One story is that the wolf ate his donkey, so he commanded it to serve him and stabled it with his sheep.

Hervé was born blind because his mother had prayed that he should not be deceived by the outside world but live by the inner light within himself. Her prayers were certainly answered in a cruel way. He was a bard as well as a monk. Most remarkable of all, Breton legend and poems say that Hervé was a horse-thief! Perhaps he stole that donkey. There is also an old myth that devils appeared at funeral services at the chapel to grab the souls of the dead, and priests said mass backwards.

MERDRIGNAC
[CÔTES-DU-NORD]

Little town 17km west of St Méen on N164 beside Hardouinais forest, it is growing as an inland resort among French 'fresh-air' holidaymakers getting away from other tourists. Quite a beautiful, wild area to the south around Gomené. Merdrignac has a youth hostel and campsite as well as hotels, and is the centre of six small places making up the 'green resort' of Merdrignac-La Hardouinais, with forests, the rivers Hivet and Meu, a forest lake, good fishing and a swimming pool.

TOURIST INFORMATION Hôtel-de-Ville (96.28.41.11)
MARKET Wednesday

HOTELS

Univers, 1 rue Nationale (N164) (96.28.41.15). In country. Patron cooks. Known for shellfish and pâtisserie. ROOMS A–C. MEALS A–E. Shut Tuesday in season; Friday, Saturday in winter; 1–15 July.

Madeleine, 29 rue Dr Moisan (96.28.40.78). Very cheap, popular. ROOMS A–B. MEALS A–C. Shut 20 September–12 January. Restaurant shut Sunday.

Auberge de la Hardouinais at Saint-Launeuc, 6km NE through forest (96.56.14.59). Good cooking by patron, especially fish cooked over wood. Rustic, near lake. ROOMS A–B. MEALS A–F. Shut Monday off-season.

MISSILLAC
[LOIRE-ATLANTIQUE]

I love Château de Bretesche and I am delighted that I saw inside it before it was converted into what must be some of the most desirable apartments in Brittany. We must now be content with the lovely view of it across the bridge from the charming Hotel du Golfe de la Bretesche which was made in its stables and barns originally to serve the excellent golf course.

The 14th-century château, among trees by a big lake, is a

delight – a real fairy-tale castle of Renaissance towers with witches' hat roofs, often reflected in the water. It is well worth having a meal at the hotel just to see it. The old stable yard is usually bright with flowers.

The castle was built by the de Montfort family. Kings of France stayed to hunt in Bretesche forest alongside. Much damaged in the Revolution, it was sold afterwards to a butcher for £400. The Marquis de Montaigne bought it in 1847, restored it, and his descendants own it. The estate including the international golf course covers 200 hectares.

HOTEL
Golfe de la Bretesche (40.88.30.05). Good classic meals served in old dining-room with views of castle. Rooms comfortable and tasteful. Pool, tennis, golf. Menus include one cheap one. ROOMS E–F. MEALS C–F. Shut February.

ÎLE AUX MOINES
[MORBIHAN]

Longest and most popular island among forty inhabited isles of the Gulf of Morbihan – not to be confused with the bird sanctuary Île aux Moines off Perros Guirec on the north coast. 'Moines' means monks and the monks who came over to Brittany from Britain often settled on islands at first – probably for safety. This one was owned by the Abbey of Redon. It is 6km long, with pine woods and beaches, but is no longer the 'haven of tranquillity' it was called ten years ago. It is easily reached in five minutes by frequent crossings from Port-Blanc at the end of D101, south-west of Vannes. But it is still very charming and very quiet off-season. Its beaches make it a pleasant seaside resort. Mimosa and camellias grow. Its woods have romantic names: Bois des Soupirs (Wood of Sighs), Bois d'Amour (Wood of Love), and Bois des Regrets (Wood of Regrets). Sailing is good and there are interesting walks to prehistoric sites, such as the half-circle of standing stones at Kergonan (1km south from the landing stage) and the dolmen at Boglieux (3km) where views stretch beyond islands to the Atlantic.

From Easter to September, return trips sail from Vannes.

MONCONTOUR
[CÔTES-DU-NORD]

Very attractive 11th-century fortified town in a fine setting on a spur where valleys meet, south-east of St Brieuc and south-west of Lamballe. In lovely countryside. Intriguing narrow alleys and staircases descend from the church to the ramparts, which were partly dismantled on the orders of Richelieu in 1626. They still have ancient charm. The old Château des Granges, reconstructed in the 18th century, is on a hill to the north. The church of St Mathurin (16th to 18th centuries) has six fine Renaissance stained-glass windows, good paintings and woodwork.

Moncontour is built in granite, but has some timbered 18th-century houses. It is one of those old, hidden Breton towns which few tourists visit. There are quite a few like that.

Just outside the village of Trédaniel, 3km south-east, is the Chapel of Notre-Dame-du-Haut, the centre of Brittany's ancient 'alternative medicine' – healing saints. The little chapel contains seven polychrome wooden statues of these saints to whom people went to pray for cures. St Lubin looked after blindness and rheumatism. St Yvertin (Livertin) holds his head to show he cares for headaches and migraine. Ste Eugénie looks after headaches but also promises easy childbirth. St Méen is invoked for madness, St Hubert for sores and dog-bites. St Mamert holds open his intestines to show that he can cure digestive problems. St Léobinus must be very busy, for he is the rheumatism saint. St Hubert cures wounds. And St Houarniaule is our old friend St Hervé from Ménez-Bré (page 181) curing fear.

It seems that the saints are still doing their good work, for new 'Merci' votive plaques appear and the register of medical complaints is still used.

Château de la Touche-Trébry (5km east) was built in the

16th century but looks like a true medieval castle with its domed turrets, main wing and two wings at right angles forming a courtyard for jousting. The courtyard has a handsome well. Two towers protect the entrance, but the ramparts were for decoration, to show the importance of the Governor of Moncontour, who built it. The castle is hidden behind a screen of trees beside a small lake. It is open afternoons in July, August except Sundays.

FESTIVAL Whitsun – Pardon of St Mathurin; 15 August – Pardon of Notre-Dame-du-Haut (both big and important)

MORGAT
[S. FINISTÈRE]

Discovered between the wars by British families who went there every year, this pretty resort on the south of the Crozon peninsula now attracts a lot of French tourists, including families from Brest. Its great sandy beach is sheltered by a pine-covered point Beg-ar-Gador to the south and a spur of rock to the north separating it from Portzic beach. Only 3km from Crozon, it is now often called Crozon-Morgat.

An enormous sweeping jetty into the Bay of Douarnenez protects its harbour, making it very popular for pleasure boats, especially small sailing boats. It can take more than 400 pleasure boats. It still has fishing boats, and tunny boats use the jetty. Morgat is extremely popular with amateur sea fishermen.

You can reach at low tide the small caves at the foot of the spur between the beach and Le Portzic. For les Grandes Grottes you must catch a motor boat on a fine day from Morgat harbour. They are beautiful, especially l'Autel (the altar), 80 metres deep and 15 metres high, with curious mineral colourings on its roofs and walls. Chambre du Diable (Devil's Chamber) has a chimney emerging at the clifftop. There are good views from the lighthouse, reached by a hill path from Morgat. Other clifftop paths are interesting.

TOURIST INFORMATION boul. Plage (1 June–15 September–98.27.07.92)

HOTELS

Ville d'Ys (98.27.06.49). Holiday hotel. ROOMS D–E. MEALS B–E. Open 19 March–end September.

Kador, 42 boul. la Plage (98.27.05.68). First-floor restaurant gives panoramic views over beach and port. Fish and shellfish. ROOMS B–C. MEALS A–E. Shut Monday low-season; November.

RESTAURANT

Roof, boul. France Libre (98.27.08.40). Nautical décor. Very good classical cooking of fish. Good menu choice. MEALS B–F. Shut Monday low-season; 15 November–15 December.

MORLAIX
[FINISTÈRE]

In 1943 the RAF attacked, and for once missed, the two-tiered viaduct which carries the Paris–Brest railway across the deep-sided valley in which Morlaix has grown up. Bad show, chaps! That viaduct is the one blotch on a most attractive scene – streets of fine old buildings sloping down the side of a valley to a charming estuary port packed usually with bright yachts and cruisers. Still, the French would only have put the railway back – probably on an even uglier bridge of reinforced concrete with great piles in the hillside and river. That was the fashion post-war.

It is still a most likeable port. Two rivers, the Jarlot and the Queffleuth, join to form the river Dorsen (often called the river Morlaix) which flows on, widening, into the Bay of Morlaix just round the corner from the ferry port of Roscoff. The two roads alongside the river banks here are most attractive. Some old houses have been knocked down in recent years and they have even covered part of the river, but the steep cobbled streets are still rich in old buildings. In rue Ange-de-Guernisac are beautiful houses, corbelled and with wooden tiles, and Grand' Rue, for pedestrians only, has some picturesque old houses ornamented with statues of saints and grotesque animals. The shops with large windows are known as *maisons à lanterne*. The central hall was lit from a glass ceiling and rose to roof height. A spiral staircase led to a gallery from which rooms opened.

Maison de la Duchesse Anne is a corbelled half-timbered mansion of three storeys with a beautiful staircase. The Duchess stayed there when she was Queen of France in 1505 after King Louis XII had recovered from a grave illness. Morlaix was rich then and treated her to sumptuous entertainment, including a live Tree of Jesse representing her ancestors. They gave her a model golden ship studded with jewels and a live ermine wearing a diamond-studded collar because the ermine was her emblem.

Much of Morlaix's wealth from the 15th century came from the activity known as privateering if it was done by your side and piracy if done by anyone else. In the 18th century the port was even more important as a corsair base than St Malo ('corsairs' were pirates licenced by the king). Jean Bart and Duguay-Trouin (*see* St Malo, page 32) sailed from Morlaix and their loot led to the creation of a prosperous Commercial Exchange in the town.

In 1522 the Morlaix pirate commander John der Coetanlem raided Bristol and looted the city. Henry VIII of England was very cross and sent eighty ships to Morlaix. The Morlaix citizens were away at a festival and the English sailors ransacked the town. Alas they found the wine cellars. The returning men of Morlaix found the drunken English lying in streets and in nearby woods. They massacred them. Morlaix celebrated by adding to its coat of arms the motto 'If they bite you, bite them back'. Then they prudently built Château du Taureau at the narrow arm of the estuary to tackle future invaders.

Charles Cornic, one of the greatest corsair captains, was born at Morlaix in 1731 and was so successful that the King put him in charge of protecting convoys. Being a bourgeois, he was only an 'officer of the Blue', not of the Red (aristocrat), so he remained a lieutenant until the Revolution, when, too old to go to sea, he was put in charge of Morlaix harbour.

Smuggling followed piracy. Morlaix built the biggest tobacco factory, with a monopoly of sales. Prices became exorbitant. So ships were loaded with tobacco and snuff in England and it was landed at night on the coast. Pitched battles were fought between smugglers and tobacco men.

One of France's most successful generals was born at Morlaix in 1763 and died of wounds fighting against Napoleon for the Russians. Jean-Victor Moreau was a lawyer at first, then became a Revolutionary general commanding an army. He won victory after victory. He drove the Austrians to the Danube. The party which overthrew the Directory offered him dictatorship of France. He declined but offered assistance to Bonaparte. He gained victories from the Rhine to the Inn and then won the decisive battle of Hohenlinden. Napoleon didn't like other heroes. He accused Moreau of conspiring against him, and sentenced him to prison, commuted to banishment. Moreau fled to New Jersey. In 1813 he joined the Russians in a march against Napoleon at Dresden, got a cannon ball through both legs and died shortly thereafter. He was buried in St Petersburg (Leningrad).

The museum, in an old Dominican convent in place des Jacobins, has rooms of local arts and crafts and a good collection of 19th-century paintings, including portraits by Courbet, the artist of realism, and Thomas Couture (1815–79) who taught Manet. The great critic, Gustave Geoffroy, friend of the Impressionists, was a Morlaix man. He introduced Monet to Côte Sauvage on Belle-Île and as a result Rodin and Matisse were attracted to the island. One of Monet's Belle-Île paintings is in the museum, also two of Boudin's Trouville beach scenes and several by Maurice Denis (1870–1943), central figure in Nabis and Symbolist movements. Museum shut Tuesdays.

3km north of Morlaix at Ploujean were born the writer Tristan Corbière (1845–75), author of *Amours Jaunes* (Yellow Love Affairs), and Jean-Loup Chrétien, first Frenchman in space (1982), called in France a *spacionaut*.

TOURIST INFORMATION place Otages (98.62.14.94)
MARKET Saturday
FESTIVALS mid-October – Commercial Fair

HOTELS

Europe, 1 rue d'Aiguillon (98.62.11.99). Alas, brilliant chef

Patrick Jeffroy has taken his Michelin star to his own restaurant at Plounérin, 25km away, and has left behind a pupil at l'Europe. Too early to judge the cooking. Fine old renovated hotel with some very big rooms – good value. Also has a brasserie-bar Le Lof with good value (jazz in evenings). ROOMS D–E. MEALS B–E. Lof meals A–D. Shut Christmas holidays.

An Ty Korn, at Plouigneau, 10km east by N12, pl. Église (98.67.72.72). Attractive old place with really good traditional cooking. ROOMS D–E. MEALS A–F. Shut Sunday evening, Monday except July, August; 15–28 February; 1–15 July.

St-Antoine at Plouézoch, 6km north by D786, D46 (98.67.27.05). Simple auberge; good shellfish. ROOMS A–D. MEALS A–F. Shut Monday low-season.

RESTAURANT

Marée Bleue, 3 rampe St-Mélaine (98.63.24.21). Old stone house up an alley leading to St-Mélaine church; good traditional cooking. MEALS A–E. Shut Monday except July, August; 15–30 November.

MUR-DE-BRETAGNE
[CÔTES-DU-NORD]

An inland resort only a mile from Lake Guerléden and near the Forest of Quénécan, so very busy in summer with active and mostly young French holidaymakers. They go walking, windsurfing, sailing, water-skiing, canoeing, rowing, fishing, horse-riding or take motorboat trips on the lake, Guerléden (*see* page 143), which covers 400 hectares. It is the best organised lake for holidays in Brittany, and Mur-de-Bretagne has the major nautical base (tel. 96.28.50.07), and two riding schools.

There's a signposted walk round the lake (48km – at least two days).

Mur has a 17th-century chapel, Ste-Suzanne, in a green setting with superb oaks which inspired Corot to paint the scene.

TOURIST INFORMATION place l'Église (15 June–15 September – 96.28.51.41)

HOTELS

Auberge Grand'Maison, 1 rue le Cerf (96.28.51.10). New décor. Very modern cuisine earns Jacques Guillo continued praise from Gault-Millau and a star from Michelin, but my readers have found it too traditionally 'nouvelle' with portions too small. But Jacques has introduced a Breton regional meal based on old recipes with his own ideas. ROOMS C–F. MEALS D–G. Shut Sunday evening, Monday; February holidays; 23–30 June; October.

Beau Rivage at Caurel, 6km north-west by D767, N1264 (96.28.52.15). Quiet, friendly Logis de France on the lake 2km S of Caurel by D111. Charming spot with lovely views. Good value. ROOMS C–E. MEALS B–F. Shut Monday, Tuesday low-season; 10 January–15 February.

RESTAURANT

Rock Tregnanton at Caurel (96.36.92.67). Superb position overlooking Lake Guerléden; patron's own cuisine. MEALS A–E. Shut January.

NANTES
[*See* Major Towns, page 55]

ÎLE D'OUESSANT (USHANT)
[N. FINISTÈRE]

If you are a fairly good sailor, you will love the two-hour sea voyage from Brest to the isle of Ushant. The passage through Goulet de Brest is a delight. Lampaul, where you land, is in a deep, lovely cove. There are few trees except around the village but the low, bare outline is attractive and the sea birds on the cliffs and islets are a joy, especially in autumn when the migrating birds from northern Europe fly in.

Ushant looks tranquil in summer. In winter, I am told, the wind hurling the Atlantic waves against the broken and rocky shores is awesome. Fog has been a hazard to shipping for centuries. Yet, thanks to the Gulf Stream, January and February are mild – some of the mildest weather in France.

The isle is 7km long and 4km wide and now has a number of roads. The old houses in the little capital Lampaul are well preserved. The port is photogenic, with a sandy beach stretching to the south, and a road round the bay to Ty-Corn which is twisty, hilly and picturesque. 1200 people live on the island. Most of the men still go to sea and the women look after the small sheep, some brown, which crop the rather sparse salt pastures. Low walls are built in star-formation to ensure their shelter from Atlantic winds. Only 1/50th of the isle can be dug. That produces a few potatoes and some wheat. Women have always been very important on Ushant and until quite recently it was the girls who proposed marriage. Now they have Men's Lib. One of the beauty spots is Arland Point on the east coast.

In the hamlet of Niou-Uhella two old houses have been preserved with furniture and fittings.

Boats from Brest are called Vedettes San Corentin (3 rue du Frégate-la-Boussole–98.05.01.26). There are two flights daily from Brest-Guipavas airport (98.84.64.87).

PAIMPOL
[CÔTES-DU-NORD]

Frenchmen brought up on Pierre Loti's masterful novel *Pêcheur d'Islande* (*Icelandic Fisherman*), set in Paimpol in 1886, and on Théodore Botrel's song 'La Paimpolaise' may be disappointed when they see the modern port. You no longer see adventurous cod-fishing boats which used to work the banks off Iceland, but inshore fishing boats, yachts and pleasure boats. Oysters cultivated in beds in the bay are landed on the quayside. Some romance has gone but life is better. Oysters have brought prosperity and Paimpol is a pleasant, bright living port with a charming town centre and nice bars there and on the quayside. It has a National Merchant Marine School, properly placed in rue Pierre-Loti, and on quai Loti, a Musée de la Mer showing

Paimpol's seafaring story from the times of the cod-boats to today (open 1 April–mid-September).

It is an excellent centre for exploring the cliffs, creeks, little harbours and estuaries of the north coast. The attractive road north takes you to Pointe de l'Arcouest with wonderful views of Paimpol Bay and of Île de Bréhat (page 85) across a passage very narrow at low tide. On the way you pass Ploubazlanec, with a sad cemetery recording the names of the men lost at sea. A mile east of Ploubazlanec is Pors-Éven, the still quaint village with lobster pots where the fisherman lived who was Yann in Loti's novel. Nearby is Widows' Cross from which women waited in fear and hope to see which boats had come back from the long fishing voyages. From Arcouest in the creek below Arcouest Point boats cross Bréhat in ten minutes. In season you can take a boat round the island or along the coast and up the river Trieux to Lézardrieux – a lovely trip passing Loguivy-de-la-Mer, a tiny lobster port which is really just a creek below a cliff from which are views of the Trieux river and Île de Bréhat. You can drive direct from Paimpol to Loguivy (5km) or take a clifftop walk from Arcouest.

Arcouest's hotel Le Barbu was recommended to me in the early 1950s by the writer Eric Whelpton, but he warned me that 'Nobody speaks English'. Then it had a small exclusive summer invasion of Parisian artists, writers and academics. Now people making for Bréhat come in their cars in dozens in summer and Le Barbu has a swimming pool. We love it in spring and in autumn. South from Paimpol, another delightful road passes the considerable ruins of the 13th-century Beauport Abbey in lovely green setting, then Ste Barbe, with a statue of Ste Barbara by the church. Take a path to the viewing table from where you can see Paimpol Bay, many little islands, the oyster beds, and Lost-Pic lighthouse. The little road round the bay passes Port Lazo to Bilfot Point, with fine sea views, often with trawlers and pleasure yachts on their way towards Bréhat.

Another attractive road from Paimpol is D786 west for 5km to Kergrist, the suspension bridge and Lézardrieux (page 171). Paimpol is a sailing centre.

TOURIST INFORMATION Paimpol Syndicat d'Initiative, rue P.-Feutren (shut October – 96.20.83.16)

PAIMPOL

MARKET Tuesday

FESTIVALS mid-July – Fête of Newfoundland Banks and Iceland (old fishermen's festival); second Sunday of December – Pardon of Our-Lady-of-Good-News (old fishermen's pardon)

HOTELS

Relais Brenner, 5km at pont de Lézardrieux (96.20.11.05) – (*see* Lézardrieux, page 171).

Marne, 30 rue Marne (96.20.82.16). Attractive little Logis de France run by young couple. Good value. ROOMS B–D. MEALS B–F. Shut Friday low-season; 15–30 October.

Repaire de Kerroc'h, 29 quai Morand (96.20.50.13). Elegant old house on harbour front built by the old pirate and French Revolutionary Pierre Corouge Kersaux in 1793. Rooms overlook port. Excellent value meals. ROOMS E. MEALS A–E. Shut Tuesday, Wednesday lunch.

Bocher at Pors-Even, 5km north-east (96.55.84.16). Delightful simple pension reminding me of visits past. Creeper-clad stone house on road down to the port. Superb value meals with excellent seafood. Book ahead in summer. ROOMS vary, A–E. MEALS B–E. Open mid-March–early November.

Le Barbu at Arcouest, 6km north (96.55.86.98). *See above*; garden with swimming pool; views to Bréhat isle. Fine traditional cooking. Book ahead. ROOMS E–F. MEALS C–G. Open 15 March–15 November.

Château de Coatguélen at Pléhedel, 10km S by D7, D79 (96.22.31.24). Fine old turreted castle in a park with its own golf courses (9 and 18 holes). Relais et Châteaux hotel. Still owned by the Marquis de Boisgelin, with Louis Le Roy ('King Louis'), one of the greatest Breton chefs, in charge of cuisine. All very splendid and pricey. Cooking courses by Louis Le Roy off-season. ROOMS G+. MEALS F–G. Open 15 March–15 November; 15–31 December.

RESTAURANT

Vieille Tour, 13 rue Église (96.20.83.18). Up steep cobbled hill. Good value menus. Local favourite. Nearly all fish but some alternatives. MEALS B–F. Shut Sunday evening, Wednesday except July, August; mid-November–early December.

PAIMPONT
[Ille-et-Vilaine]

The forest of Paimpont, 35km south-west of Rennes, was called Brocéliande in the Middle Ages and was the home of the wizard Merlin and the fairy Viviane, whatever they tell you in Cornwall! But then the Bretons say that King Arthur was a Breton. When Merlin and Viviane fell in love, she enclosed him in a magic circle to keep him. Being a wizard, he could have easily escaped. But he didn't want to. He is still there. Once the forest stretched 140km from Rennes to Carhaix. Now it is down to 6,600 hectares but in recent years conifers were planted to increase it. Some of the lovely older trees have survived, especially around pools, of which there are fourteen. Sometimes you find yourself in open heathland.

This is truly the land of ancient legends, but since World War II the French Army have taken over the heathland at the southern tip of the forest for Coëtquidan-St Cyr camp, where cadets of the great St Cyr military academy, the equivalent of Sandhurst and West Point, hold exercises – tanks and armoured cars – and there is also an Inter-Arms School. St Cyr moved here from Paris in 1959 and fittingly the statue at the entrance is of Général Leclerc, commander of the Free French Forces who invaded with the Americans in Normandy in 1944 and won famous victories over the Nazis.

John Fowles' novel *Ebony Tower* was about an English artist who came to the forest to gain knowledge from a Merlin-style man, with two Viviane-like mistresses. You meet Merlin and his magic all over the forest. Water from the Fontaine de Barenton, where Viviane cast the spell around Merlin, falls over Perron de Merlin (Merlin's Steps) and as late as the 15th century stories were told of the Seigneur de Montfort tipping water over the steps to bring instant rain to thirsty crops and make abundant harvests.

Château de Comper by a vast attractive lake in the north-east corner of the forest, is where Viviane was born – though not in the present rugged château built mostly in the 19th century. Her castle is buried under the lake. Here, she swam across the lake with the infant Sir Lancelot under her arm after she had found him abandoned by the roadside, which is why he was called Sir

Lancelot of the Lake. Pas du Houx lake just south has two châteaux built in 1912.

In Val-sans-Retour, a wild narrow valley with overhanging rocks in the south-west of the forest, Morgane the witch lived. If a knight was unfaithful to his lady, she lured him there and punished him. Nobody knows how. Sir Lancelot broke her spell. 1km away the village of Tréhorenteuc has a restored church with rather rustic mosaics and pictures showing the legends of King Arthur, Merlin, the Knights and the Holy Grail. South of Val-sans-Retour is the elegant 15th-century château, de Trécesson, surrounded by a lake and looking very medieval in reddish stone, built round an inner courtyard, its gateway flanked by two pepper-pot turrets. You cannot go inside.

On the south edge of the forest, between Beignon and Plélan-le-Grand, is the bridge over the river Aff called Pont du Secret, where Queen Guinevere told Sir Lancelot that she loved him.

The tiny market town of Paimpont in the middle of the forest beside another pleasant lake, has one road running under a medieval arch, with a war memorial at the other end. Its large 13th-century church was the church of an abbey founded in the 7th century. The abbey was restored in the 18th century and is now the municipal offices. Though there are forest roads, quiet and pleasant, the best way to explore is by well-marked footpaths.

HOTELS

Relais de Brocéliande de Paimpont (99.07.81.07). Prettily sited by the lake, old-style stone inn used by lake fishermen with comfy, spacious rooms in adjoining annexe. Hearty meals of fresh food. Cheerful. ROOMS B–C. MEALS A–F.

Manoir du Tertre, at Le Tertre 4km south-west of Paimpont by D71 and local road right (99.07.81.02). 16th-century farmhouse on a hill in quiet country. Lovely dining-room with antiques; local produce. Simple old farmhouse bedrooms; WC down corridor, rickety stairs. ROOMS B–C. MEALS A–F. Shut 1–21 February; 1–8 October.

PERROS-GUIREC
[CÔTES-DU-NORD]

One of the most popular and nicest resorts in Brittany. Biggest resort in the north. It is built like an amphitheatre above a fishing and pleasure boat harbour and two well-sheltered beaches. Opposite is Île Tomé. Trestraou and Trestrignel beaches are of fine sand and are sheltered by trees, and there are a lot of pleasure activities, so the resort is very popular with families. Despite the summer visitors, it never seems overpacked because of the serrated coastline which has many separate beaches. Off-season, in the evenings, despite some nightlife, Perros-Guirec can seem dreamy and romantic.

The only snag with small children is the long steepish climb from the wide boulevard de la Mer which runs north from the port to the main town, and many of the hotels are up there. From Pointe du Château at the north-east end of the port are fine views along the beaches, the coast eastward and the islands. The lovely sandy cove of Trestrignel beach is west of the point. Beside the long, curving, popular Trestraou beach further west are the casino, conference centre, bigger hotels, restaurants, bars and entertainments. At the far west end is a sailing school and a little point of land from which boats go in summer for trips round the Sept-Îles (Seven Isles), sanctuary for tens of thousands of sea birds – gannets, gulls, cormorants, fulmars, puffins and oyster-catchers. Landing is forbidden except on Moines (one hour's stay) but the boats go near enough to photograph birds and record their cries. The bird population was very badly depleted by the two oil-ship disasters, *Torrey Canyon* in 1962 and *Amoco Cadiz* later, but has much recovered.

Steps from the sailing school lead to the old Sentier des Douaniers, the customs officers' path, which goes right round the Ploumanach peninsula. At first it follows the cliff-line giving splendid views of the Seven Isles. The granite rocks are of colours from vermilion to grey and are in strange shapes which have been given imaginative names.

The 18km stretch of D788 road westward from Perros-Guirec is called Corniche Bretonne and overlooks a delightful coastline of rocks sculptured by the waves, pools, creeks, lagoons and caves.

Dominating the town of Perros-Guirec is Colline de la Clarté, a hill of pilgrimage with a celebrated pardon on 15 August around the beautiful 16th-century rose-granite chapel. This chapel was built by a local lord who was saved when his boat was lost in fog off the coast.

Perros-Guirec is a good centre for deep-sea fishing off Sept-Îles, deep-sea diving, windsurfing, sailing (Centre Nautique, 96.23.25.62 – open all year) and tennis. There are three children's beach clubs, a seawater therapy centre with seawater pool (Trestraou beach, 96.23.28.97). Trips to Seven Isles take about three hours (Les Vedettes Blanches, Plage de Trestraou, 96.23.22.47).

Tourist Information 21 place Hôtel-de-Ville (96.23.21.15)
Market Friday
Festivals 15 August – Pardon of Notre-Dame-de-la-Clarté; 16 August – Fête

HOTELS

Printania, 12 rue Bons-Enfants (96.23.21.00). One of my favourites in Brittany. Large white old Grand Hotel with nice gardens and views over sea, islands and town. Modernised, individually decorated bedrooms. Get a room with a balcony overlooking the sea – very romantic at night. Sun terrace. Rooms E–F. Meals D–E. Shut 15 December–15 January. Restaurant shut Sunday evenings 1 October–1 May; Monday lunch.

Sphinx, 67 chemin de la Messe (96.23.25.42). Fin-de-siècle villa turned into a modern hotel. Direct access over rocks to Trestrignel beach. Views of sea and isles. Rooms E. Meals C–F. Open 15 March–20 November, 20 December–15 January.

Trestraou, boul. J.-Le-Bihan (96.23.24.05). Old Grand Hotel opposite beach. The Centre de Thalasso Thérapie (sea cures). Restaurant for residents only. Rooms D–F. Meals C–E. Open all year.

Feux des Îles, 53 boul. Clemenceau (96.23.22.94). Converted villa. Outstanding food. Rooms (smallish) D. Meals C–F. Shut

Sunday evening, Monday off-season; 10 January–28 February; 15 November–15 December.

PIRIAC-SUR-MER
[LOIRE-ATLANTIQUE]

Pleasant tiny resort and fishing village 13km north-west of Guérande (*see* page 139). 17th-century houses in the square by the church. 1km south-west is Pointe du Castelli, from which you can see Rhuys peninsula and Îie Dumet to the right, Croissic approaches and church tower to the left.

PLANCOËT
[CÔTES-DU-NORD]

It could only happen in France. In this tiny port on the river Arguenon 17km north-west of Dinan, with the river running through the town and crossed by a little wooden bridge, is a little station restaurant with a Michelin star! And its patron-chef has been there for more than forty years. The attractive ancient port is now used by pleasure craft and is famous for fishing excursions. Only 10km from Pléven and the reservoir lake leading to Jugon-les-Lacs (*see* page 160) and its other big lake. 10km, too, from a string of sand beaches.

Pléven is a charming little place in lovely surroundings beside the forests of Hunaudaie and St Aubin. Ruins of Hunaudaie castle are 4km south-west. The lake was formed by damming the Arguenon river (*see also* Jugon-les-Lacs, page 160). Pléven's 15th-century Manoir de Vaumadeuc is now a lovely hotel.

HOTELS
Chez Crouzil, La Gare (96.84.10.24). Called Hôtel de la Gare until recently. Jean-Pierre Crouzil deserves to have it named after him for his brilliant expertise of turning fresh local products

into gourmet feasts. Superb fish from Erquy, freshwater fish and fruit and vegetables from Jugon, oysters from Cancale. Local game. He has turned his 14 bedrooms into seven apartments – rather expensive. But 'La Gare' remains a Logis de France. Terrace with river views. Apartments G. MEALS B–G. Shut Sunday evening, Monday; 11–26 June; 6–20 November.
Source (96.84.10.11). Nothing to look at but good meals at low prices. ROOMS A–B. MEALS A–D. Shut Monday.
Manoir de Vaumadeuc at Pléven, 9½km south-west (96.84.46.17). Vicomtesse de Breilde Pontbriand turned her magnificent manor into an expensive but superb hotel with magnificent furnishings, modern comfort. Good simple cooking, ingredients from own farm. ROOMS F–G. MEALS D–F. Shut 5 January–20 March.

PLEUGUENEUC
[ILLE-ET-VILAINE]

On N137 between St Malo and Rennes, just outside this village is the grandiose 16th-century Château de Bourbansais on a huge, beautiful estate with a zoo in the grounds. One apartment is let to visitors under the 'Bienvenu au Château' scheme (Seratour, 13 rue Pont-aux-Foulons, 35000 Rennes – 99.78.18.19). It is essentially a house, not a fortress, built on the site of a former Roman villa. It was modernised in 1745. Mansard pavilions were added, the park was laid out and formal French-style gardens added. Inside all the apartments were panelled. It belonged for several generations to the Huards, members of the Brittany Parliament.

Most of the furniture and decorations are from the 18th century, with 17th-century Aubusson tapestries and old porcelain (château open afternoons. Shut 1 December–1 March.)

The zoo has animals from five continents (open daily).

The apartment is let from Easter to All Saints Day (telephone 99.69.40.48). Price around 800F. There is good horse riding.

Nearby is Château de la Motte Beaumanoir (15th to 18th

PLOËRMEL
[Morbihan]

centuries) with five rooms, one apartment, two suites to let all the year. Price around 600–800F. It is in a pleasant park with woods and small lakes (99.69.46.01).

PLOËRMEL
[Morbihan]

In the very heart of farming country, Ploërmel was once the seat of the Dukes of Brittany and it was from here that the English captain Bemborough rode out in 1351 for the strange Battle of the Thirty, which he and his knights lost (*see* Josselin, page 157).

It was founded by St Armel, yet another saint who tamed a dragon and led it away by his ecclesiastical stole. You can see him leading it in St Armel church. Amusing carvings on the church doorway include a shoemaker sewing up his wife's mouth, a sow playing bagpipes, a woman pulling off a man's cap and two boys,

Marmousets

one crying, one laughing. White marble statues include Dukes John II and III.

Old houses include a 16th-century house of the Dukes and the gorgeous Renaissance Maison des Marmousets. At l'Étang au Duc, 2½km north by N8, the lake has an artificial beach and watersports centre.

TOURIST INFORMATION Syndicat d'Initative, 5 rue Val (97.74.02.70)

MARKET Monday; Tuesday – auction

FESTIVAL Mid-Lent – carnival

HOTELS

Cobh et Restaurant Cruaud, 10 rue des Forges (97.74.00.49). Reberminard restaurant has changed address and name. Rooms offered also at Hotel Commerce, 70 rue de la Gare, by Cruaud family. Classical dishes. ROOMS C–E. MEALS A–F. Shut 10–30 January. Restaurant shut Tuesday evening.

PLOUESCAT
[N. FINISTÈRE]

A small town 20km west of Roscoff among sand dunes in the Bay of Kernic which is both a fishing and agricultural centre. It has a lovely 17th-century market hall supported by oak pillars. Nearby are several good sand beaches and old manor houses. Few Britons landing at Roscoff from the ferry think to drive westward to discover this coast. It is a land of *cotriade* (Breton fish soup) and *caillebottes* (like Cornish clotted cream), of old houses and hidden-away prehistoric menhirs.

Château de Maillé, 4km south, is a 17th-century stately home in granite flanked by a Renaissance wing (visits to outside mid-June to mid-September except 14 July–15 August; other times tel. 98.61.44.68).

Kergornadeac'h Château, 7km south of Plouescat, was built in 1630, the last fortified castle built in France. Ruined, but enough left to be interesting.

Manoir de Tronjoly, 8km north-east of Plouescat, is a particularly pleasant manor house of the 16th to 17th centuries, with tall Renaissance dormer windows added, giving it extra elegance. In the main courtyard, enclosed by a terrace with a balustrade, is a massive square tower. It is the sort of house you could dream of living in (visits to exterior only).

TOURIST INFORMATION rue St-Julien (June–July– 98.69.62.18); Mairie (other times – 98.69.60.13)

HOTELS

Azou, 8 bis rue Gén-Leclerc (98.69.60.16). Simple hotel (five rooms) with smart, good restaurant. Six cheap to gastronomic menus, mainly fish. ROOMS B–C. MEALS A–G. Shut Wednesday lunch, Tuesday except high summer; 10–22 January; 25 September–18 October.

Caravelle, 20 rue Calvaire (98.69.61.75). Comfortable hotel with very good classical dishes cooked by enthusiastic young chef; garden-style dining-room. ROOMS C–D. MEALS A–F. Restaurant shut Monday low-season; February.

PLOUGASNOU
[N. FINISTÈRE]

Small resort 800 metres from a beach on the Pointe de Primel, 17km north of Morlaix. A good little hideout; built round a green, leafy square with a mostly 16th-century church. Just north is another little resort Primel-Trégastel, beside Primel Point which is a jumble of pink rocks. Fine views. Diben Point, 3km north-west of Plougasnou, is an attractive fishermen's village with lobster beds and a pleasure boat harbour. A very nice quiet little area.

4km down the coast from Diben, past the gorgeous sand beach of St Samson, is the super little fishing port of Térénez, typically Breton, popular now with amateur sailors. Just south is the tumulus of Barnenez, not fully revealed until excavations between 1955 and 1968 showed eleven burial chambers reached by 7- to 12-metre passages. It is a remarkable mound.

The D76 goes inland to the village of Plouezoch, then along

the Dourduff river to the port of Dourduff in its estuary – a tree-lined route. Dourduff is yet another delightful little place, with a viaduct over the estuary, trees lining both banks, and an attractive, protected pleasure boat harbour, once used by fishermen, still used by the men who look after the oyster beds.

The Corniche road from the bridge goes to Morlaix.

TOURIST INFORMATION Syndicat d'Initiative, rue des Martyrs (98.67.31.88)

HOTEL

France, place de l'Église, Plougasnou (98.67.30.15). Everything happens here for locals and visitors. A family-run hotel with very simple rooms, very comfortable and well-furnished rooms in annexe and good meals, excellent value. ROOMS B–C. MEALS A–F. Restaurant shut in winter.

PLOUGASTEL-DAOULAS
[FINISTÈRE]

Plougastel is the centre for strawberries, many tons of which go to Britain, and also grows melons and shallots. It is in the centre of Plougastel Peninsula (Presqu'île de Plougastel). Its famous calvary was built in 1602 to commemorate the end of a plague. The cross has 180 figures, with thieves on either side surmounted by a devil and an angel.

The big N165 to Brest runs by the edge of the town and on to Daoulas south-east, but the peninsula is a little tranquil retreat of Breton agriculture, where old Breton customs survive. Narrow winding roads run between hedges, with hamlets surrounding small chapels where truly religious little pardons are held. From Kernisi on the west coast is a knoll from which are panoramic views to Brest. Near Pointe de l'Armorique at the south at Kerdéniel is a fine view of the Faou estuary. North-east of Pointe de l'Armorique is the charming little fishing port of Lauberlac'h, popular too as a sailing centre.

FESTIVAL 15 August – Pardon

HOTELS

Kastel Roc'h (98.40.32.00). Breton house, comfortably furnished. Swimming pool in garden. Remarkably cheap, good value meals. ROOMS C–D. MEALS A–C. Restaurant shut Saturday lunch, Friday.

PLOUMANAC'H
[CÔTES-DU-NORD]

A walk west of Perros-Guirec (*see* page 196) this old fishing port is in a really attractive position at the mouth of two picturesque valleys, and not surprisingly has become a well-known seaside resort. Its piles of grey and rose rocks are some of the most photographed in Brittany.

The delightful sheltered beach is in the Bay of St Guirec, named for an Irish monk who landed here in the 6th century. There is an oratory to him on a rock washed by the sea at high tide. His wooden statue has been replaced by a stone statue to save him the indignity of having pins stuck in his nose by girls who wanted to get married; these Breton customs are certainly quaint!

The harbour has become a little touristy but is lively with boats and people and is fun. You can see it best from rocks at the end of the Bastille promenade. The path to the lighthouse passes some interesting rocks. Afternoons in July and August you can visit the lighthouse. From its terrace are views to the Seven Isles (*see* Perros-Guirec).

HOTELS

Rochers (96.91.44.49). Lovely views of port and sea, beautiful classical cuisine. Worth every centime. ROOMS D–E. MEALS C–G. Open Easter, then end April–end September. Restaurant shut Wednesday low-season.

Parc (96.91.40.80). Really good value cheaper menus. ROOMS B–D. MEALS A–E. Open 25 March–25 September.

PONT-AVEN
[S. Finistère]

Pont-Aven is still one of the most agreeable places in Brittany, despite midsummer traffic and crowds of day-visitors. Go in May, early June or autumn and you will know why artists chose it as a place to live.

In a very pleasant setting at the point where the river Aven, after being squeezed between rocks, opens into its long fjord-like estuary, it is 14km south-east of Concarneau and only 6km south of the important N165 Brest–Lorient road, so it is a little *too* easy to reach. It is associated in French guides mainly with Gauguin and the Pont-Aven school of painters, but well before he went there in 1888 (*see* Concarneau, page 111) American artists had moved in, led by Robert Wylie in 1866. They moved there from Concarneau not only for the scenery but because the peasants were patient and prepared to sit for hours as models for a few sous, and two hotels – Des Voyageurs and Pension Gloanec – were so cheap. Julia Guillou, who ran Des Voyageurs, was known as '*la mère des artistes*'. Her hotel in Place de l'Hôtel-de-Ville has gone, but there is a plaque to her. Pension Gloanec

Pont-Aven

stood in the square now called Place Gauguin, where a Maison de la Presse now stands. It was rowdy and Bohemian, it seems.

One of the first artists to discover and publicise Pont-Aven was the great British graphic artist and illustrator Ralph Caldecott, after whom America's Caldecott medal for the best illustrations for children's books is named. He died about the year Paul Gauguin went to Pont-Aven. Gauguin used the same studio as the Americans had used, a manor house called Lezaven just outside the town. Other artists who joined him there were Emile Bernard (1868–1941), painter and writer and friend of Van Gogh, Charles Laval (1862–94), Paul Sérusier (1865–1925), a founder of the Nabis movement which rejected realism for flat, pure colour, and Maurice Denis (1870–1943), another of the Nabis school.

Gauguin painted two of his best-known works here – *La Belle Hélène* and the *Yellow Christ*, inspired by the yellowish wooden 16th-century crucifixion at the Chapelle de Trémalo, a typical Breton chapel among trees 1.5km north-west of Pont-Aven. His *Green Christ* was painted at Nizon's church 3km north-west of Pont-Aven.

A path from Moulin David follows the river to Bois d'Amour, a most attractive wooded park to the north painted by several of the artists. Near Moulin David is a plaque to record that Sérusier painted his influential *Le Talisman* there. In the summer of 1889, Gauguin decided that his fellow artists at Pont-Aven were 'an abominable lot' and moved to Le Pouldu (*see* page 213) followed by lesser painters Laval, Charles Filiger, Mayer de Maan and J. F. Willumsen. From here he went to Tahiti.

The poet and songwriter Théodore Botrel who wrote 'La Paimpolaise' started the celebrated Pardon des Fleurs d'Ajoncs (Gorse Bloom Festival) in 1905 with a contest for the Festival Bard. It is still held on the first Sunday in August.

There's an interesting walk from the bridge in the middle of the town, past old water mills, to the little port, used mostly now by pleasure boats, though there are some fishing boats still.

South at the entrance to the estuary is Port Manech (page 212), where the Aven and Bélon river estuaries meet – a fishing port which has become a small resort. 4km south-east of

Port-Aven is Riec-sur-Bélon, a little market town near the Bélon oyster beds. The oyster town of Bélon itself is across the river.

The museum of Pont-Aven named after Gauguin does not include a single work by him or his Pont-Aven fellow artists. It is open only in summer and shows works of his minor followers borrowed from other collections. Occasionally it will borrow one of his paintings (open mid-June to mid-September).

TOURIST INFORMATION 5 place Hôtel-de-Ville (98.06.04.70)
MARKET Tuesday
FESTIVALS *See above*

HOTELS

Moulin de Rosmadec (98.06.00.22). In a 15th-century water mill; garden terrace. Classic menu with accent on sea-food. Michelin star. ROOMS only four F–G. MEALS C–F. Shut Sunday evening low-season; Wednesday; February; 15–30 October.

Ajoncs d'Or, place Hôtel-de-Ville (98.06.02.06). ROOMS C. MEALS B–E. Shut Sunday evening, Monday.

Auberge de Kerland at Pont-du-Guilly, 3km south of Riec by D24 (98.06.42.98). Old farm in lovely situation among pine trees and a park above the Bélon valley. Super view from the terrace. Good cooking; interesting dishes. ROOMS E–G. MEALS C–F. Restaurant shut Sunday evenings in winter.

Chez Mélanie at Riec, place Église (98.06.91.05). Historic restaurant. Curnonsky, 'Prince of Gastronomes', chose it as his bolt-hole in World War I – the victim of his pseudonym. His real name was Maurice Sailland, and the Slav name under which he wrote heaped suspicion upon him in those days. He founded the magazine *Cuisines et Vins de France*. In Riec he stayed at the tiny inn of Madame Mélanie Rouet, said to have been the best cook in Brittany. Among the pictures of ladies in *coiffes* in the fine old dark-wood restaurant is one of the great man opening oysters with Mélanie. Curnonsky died in 1956 after attending more than 4000 banquets. She died shortly after. But the waitresses still wear *coiffes*, Bélon oysters are served in mountains and *Homard* (lobster) *Mélanie* accounts for the truly gastronomic menu at around 500F! Don't worry – there's one around 100F. Rooms are attractive, too. ROOMS, seven C–D. MEALS C–G.

Hotel shut 1 October–Easter. Restaurant shut Tuesday low-season; 15 November–15 December.

RESTAURANTS

Auberge La Taupinière, 4km on Concarneau road (98.06.03.12). Excellent ingredients; imaginative cooking; local favourite. Expensive. Meals F–G. Shut Monday evening except midsummer, Tuesday; 27 February–8 March; 17 September–19 October.

Chez Jacky at Riec, 4km at Port du Bélon (98.06.90.32). Beside lovely stretch of river, oyster cultivator sells oysters retail at the back of restaurant and at table inside it. All shellfish. MEALS F–G. Open Whitsun–end September. Shut Monday.

PONTIVY
[MORBIHAN]

Set in the lovely Blavet valley in the heart of Brittany, Pontivy has two distinct towns – the attractive, very Breton medieval town and the military base with a regular 'parade ground' plan built by Napoleon and called by him Napoléonville. At the end of the first Empire it was called Pontivy again; the Emperor Napoleon III brought back Napoléonville and Pontivy lived again when he was forced to flee to Chislehurst in Kent. Pontivy was named for a Welsh monk, St Ivy, who built the first bridge over the river.

Napoleon's coastal traffic was being attacked by British cruisers in the Napoleonic Wars, so he canalised the Blavet and other rivers, built canals to join them and made a safe canalised waterway from Nantes to Brest. Pontivy was made the military and strategic headquarters of the canal and Brittany. Now it is a lively and prosperous place, but with an increasing industrial zone. A market town, too.

The town became very important in the 15th century as the base of the very powerful de Rohan family. Jean II de Rohan also owned Josselin. He built the castle at Pontivy in 1484 and made the town his capital. He sided with France against François II,

Duke of Brittany. The castle still stands, its façade flanked by two formidable towers and the ramparts, 20 metres high, are protected by a moat. A remarkable chimney inside the castle is decorated with Rohan family coats of arms. Various exhibitions are held here from 15 June to 30 September. Castle open all day (except Monday, Tuesday off-season).

The narrow streets, like rue du Fil and rue du Pont, lined with 15th- and 16th-century gabled and overhanging houses, are from the same period as the castle. The centre of the old town, place du Martray, is bright and busy and the centre of the Monday market. The Flamboyant-style church of the 16th century has a tower with a spire and a polygonal staircase turret. In the Napoleonic part of the town, the interesting Church of Saint Joseph with an ornate square tower, built in Napoleon III's reign, is in a pleasant silvery-grey stone.

Pontivy is a good touring centre, with Mur-de-Bretagne and Lac de Guerléden (*see* page 143) 14km north up the Blavet river. South-west on the Blavet is the very pleasant little hillside town of St-Nicolas-des-Eaux, with thatched-roofed houses surrounding its chapel above a horse shoe loop of the river. A superb view from Site de Castennec round the loop.

At Stival, 3½km north of Pontivy, St Mériadec church has some outstanding stained glass. A bell said to have belonged to St Mériadec is rung in front of the deaf and placed on their heads at the Pardon on the third Sunday after Trinity. A strange form of alternative medicine.

TOURIST INFORMATION 61 rue Gén-de-Gaulle
(97.25.04.10)
MARKET Monday
FESTIVALS mid-September – Pardon; end September – Fair-Exposition

HOTELS

Chez Robic, 2 rue Jean-Jaurès (97.25.11.80). Unpretentious but superb value, with some really cheap menus. Local favourite. ROOMS vary A–D. MEALS A–E. Open all year.

Rohan, 90 rue Nationale (97.25.02.01). Very near Gambetta restaurant, same ownership. Napoleonic house, medieval name. ROOMS D–E. Open all year.

RESTAURANT

Gambetta, place Gare (97.25.53.70). Known for best fish, grilled over wood fire. Rooms – *see* Rohan *above*. MEALS B–E. Shut Sunday evening, Monday; February school holidays.

PONT L'ABBÉ
[S. FINISTÈRE]

Try to be there on Thursdays when the huge market square is taken over by a real Breton market. Capital of the old Bigouden, it is famous for the old smart and rather formal Breton dress and very high, thin *coiffes* with streamers still worn on fête days or for any other excuse and by some old ladies almost every day. You can see how the *coiffes* grew tall in the museum housed in a wing of the castle. Pont l'Abbé is the centre of a thriving market garden area.

Although it is a tourist centre for visiting Loctudy (6km south-east) and the coast to Pointe de Penmarch and is 11km west of Bénodet, at the Pont l'Abbé river estuary, the town is still a peaceful port and most pleasant, though the castle by its lake, with a large oval tower (13th to 18th centuries) looks somewhat fearsome. As well as head-dresses, the museum has some fine local furniture. The 14th-century former abbey church of Des Carmes has two of the most beautiful rose windows in France. Beside the quay is an impressive monument in granite to the Bigoudens.

TOURIST INFORMATION Château (98.87.24.44)
MARKET Thursday
FESTIVALS Second Sunday in July – Fête des Brodeuses (Embroideresses); fourth Sunday in September – Pardon

HOTELS

Bretagne, 24 place République (98.87.17.22). Local choice for fish; outstanding straightforward cooking. Family hotel of charm. All good value. ROOMS C–E. MEALS B–F. Shut 15–31 October; 15–31 January. Restaurant shut Sunday evening, Monday off-season.

Tour d'Auvergne, 22 place Gambetta (98.87.00.47). Pleasant little hotel in centre. Restaurant for residents only. ROOMS B–C.

RESTAURANT

Enclos de Rosveign, 4km north-east on route de Bénodet at Menez-Kerlaourn (98.87.02.90). A truly Breton patron-chef uses local ingredients to produce classic and Breton dishes. Excellent. MEALS B–G. Open all year.

PORT-LOUIS
[MORBIHAN]

Nowadays it is almost a suburb of Lorient, and Lorient's bathing beach. At the mouth of the Blavet river, it was called Blavet for centuries and was an important trading port in medieval times. When the Duc de Mercoeur and his Catholic Leaguers were rampaging round Brittany, they took Port-Louis with the help of a particularly vicious Spanish army sent to help them. The women of Port-Louis knew what their fate would be so a lot of the young girls escaped in a boat. But the Spaniards saw them and chased them. Rather than be taken by them, forty 'Virgins of Port-Louis' joined hands and jumped into the sea to drown.

Under Louis XIII Blavet became Port-Louis and under Louis XIV Richelieu strengthened its fortifications and made it headquarters of his first India Company, which failed. When Colbert took over, he built Lorient as the company base and Port-Louis declined. Last century it became very well known for sardine fishing and canning, and that lasted until World War II, when the citadel became a Gestapo interrogation, torture and execution centre for captured Resistance fighters. Three ditches were found in 1945 with the tortured, mutilated bodies of Resistance fighters.

The 16th-century citadel and 17th-century ramparts still dominate the little port looking, from across the estuary, like a great, threatening granite wall. The citadel has a maritime museum loaded towards the India Company (closed Tuesdays). There's a gap in the ramparts to the excellent beach of fine sand, with views of Groix Island to which you can take boat trips in season, and Larmor-Plage across the narrow estuary entrance. Out of season the beach virtually shuts down – cafés, bars and all. Boats run between Lorient and Port-Louis. Port Louis is at the entrance to the 'little sea' of Gâvres – an almost landlocked sea-lagoon.

MARKET Saturday

HOTEL

Commerce, place Marché (97.82.46.05). In the market place, surrounded and crowded on Saturdays, 200 metres from the beach. Garden. Rooms vary. Good menu range. ROOMS A–E. MEALS A–E. Shut Sunday evening, Monday in winter; 15–31 October; part February.

RESTAURANT

Avel Vor, 26 rue de Locmalo (97.82.47.59). New building facing Mer de Gâvres with big terrace. Known already for good cooking, especially of fish landed that morning. MEALS B–F. Shut Sunday evening low-season.

PORT-MANECH
[S. FINISTÈRE]

Pleasant bathing beach south of Pont-Aven at the edge of woods at the mouth of the long Aven and Bélon estuaries. A corniche path with nice views joins the beach and the port.

FESTIVAL 15 August – Folklorique Festival

HOTEL

Ar Moor (98.06.82.48). Seasonal. ROOMS B–E. MEALS B–F. Open Easter–end September.

LE POULDU
[S. Finistère]

The Laïta river wanders down 16km from Quimperlé past Forêt de Carnoët to reach the sea here, right on the borders of Finistère and Morbihan, and the little D49 through the forest is an absolutely delightful road. It must have been even better when Paul Gauguin and a few of his lesser-known artist friends came here in 1889 to get away from artists he had tired of in Pont-Aven.

More than Pont-Aven little Pouldu has really remembered Gauguin with a monument at the side of the chapel of Notre-Dame-de-la-Paix which was transported 26km and rebuilt here in 1957. The chapel has some fine stained glass by Manessier and Le Moal.

The beach is of fine sand with a good view of Groix Island and the coast. It is an old fishing port and now has a sailing school. Big hotels overlook the sea but there are nice scenes from the port overlooking the river Laïta.

TOURIST INFORMATION boul. Océan (2 January–September – 98.39.93.42)

HOTELS

Ar Men, route du Port (98.39.90.44). Our old friend Quatre Chemins renamed after 'total' reconstruction' to modern comfort but still looks like a big old Breton house. Terrace, garden. Very nice cooking. ROOMS C–E. MEALS A–E. Restaurant shut end September–1 May.

Bains, plage Grands Sables (98.39.90.11). Traditional 'Grand' beach hotel with fine sea views. ROOMS B–E. MEALS A–F. Open end April–25 September.

Panoramique, route plage de Kéron (98.39.93.49). No restaurant but half-board for residents. Little hotel in Breton style with views of sea and country from its terrace. ROOMS B–E. Demi-pension C–E. Shut early November–mid-January.

QUESTEMBERT
[Morbihan]

Likeable small market town in the countryside 28km east of Vannes, 32km west of Redon. It has a special place in Breton history, for here in AD 888 Alain-le-Grand took on 15,000 Norsemen who came annually to pillage, rape and burn and beat them so seriously that only 400 escaped to their ships. A monument commemorates the victory. The town has a covered market from 1675 and a few old houses. In the churchyard is a calvary and 16th-century chapel.

Questembert was little known until thirty years ago when Georges Paineau took over the Hotel Bretagne. Now tourists are lured to his restaurant – two Michelin stars and three toques and 18/20 from Gault-Millau.

HOTELS
Bretagne, 13 rue St-Michel (97.26.11.12). *See above*. French guide books rave about Georges Paineau's cooking but several customers have complained to me very recently about pallid tastes, too many mousses, limpid sauces, small portions at astronomical prices – the usual complaints about nouvelle cuisine. But no one has complained about the artistic décor of the dishes. I stay neutral – I have never had the luck to eat there. And my favourite French critic, Marc Champérard, loves the food. Rooms (six) have been improved but are very pricey. ROOMS F–G. MEALS E–G. Shut Sunday evening, Monday except July, August; 15 January–1 March.
Auberge Bretonne, 6 place du 8 Mai, 1945 (97.26.60.76). Unlikely to be mistaken for the other Bretonne! Fish specialities. ROOMS A. MEALS A–D. Shut Sunday evening, Monday.

QUIBERON
[Morbihan]

I saw the Quiberon peninsula first in the late 1950s and it seemed to be an agricultural poverty belt – fields surrounded by tumbling drystone walls and flaking low houses, tumbledown mills, and half-neglected chapels. The maritime pines of the isthmus which held the sand dunes had been decimated during German occupation. In the bay warships practised firing, so there was little sustained peace.

Quiberon itself was quite busy with passengers making for Belle-Ile, and Houat and Hoedic Islands, but the sardine fleet was diminishing, the canneries in recession, and I saw hardly any visitors on the fine sand beach or exploring the spectacular Côte Sauvage down the west side, where rocks of a million shapes and sizes hide caves, crevasses and tiny sand beaches.

In summer at least, the scene has changed quite dramatically. The campers and caravanners have come to high-starred sites. Attractive small blocks of holiday flats have been built. Fishing boats have returned. Quiberon has become *une station balnéaire très recherchée* – a much sought-after resort, especially for families. Though much livelier, with a lot more bodies on the super wide sands, it is not too crowded outside French school holidays (July–early August) and nearly all the visitors are French. Apart from family-run hotels, it has about ten campsites from two to four stars and a youth hostel. Its original lure for the French was the sea-treatment station (Institut Thalasso Thérapie) founded in 1964 with its own very expensive Sofitel and equally pricey Sofitel Diététique attached. The Institut swimming pool, with sea views, is attractive.

The harbour from which the island boats go is spacious Port-Haliguen 1½km east, a port for fishing boats which has been enlarged for pleasure boats, with regattas in summer. The corniche road starts here, with good views of the airfield and plage de Pierre Percée from where you can walk to Pointe du Conguel, giving excellent views from a viewing table to the three isles, the Morbihan coast and of Quiberon Bay. The Côte Sauvage really can be savage, with the sea boiling and beating against the rocks combining with the wind to make a fearsome din. Take D186 all the way round the coast, and walk down to the seashore to see the coastline. Understandably bathing is forbidden on the tempting little beaches. Anyone who does it and lives needs a thorough examination, especially of the head. The views from Pointe du Percho are to the Côte Sauvage on one side, the fort and beach of

Penthièvre on the other. On the other coast is Beg Rohu with a national sailing school and St Pierre-Quiberon with two bathing beaches on either side of a little port called Orange, for fishing and pleasure boats. The peninsula is famous for sailing. St Pierre holds regattas and has eight good hotels.

Quiberon was once an island, but is now joined to the Penthièvre peninsula by a landstrip little wider than the road. On the left just before you cross is the fort which once defended the causeway, Fort de Penthièvre, rebuilt in the 19th century. A monument and tomb recall the murder here of fifty-nine Resistance men caught by the Germans in 1944.

Much earlier Resistance fighters were shot after landing in Quiberon. In 1795, when the Chouans in Brittany and Vendée were revolting against the excesses of Revolution, the aristocrats who had fled to England and the German states thought that the time had come to return and reclaim their power and lands. The idea was for 100,000 to land in Brittany, led by their princes. In fact 10,000 were prepared to be brought over by the British fleet. The princes and higher-ranked aristocrats thought it prudent to stay behind. The troops were led by less important counts who could not agree on a plan and who had different goals from the Chouans. Furthermore, the very competent Revolutionary Général Lazare Hoche knew that they were coming. He drove them back up the Quiberon peninsula. Some reached the British fleet, anchored offshore, by small boats. Those who surrendered were summarily shot (many at Auray) by order of the Revolutionary Convention and against Hoche's wishes.

Penthièvre has two very fine beaches, one on each side of the isthmus.

For boat trips see under isles of Belle-Île (page 76) and Houat and Hoedic (*see* page 152).

TOURIST INFORMATION 7 rue Verdun (97.50.07.84)

HOTELS

Most hotels insist on demi-pension in high summer.
Sofitel – Thalassa (97.50.20.00). *See above.* Corridor to the Thalassapeutic Institute. Rooms very pricey indeed. MEALS E–F. Shut January.

Ker Noyal, rue St-Clément (97.50.08.41). Big high quality hotel; flower garden. ROOMS F–G. MEALS E. Open 1 March–31 October.

Neptune, 4 quai de Houat, Port Maria (97.50.09.62). Very pleasant, family run; facing sea. ROOMS D–E. MEALS A–E. Shut Monday in winter; 20 December to mid-February.

Beau Rivage, 11 rue Port-Maria (97.50.08.39). Direct access to beach; faces south; panoramic restaurant. Very good fish. ROOMS D–E. MEALS B–D. Open 1 April–20 September. Restaurant open 1 May–20 September.

Pension de Famille, 1 rue des Tamaris (97.50.10.26). Simple, excellent value; in gardens 200 metres from sea. Family cooking. ROOMS A–B. MEALS A–C. Shut October–April.

Plage at St. Pierre-Quiberon, 4½km north (97.30.92.10). Restaurant and some rooms have sea views. Some self-catering suites in low season. ROOMS D–G. MEALS B–D. Shut mid-October to end March; 15–30 April.

RESTAURANTS

Goursen, quai Ocean, Port Maria (97.50.07.94). Some of the best fish in Morbihan or even Brittany – not cheap. MEALS D–F. Shut lunch in July, August; Tuesday low-season; mid-November to mid-March.

Relax, 27 boul. Castero, plage de Kermorvan (97.50.12.84). Good classic cooking, Circular restaurant half open to the bay. Good fish; good value. MEALS A–E. Shut Sunday evening, Monday off-season; January.

QUIMERC'H
(S. FINISTÈRE)

Hamlet on D770 between Le Faou and Port Launay with remarkable views from Ménez Hom to Cranou forest, over Plougastel peninsula and Rade de Brest.

QUIMPER
[S. Finistère]

I have grown to like Quimper more and more over the years. It is a higgledy-piggledy place, lighthearted, lively and sometimes crowded, especially in market hours or with midsummer day visitors, but can be gentle and tranquil in spring or autumn evenings. Two rivers reflect the town's two characters – the gentle, pretty Odet, flowing through hills, meeting the lively river Steir.

The long quays of the Odet divide the town and everything of real interest is on the north side. The quays border a shopping centre. The other most interesting areas are the cathedral, the market, the town hall and rue Kéréon running from the east bank of the river Steir, with shops beneath overhanging storeys opening up to give a fine view of the cathedral. The Steir river has been covered before its meeting with the Odet but there is a good view from its bridge of the river and the old houses with flower window boxes alongside it. The other way is the market hall and place Terre-aux-Ducs, with some lovely old houses. In the old days, this area was the lay town, apart from the ecclesiastical city around the cathedral.

The town was for long called Quimper-Corentin after the first bishop, St Corentin. The story of its founding is typical of the Cornouaille, this part of Brittany. After the town of Is had disappeared beneath the waves of the Bay of Douarnenez, King Gradlon, who had escaped on his horse, set up a new capital called Kemper-Odetz, now Quimper. He was out hunting in the forest near Plomodiern when he asked the hermit Corentin for something to eat. The hermit caught one little fish that was swimming in his spring. He cut a small piece from the fish's back and gave it to the King's Master of the Household to share with King and courtiers, who roared with laughter. To their amazement, there was not only enough fish for all of them but Corentin threw the fish back and it was immediately whole again, with no wound or scars. Gradlon was so impressed that he gave him a monastery, then made him bishop of his new capital.

Gradlon, on the horse which rescued him from the floods, stands in statue on the parapet between the towers of the cathedral. Before the Revolution, on 22 November, eve of St Cecilia's Day (patron saint of Music), the cathedral choir would sing an anthem from the balcony by the statue. Meanwhile an official climbed on the horse behind King Gradlon, tied a napkin round his neck, put a glass of wine to the King's lips, then drank the wine himself and hurled the glass to the crowd in the square below. If anyone could catch the glass unbroken, the town would pay them a hundred gold écus, a fortune to citizens in those days. No one ever did. Rumour has it that the town officials made several saw-cuts in the stem of the glass before the ceremony.

The cathedral, started in the 13th century, is known for its graceful twin spires, which can be seen from outside the town. They were not built until 1856, modelled on the Breton steeple of Pont-Croix's Notre-Dame-de-Roscudon, near Audierne. Perhaps the people of Quimper were smarting under the sneers that the roofs of their towers were like candle-snuffers (*éteignoirs*). The sea toned down their colour and they look as old as the rest. It is one of the earliest Gothic churches in Brittany, made more sophisticated by the 15th-century buttressed nave with soaring arches. The 15th-century stained-glass windows are fine but of such dark colours that the inside of the cathedral looks sombre. The organ was built in 1643 by Robert Dallam, 'freshly emigrated from England'. A member of a famous family of organ builders, he was the son of one of Queen Elizabeth I's organ makers. Robert went to France to get away from the Puritans, who did not approve of church organ-playing. He rebuilt the organs of many churches in Brittany before returning to England to work at New College, Oxford, where he is buried. His sons became famous in France.

The former Bishop's Palace (early 16th-century) has a charming close from which the Bishop could enjoy river views without being bothered by his flock. You reach the palace up a fine 16th-century spiral staircase. Inside is an interesting Breton museum which includes an old Breton house interior, historic wood carvings, including furniture, traditional costume and Quimper *faience* (pottery), for which the town has been known since 1690 (shut Tuesday).

Pottery was brought from Provençe by Jean-Baptiste

Bousquet. Through marriage, Rouen techniques and designs were introduced. Blue was the main colour with human figures until recent times when more modern designs of flowers and marine fauna were brought in. There are working potteries including one with a museum which you can visit in Locmaria area at the south-west of town (most shut Saturday afternoons, Sundays).

The Beaux-Arts museum, in part of the former town hall in place St-Corentin, is outstanding for its collection of paintings, built on the collection of a 19th-century connoisseur Comte de Silguy (closed Tuesday; January). The 16th- and 17th-century collection of foreign works has a sketch by Rubens and paintings by Carracci, Van Haarlem and Jacob Jordaens. 18th- and 19th-century French paintings include works of Boucher, Fragonard, and Corot, with Boudin's fine *Le Port de Quimper*, and the so-called Pont-Aven artists have many paintings, including pictures of Breton women by Emile Bernard, Paul Sérusier's *La Vieille du Pouldu*, which, although it has one old woman in it, is really a mystical rocky seascape. There is an enormous Pont-Aven landscape by Maxime Maufra and an interesting small sketch by Clarin of Lezaven, the manor used as a studio by Gauguin and the others. Of special interest to me are the pictures by the Americans in Pont-Aven before Gauguin – Henry Mosler's *Breton Fortune Teller* and a pastel *Concarneau Seascape* by Charles Fromuth, a Philadelphian little known in Europe though respected by Rodin. Charles Cottet (1863–1924), who specialised in Breton paintings, has four, including a symbolic *Burnt Church* showing peasants kneeling before the charred remains of their church – an insight into Breton history.

A room is given to the drawings and manuscripts of the poet and painter Max Jacob, friend of Picasso and Cocteau, now becoming more highly recognised. Jacob was born in 1876 in rue du Parc, Quimper, a shopping street overlooking the river, the son of Jewish shopkeepers. Brilliant as a child, he went to Paris at age twenty to become an artist. There he starved, sharing a room with Picasso. Max worked in a shop by day and slept in the only bed at night. Picasso slept during the day and painted at night. He had his first writing published in 1904 but continued painting. In 1907 he moved to a little slum room in

Montmartre. There one day he saw Christ in a landscape he had painted. Like St Paul, his conversion to Christianity was instant.

His first major work was a novel on life in Quimper, *Le Terrain Bouchaballe*. He was famous in Paris as a wit and raconteur. He was baptised into the Roman Catholic church in 1915, with Picasso as godfather. Suddenly in 1921 he cut himself off from a hectic life in Paris to hide himself in a monastery at St Benoît-sur-Loire near Orléans to paint but mostly to write. 'Now I am a Catholic, there is no fun in sinning any more,' he said.

After seven years he tired of the monastic life and moved back to Paris, living luxuriously on the sales of his gouaches – water colours mixed with a pigment. He was made a *Chevalier* of the *Légion D'Honneur*. But he seems to have tired of sinning again and in 1936 returned finally to St Benoît. When France was occupied, his family were sent to concentration camps. His sister and brother died in Auschwitz. He was made to wear the yellow star of David to show that he was Jewish. In February 1944 the Gestapo took him to Drancy in the Paris suburbs – Nazi transit camp for the gas chambers. Cocteau and all his friends

except Picasso fought to get him freed. They were too late. The Gestapo said that he had died in Drancy of pneumonia. On his centenary in 1976 Quimper named the main bridge over the river Odet 'Pont Max Jacob'.

800 metres from the bridge is the beautiful, restored Romanesque church of Locmaria.

After a fire in 1976, Quimper built a fine new market hall near the cathedral. Markets are held here every morning, with a street market on Saturdays. The Cornouaille folklore festival in July is one of the biggest in Brittany (*see* Festivals, *below*).

The boat trip down the Odet to Bénodet is delightful with woods and parks of many manor houses and a lake where the river widens at Kérogan (ask Tourist Office for timetable, times depend on tides in the estuary).

TOURIST INFORMATION 3 rue Roi Gradlon
(98.95.04.69)

MARKETS *See above*

FESTIVAL Les Grandes Fêtes de Cornouaille – lasts six days from Tuesday to the last Sunday in July. Started 1923. More than a thousand musicians and three thousand people in full costume – many from other Celtic countries. Great procession on final day.

HOTELS

Tour d'Auvergne, 13 rue Réguaires (98.95.08.70). *Souvenirs des temps perdus!* I used to love this typical old French provincial hotel, with a bird-cage lift and atmosphere of yesteryear. Not much changed but the restaurant shuts in winter when you want to stay in. But Capucin Gourmand is down the street (*see below*). France Accueil. ROOMS B–E. MEALS B–E. Shut 23 December–8 January. Restaurant shut 1 October–30 April.

Moderne, 21 bis ave Gare (98.90.31.71). Old 'Grand Hotel' modernised; some rooms modern, some rustic. Good reputation for food. ROOMS B–E. MEALS B–E. Shut mid-December to mid-January. Restaurant shut Saturday in winter.

RESTAURANTS

Quimper has many good-value, cheap restaurants.
Capucin Gourmand, 29 rue Réguaires (98.95.43.12). Doesn't look

much but don't be misled. Michelin star cooking at reasonable prices and sensible portions. Inconvenient closing. MEALS D–E. Shut Saturday, Sunday; mid-July to mid-August; part February.
Tritons, allées de Locmaria (98.90.61.78). Good value for evenings – open until 1 a.m. Old-fashioned Breton family dishes (*potée bretonne*); excellent value. MEALS B–C. Shut Monday.

QUIMPERLÉ
[S. FINISTÈRE]

A beautiful town in a pretty position in a deep valley where the rivers Ellé and Isole meet to form the Laïta, Quimperlé is an excellent centre for discovering the attractive countryside around the forest of Carnoët and little coast villages such as Le Pouldu (*see* page 213). The forest road south D49 to Pouldu and back inland to Landlaric is especially attractive, and at Pouldu it joins the attractive coast road south-east D152. The traffic from Brest and Quimper to Lorient 16km south-east bypasses Quimperlé.

Quimperlé is a lovely town for wandering, looking and stopping at a pavement café just to watch the world go by. The cobbled quaysides of the river are a delight for lingering. Walk down the very narrow rue Dom Morice past 16th-century houses with overhanging storeys and wooden tiles, and rue Brémond Ars with wooden houses.

The upper town is dominated by St Michel church, 13th to 15th centuries, Gothic, with a great square tower and a beautifully sculptured porch. It looks down on the lower town, the old part of which is huddled between the two rivers around the abbey church of Ste Croix, attractive and remarkable. Steps join the two towns.

Ste Croix church was built in the 11th century and partially rebuilt on the original plan in 1862 after the belfry collapsed. The new belfry stands alone. The church was based very closely on the Holy Sepulchre in Jerusalem – circular with a rotunda and round tower, with a porch in the shape of a Greek cross. Inside this is a beautiful Renaissance screen with Christ and the Evangelists with crowds of carved figures.

In the War of Succession Jean de Montfort and the English held Quimperlé until du Guesclin took it in 1373.

The forest of Carnoët, mainly beech and oak trees, and bounded by the river Laïta, has some fine walks on forest-ways reserved for walkers and horse-riders.

This was the forest of the Count of Comorre, the Bluebeard of Cornouaille who had his wives killed as soon as they were pregnant because it had been predicted that his son would cause his death (*see* Iles de Houat et Hoëdic, page 152). Rocher Royal (Royal Rock) has views over the Laïta and some remains of Château de Carnoët where Bluebeard is supposed to have lived.

St Maurice, reached by D224 left off the attractive D49, is prettily placed between the river and a lake.

TOURIST INFORMATION Pont Bourgneuf (June–October–98.96.04.32)

MARKET Friday

FESTIVAL Whitsun – Grande Fête de Toulfoën (Feast of Birds)

HOTELS

Hermitage at Manoir de Kerroch, 2km south by D49 (98.96.04.66). Manor house on a hill with views over its own park; swimming pool. Rooms in buildings around the grounds vary but are all comfortable. ROOMS D–F. MEALS B–D. Open all year.

Auberge de Toulfoën, 3km south by D49 (98.96.00.29). Old forest coaching inn with good country cooking. Nine rooms B–D. MEALS C–E. Shut Monday except July, August, September; 25 September–31 October.

RESTAURANTS

Bistro de la Tour, 2 rue Dom Morice (98.39.29.58). Delightful old restaurant with authentic antiques. Two dining-rooms. Imaginative dishes at sensible prices. MEALS B–E. Shut Monday, Saturday lunch and Sunday evening.

Relais du Roch, 2km S by D49 (98.96.12.97). At end of drive of Hermitage (above) but no connection now. MEALS B–G. Shut Monday, Sunday evening low-season; January.

La Vache Enragée, 5 rue Jacques Cartier. I haven't met the patronne of this 'Angry Cow' but I am told that she serves good family meals at low prices. MEALS A–C.

Ty-Gwechall, 4 rue Mellac (98.96.30.63). One of the best crêperies in Brittany, with lots of choice. In fine old building. Try a bolée of cider. MEALS A–C. Shut Wednesday low-season.

QUINTIN
[CÔTES-DU-NORD]

Charming old town with houses rising in terraces from a pleasant stretch of the river Gouët. Some traces remain of its old ramparts, such as the delightful Porte Neuve of square towers with pointed roofs. It is 20km south-west of the beaches of St Brieuc. It took me years to discover Quintin but I find the whole town peaceful and delightful, with attractive old houses, many of them mansions, in squares such as place du Martray and place du 1830, and in Grande-Rue, and grassy banks to the river. The remains of Château de la Noée-Sèche have a 17th-century wing, a fine terrace overlooking the river and a delightful doorway with pointed turrets. The basilica has what is said to be a piece of the Virgin's girdle brought back from a 13th-century crusade by the first Lord of Quintin, Geoffrey. Until the Revolution the town was famous for making veils, exported as far as America for women's hats. There were 30,000 workers in the industry. Now the population is only 3,500. There are some treasures in its winding streets left from those prosperous days, like Grande Maison, once a post-inn and headquarters of the Chousans in 1795, and old fountains like those from the 17th century in Jardin des Carmes. The river is used particularly for canoeing.

The austere 17th-century Château de Robien, 2km south on D790, has a monumental staircase. You can visit the park from early March to end August. The D7 south-east has a pleasant stretch through Forêt de Lorge.

MARKET Tuesday
FESTIVAL Second Sunday in May – Pardon

HOTEL

Commerce, rue Rochonen (96.74.94.67). Quiet Logis. Rooms B–D. Meals C–E. Shut Sunday evening, Monday lunch except July, August; mid-December–mid-January.

RAZ, POINTE DU
(S. Finistère)

One of the most exciting places in Brittany. It is France's Land's End, sticking into the Atlantic between the Bay of Douarnenez and Bay of Audierne, 15km west of Audierne. In summer the huge car park is packed amidst souvenir stalls, crêperies and hot dog stands as well as restaurants and cafés. But still the cliffs 70 metres above the water make you feel dizzy, the seas roar as they hit the sheer walls of the great chasm – Enfer de Plogoff – and you can hear the strange moaning that the Bretons say is the souls of the dead. If you are a little dodgy on your legs or just hate heights, stay at the top with Notre-Dame-des-Naufragés (Our Lady of the Shipwrecked) and take one of the simpler paths. You will still have a fine panoramic view.

But if you have sensible non-slip shoes and do not mind heights, join the guide on the more adventurous path, keeping to the safety rope, and you will have a superb one and a half hour trip around the edges of the deep chasms.

The panoramic view from the top beyond the semaphore looks over a chain of reefs to Sein island (*see* page 251) and on clear days to the Ar Men lighthouse. The bodies of druids were rowed across to Sein to be buried, and the little bay along the north of Pointe du Raz is called Baie des Trépassés (Bay of the Dead). But some believe that the name comes from the number of bodies of drowned people which were washed by the current to the coast of the bay. The drowned town of Is is said to be buried under the marshy coast.

North of Baie des Trépassés is another point, Pointe du Van, with a chapel and a path round it with views not quite so spectacular as from Raz, but you can see Sein island, and there are not so many tourists.

HOTELS

Baie des Trépassés (98.70.61.34). Famous for shellfish, especially the platter. New rooms with good views. ROOMS D–E. MEALS A–F. Shut 5 January–early February.

REDON
(ILLE-ET-VILAINE]

Here the river Vilaine and the Nantes–Brest canal are linked by a dock with a port serving both and the railway runs through, so Redon was once very important commercially. It is still the centre of several small industries – mechanical engineering, plastics, refrigerator depots, foundries. It is also an agricultural market centre with a big, important market on Mondays and various fairs, including the Foire Teillouse, famous for chestnuts (fourth Saturday in October).

Redon did not lure many tourists until recently. Now it has become popular for sailing and canoeing, mainly because of its pleasure marina on the Vilaine. There are boat excursions on the river and some coasting vessels still come up river.

The former abbey church of St Sauveur was cut off from its 57-metre, 14th-century Gothic bell-tower by a fire in 1780. But the church still has a 12th century Norman tower with rounded angles.

There are fine houses from the 15th and 16th centuries in the old town, on quai Duguay-Trouin on the river and on quai St-Jacques. Alas, huge trucks can jam the narrow streets.

TOURIST INFORMATION place Parlement (99.71.06.04)
MARKETS Monday; daily in market hall
FESTIVALS July–August – Petite Ville Grand Renom;
mid-May – Commercial Fair; fourth Saturday in
October – Foire Teillouse (especially chestnuts)

HOTELS

Chandouineau, 10 ave de la Gare (99.71.02.04). The Relais de la Gare has taken the name of its owner, and gone upmarket in elegance, comfort and price. It still has one good cheap menu.

Very nice rooms. ROOMS E–F. MEALS C–G. Shut Saturday lunch, Sunday evening except in summer; end July–middle August.

Auberge du Poteau Vert, 6km S by D164 at St-Nicolas-de-Redon (99.71.13.12). Big country restaurant, very respected locally. Six rooms C. MEALS C (weekdays), D–G. Shut Sunday evening, Monday; 23–30 September; 1–7 January.

RESTAURANT

La Bogue, 3 rue des États (99.71.12.95). Happy place, excellent value, especially cheaper menus. MEALS A (weekdays), C–F. Shut Tuesday evening, Wednesday; 1–20 January; 3–15 July.

Moulin de Via, 3km on route de la Gacilly (99.71.05.16). Big 19th-century stone house; good professional cooking. MEALS D–F. Shut Sunday evening, Monday; 1–9 September.

RENNES
[See Major Towns, page 44]

LA ROCHE-BERNARD
[MORBIHAN]

A charming old town prettily placed on a spur of La Garenne overlooking the river Vilaine, lively in summer with pleasure boats and their 'crews'. The Vilaine is pretty here, wide, tree-lined, with old and new harbours. The superb modern suspension bridge, 50 metres above the water, blends very nicely into the landscape.

The shipyards of La Roche-Bernard were famous in the 17th century. Some coastal boats do go through here and up the Vilaine to Redon, but it is the 'pleasurers' who regard it as their home port now. Many years ago I took a boat through Brittany from here to Redon, Josselin back to Rennes and the villagers came down to the banks to talk to us. Now there is quite a traffic in pleasure boats.

The old town begins at Promenade du Ruicard and climbs in small cobbled streets and steps past 16th- and 17th-century houses to place Bouffay, where the guillotine stood in 1793. La Roche-Bernard was a strongly Republican town. Defended by 150 men, it was attacked in 1793 by 6,000 Chouans who easily defeated the 150 'Blues'. The mayor, named Sauveur, was ordered to shout *'Vive le Roi'* – 'Long Live the King'. He shouted *'Vive la République!'* and was shot down and badly wounded. The Chouans set light to the Tree of Liberty and threw the dying man into it. His father wrote next day to the Republican authorities at Rennes: 'My son died at his post. The Barbarians could not rise to the level of a true Republican.'

A small Musée de la Vilaine Maritime is in the attractive Château des Basses Fosses (16th to 17th centuries) where James II of England and Queen Henrietta stayed in exile. It includes a lovely model of a ship made in La Roche-Bernard in 1629 (a man-of-war ordered by Richelieu), also folk costumes (open daily 1 June–30 September; weekends rest of year).

Downstream the Vilaine is controlled by Arzal Dam, which forms a freshwater reservoir, controlling the tides and making navigation easier for all boats up to Redon. Upstream is the little port of Foleux used by pleasure boats – a charming spot. You can reach it by the attractive D148, right on D20 then right at Château Léhélec, a 17th- to 18th-century manor with three courtyards, in a woodland setting. You can visit four rooms in July, August afternoons except Tuesday.

To the north-west near Le Guerno, which has a 16th-century church which was once a place of pilgrimage, is a zoo among ponds and trees in the big grounds of Branféré Château, with two hundred exotic birds and animals living semi-free. (Open Easter to mid–November). River trips in the *Anne de Bretagne* go to Arzal, Foleux and on to Redon (telephone at Arzal, 97.45.02.81).

TOURIST INFORMATION Mairie (15 June–15 September – 99.90.67.98)
MARKET Thursday

HOTELS

Auberge Bretonne, 2 place du Guesclin (99.90.60.28). Young

Jacques Thorel has won a star from Michelin and all-round praise for good simple dishes, regional and modern but not nouvelle. He learned from the great Boyer of Reims. He remains modest and unruffled, and keeps sensible prices except for a feast based on a theme, often built round a good bottle of wine. He has a passion for wine. Only five bedrooms, reserved well ahead. Talk in 1989 of two more houses for more rooms. ROOMS D–E. MEALS C–G. Shut Thursday; Wednesday lunch; 15 November–15 December.

Deux Magots, 1 place Bouffay (99.90.60.75). Excellent value meals; fifteen rooms in house built in 1700. Pleasant rooms D–F. MEALS A–E. Shut Sunday evening low-season, Monday; 15 December–15 January.

Armor Vilaine, at Péaule, 9km north-west, place Église (97.42.91.03). Nice comfortable Logis. ROOMS C–D. MEALS A–E. Shut Sunday evening, Monday except July, August; February.

ROCHEFORT-EN-TERRE
[MORBIHAN]

A truly pretty village, especially when the window boxes and the stone troughs are ablaze with flowers. It looks down on the wooded deep valleys of the little Arz and Gueuzon rivers. The old streets in the centre are lined with beautifully preserved 16th- to 17th-century houses. The church, 12th to 16th century, is well tended, too. On a 17th-century altar is the statue of Our Lady of La Tronchaye, believed to have been hidden in a hollow tree from looting Norsemen and found there in the 12th century. A pardon is held on the third Sunday in August.

The remains of the 12th-century castle were incorporated into the present château by the American artists Alfred and Trafford Klots in the early part of this century. New rooms were made from stones of other ruined castles. The Klots decorated a complete room with paintings. Now the building belongs to the Morbihan council (open 1 June–30 September daily; weekends

April, May). From its terrace are superb views of the Gueuzon valley.

Rochefort has many day visitors and has a lot of crêperies and antique shops. Good trout fishing in nearby rivers.

FESTIVAL Sunday after 15 August–Pardon

RESTAURANTS

Lion d'Or, rue Pélican (97.43.32.80). Most attractive 16th-century coaching inn – alas, no bedrooms now. Mostly classic dishes. MEALS C–F. Shut Sunday and Monday evenings, Tuesday except in July, August; 4 January–15 February.

Auberge du Moulin Neuf, 1km S by D774 (97.43.32.19). Restored old watermill by a small lake; very good value; dishes slightly modernised. MEALS A–E. Shut Monday; part February.

ROCHE-JAGU, CHÂTEAU
[CÔTES-DU-NORD]

Just off D787 north of Pontrieux, the castle was built in the 15th century at the top of a steep wooded hill sloping to the river Trieux. It was restored in 1967. Gorgeous views down to the river where it forms a steep-sided loop. Rooms have superb French-style decorated ceilings and fine chimneys. Visits daily Easter to end September; Sundays rest of year.

LA ROCHE-MAURICE
[N. FINISTÈRE]

Village high on a rock above the Élorn river north-east of Brest and 5km from Landerneau, with a beautiful parish close from the 16th century. At the entrance are three crosses showing the crucifixion of Christ and the two thieves, and inside the church are interesting statues and a great window of 1539 showing the Passion and the Resurrection. The ossuary has a fierce-looking skeleton warning us: *Je vous tue tous* – 'I shall kill you all'.

RESTAURANT

Auberge Vieux Château (98.20.40.52). Serves only lunch, but good value. MEALS B–F. Shut Monday; 1–21 November.

ROSCOFF
[N. FINISTÈRE]

For a town of around 4,000 people, Roscoff plays many parts in the life of Brittany and France. A seaside bathing resort, a great market for vegetables and fish, a fishing port, a ferry port, a commercial port and a very important medical centre where the University of Paris has a laboratory to experiment in seawater treatments and marine biology. And there is a port from which boats go to the isle of Batz (*see* page 69) which you can see offshore.

Pirates (or corsairs, if you wish) and smugglers made the original prosperity of Roscoff. A shipowner and farmer, no pirate but just as adventurous as they were, has made it prosperous today. Alexis Gourvennec was one of the young peasant farmers who got tired of having the market rigged against them by wholesalers. They formed JAC (Jeunesse Agricole Catholique) in the late 1950s. They set up a village-by-village organisation of growers and when the Ministry of Agriculture in Paris stalled at their demands, three thousand of them gathered in Morlaix and occupied the Sous-Préfecture, for which Gourvennec got three weeks in jail. But their movement grew into the powerful SICA (Societé d'Intérêt Collectif Agricole) with big headquarters at Kérisnel, outside the market town of St Pol-de-Léon, 5km from Roscoff, and a sophisticated auction system with whole lorry-loads of vegetables sold without unloading.

Gourvennec knew that Finistère's traditional trade with Britain in onions and early vegetables was dying because of the high cost of transport by the long routes through St Malo and Cherbourg. A typical tough, militant Breton, he bullied and cajoled Paris into allocating six million francs for building a new deep-water port at Roscoff. Then he canvassed shipping firms and brokers all over Europe to set up a ferry to carry freight from Roscoff to Plymouth. They all scoffed. One London broker said: 'Roscoff? No, we *never* do business with the Russians.'

So he persuaded the farmers' cooperative SICA to start Brittany Ferries. He gambled on Britain joining the EEC. No one except the Bretons believed it could last. It has, in fact, revolutionised not only trade between Britain and Brittany, but tourism. The second ferry to St Malo especially drew millions of British tourists to France. And Brittany Ferries now has services Plymouth–Roscoff, Portsmouth–St Malo, Portsmouth–Caen, Plymouth–Santander in Spain, Roscoff–Cork in Southern Ireland and a truck 'Routiers' route, Portsmouth–Cherbourg which carries cars and passengers in modest comfort at low rates in summer.

In August 1548, Mary Queen of Scots landed in Roscoff to be engaged to the Dauphin François, son and heir of King Henri II of France. A tower is named after her and an old stone house is called 'Maison Marie Stuart' though the connection is doubtful. Mary was five years of age and had been Queen of Scotland since five days after she was born, when her father James V of Scotland was defeated and killed by the English at the Battle of Solway Moss. The Dauphin was three years of age. The marriage was arranged as an alliance between France and Scotland against England. The journey from Dumbarton took eighteen days through terrible storms.

Mary spent the next thirteen years of her life in France. She married François in 1558 and next year he was King of France and she was Queen of France and Scotland. He was a sickly boy and died six months later. Mary went home to Scotland.

Near the ferry harbour and the 16th- to 17th-century church of Notre-Dame-de-Kroaz-Batz is the Aquarium Charles-Pérez where reservoirs contain sea creatures and fish in their natural surroundings. On Pointe de Bloscon beside the tiny fishermen's chapel of Ste Barbe, with fine views, are the *viviers* containing lobsters, crabs, salmon and salmon trout. The bays and cafés of the quays are the favourite evening spots for locals and tourists. With sea on three sides, Roscoff has a choice of sandy or shingle beaches. The best of fine sand is at Laber.

TOURIST INFORMATION rue Gambetta (98.69.70.70)

HOTELS

Brittany et Restaurant Ar Maner, boul. Ste-Barbe, Hotel (98.69.70.78). Restaurant (98.69.20.34). Luxurious hotel of character in a 17th-century mansion, facing the pleasure boat harbour. Lovely bedrooms, swimming pool, garden to the sea-shore. Restaurant with views run separately. ROOMS E–F. MEALS C–G. Open 10 March–10 November. Restaurant shut Sunday evening, Monday low-season.

Gulf Stream, rue Marquise de Kergariou (98.69.73.19). Facing Laber beach, lovely position but outside town. Very good cooking. Very fresh ingredients. ROOMS E–F. MEALS C–G.

Corsaire, pl. Lacaze-Duthiers (98.61.22.61). New; big, comfortable rooms. For restaurant *see* Temps de Vivre, *below*. ROOMS D–E. Shut 15–30 November.

RESTAURANT

Temps de Vivre, in Corsaire Hotel above (98.61.27.28). Good meals; wide menu choice. MEALS C–F. Shut Monday, Sunday evening in winter; February.

ROSPORDEN
[S. FINISTÈRE]

13km north-east of Concarneau beside a lake formed by the river Aven, it is a typical small Breton town with the bell-tower of its ancient church reflected in the water. It is known for hydromel, a type of mead made with honey since ancient times (called *chouchen* in Brittany).

TOURIST INFORMATION rue Le Bas (July–August 98.59.27.26)
MARKET Thursday

HOTELS

Bourhis, place Gare (98.59.23.89). Two restaurants – a grill called Le Jardin and a distinguished restaurant with elegance, comfort and Grande Cuisine, imaginative and beautifully presented. Michelin star. Comfortable modern rooms, well

sound-proofed. ROOMS E. MEALS D–G. Shut Sunday evening, Monday in winter.
Gai Logis, 5 route Quimper (98.59.22.38). Two-star Logis. ROOMS B–D. MEALS A–F. Shut 15 February–15 March. Restaurant shut Saturday off-season.

SABLES-D'OR-LES-PINS
[CÔTES-DU-NORD]

The fine sand beach and the pine trees say it all. One of the best beaches in Brittany. In the protection of a bay down the west coast from Cap Fréhel, it has a main beach facing north which can be windy, so climb the sand dunes or go round the road to the other beach facing south. The town is modern, built up as a resort with seasonal entertainment and sport but nothing of special interest except the villa gardens filled with hydrangeas in summer. Good sailing and horse riding in the pines and dunes.

Pléhérel-Plage is another tinier beach resort up the coast. Sables d'Or is an excellent holiday spot for families who like beach lounging, picnics in the woods and comfortable, fairly inexpensive hotels.

HOTELS
Voile d'Or, allée des Acacias (96.41.42.49). Well-run hotel with renovated rooms and sensible range of menus. ROOMS B–D. MEALS A–F. Shut Tuesday lunch and Monday off-season; mid-November–mid-March.
Bon Accueil (96.41.42.19). Family seaside hotel, well run by same family for decades. ROOMS C–E. MEALS A–D. Open Easter; end April to end September.

RESTAURANTS
Duchesse-Anne, boul. de la Mer (96.41.49.05). Simple restaurant with good value meals, overlooking the beach. Large choice, old-style cooking. MEALS B–E. Shut 2 January–end March; mid-November–23 December.

ST BRIAC-SUR-MER
[ILLE-ET-VILAINE]

A delightful little fishing port and beach resort only 18km west of St Malo and 9km west of Dinard yet quiet and at times sleepy. It is on the east bank of the river Frémur estuary with a suspension bridge to Lancieux which has a long sandy beach (*see* page 165).

St Briac has several beaches, including two in delightful horseshoe bays, facing south and west, with fine sand, shelving safely into the sea, fringed by pines. The views of islands and other beaches are splendid. The harbour is delightful, too – fishing boats and pleasure yachts and enough action to be interesting. The estuary drains at low tide. Narrow streets with little granite houses hide in the town. The thirty-three-hole golf course on a headland is used for competitions and lures many of the visitors. There are few hotels or pensions.

FESTIVAL second Sunday in August – Festival des Mouettes (Seagulls)

HOTEL
Houle, in main street (99.88.32.17). Nice modest little hotel but awkward opening and closing times. ROOMS A–D. MEALS A–D. Shut Wednesday March–mid-June; January; February. Restaurant open only 1 March–30 September.

ST BRIEUC
[CÔTES-DU-NORD]

Busy commercial and administrative city of wide boulevards, tall modern buildings, it is built on flat land between Gouedic and Gouet rivers, with imposing viaducts across them. Only 4km from the sea, it must have been a good defensive port in old times. Its cathedral, St Étienne, built in the 13th to 14th centuries, looks like a fortress – which it was. Its two great towers have loopholes and machicolations for defence.

St Brieuc is usually regarded by tourists as a good shopping centre or centre for exploring other places. The river Gouet is canalised and leads to the commercial and fishing port of Légué. The industrial zone, mostly post-World War II, includes huge refrigeration stores for meat and vegetables of the area. But the city has some fine old streets and houses, some for pedestrians only, with pavement cafés. Rue Saint-Guillaume is very pleasant. There are old houses in streets around the cathedral, especially in rues Fardel and Quinquaine. No. 15 rue Fardel is Hôtel des Ducs de Bretagne where James II of England hid after he lost his throne to William of Orange in 1688. The beautifully ancient Fontaine de St Brieuc north-west of the cathedral is protected by a 15th-century Flamboyant portico, built on to a restored chapel.

The local cultural office organises many events of music, theatre and art, and there are several important festivals and fairs (*see* Festivals).

There are many interesting walks in and around town.

TOURIST INFORMATION 7 rue St-Gouéno (96.33.32.50)

MARKETS Wednesday, Friday, Saturday

FESTIVALS April – Commercial Fair of Côte d'Armor; Last weekend in May – Pardon with processions; May – Festival Mai Breton; early July – Festival Breton music; late September – Michaelmas Fair (very important)

HOTELS

Griffon, rue Guernsey (96.94.57.62). In attractive grounds; modern, comfortable. ROOMS D–F. MEALS B–F. Shut 23 December– 8 January. Restaurant shut Sunday in winter.

Ker Izel, 20 rue Gouet (96.33.46.29). No restaurant but in quiet side street near pedestrian quarter. ROOMS D–E. Open all year.

RESTAURANTS

Vieille Tour, 3km north-east by D24, 75 rue de la Tour (96.33.10.30). Facing the port of Légué, charming restaurant with outstanding cooking by Michel Hellio, a talented 'Jeunes Restaurateurs de France'. Seafood and Breton dishes, sensibly modernised with excellent presentation. Superb desserts. Lovely views over bay. Pricey. MEALS F–G. Shut Sunday, Saturday lunch; 23 December–4 January; 15–30 June.

Printania, very near Vieille Tour, *above*, at end of port overlooking sea (96.33.27.36). Pierre Deschamps is second only to Hellio (Vieille Tour) and some menus much cheaper. MEALS C–F. Shut Thursday.

Amadeus, 22 rue Gouet (96.33.92.44). Warm, intimate restaurant in town. Classic cooking with slight modern touches. Good value. MEALS B–F. Shut Sunday evening, Monday.

ST CAST-LE-GUILDO
[CÔTES-DU-NORD]

St Cast itself is one of the most popular seaside resorts in Brittany, round the big bay west of Dinard, with one of the longest beaches. St Guildo was joined to it in 1972. Together they cover the peninsula to the Pointe de St Cast.

St Cast has four main districts. Hotels and shops are mostly in Les Mielles. L'Isle, north of the 2km-long sandy beach, has a lively fishing and yacht harbour. Le Bourg, the administrative centre, has an interesting modern church with a window showing the defeat of the English in the Battle of St Cast in the Seven Years War, when the French and Bretons threw back English troops who had landed there to take St Malo. La Garde is a well-wooded, attractive residential area, carefully laid out. From Pointe de la Garde is a good view across the bay, and to the fine sand beach of Pen-Guen around the point.

From the tip of Pointe de St Cast is a fine view both ways along the Emerald Coast. In the centre of St Cast is a tall monument in Rue de la Colonne commemorating that same victory. It shows a French greyhound trampling an English leopard. St Cast has a sailing school. The fishing fleet of St Cast is now devoted almost entirely to bringing in *coquilles St Jacques* (scallops) and *praires* (clams).

Le Guildo is on the shore of the Arguenon estuary south of Pen-Guen. It has a small harbour. Here are the ruins of the castle of Gilles de Bretagne, where he lived it up. Cousin of Henry VI of England and son of Duke Jean V of Brittany he was inevitably involved in political intrigue and power-grabbing. He had spent his childhood in England from the age of eight and was such an anglophile that he hired an English garrison for Le Guildo and corresponded with Henry VI of England by secret ships slipping into Le Guildo. This was asking for trouble, as his brother the Duke of Brittany was allied with France against England. He was finally murdered after arrest at Le Guildo by the Duke's men. He died at Château de la Hardouinais near Moncontour (*see* page 184) in 1450 and Duke François was so tormented by guilt that he died very shortly after. Of the castle at Le Guildo, little is left except a strong tower.

TOURIST INFORMATION place Gén-de-Gaulle, St Cast
(shut afternoons in winter – 96.41.81.52)
MARKETS Tuesday; also Friday June–September
FESTIVALS mid-August – Pardon and Fête-de-la-Mer;
also horse-races

HOTELS

Ar Vro, Grande Plage (96.41.85.01). Attractive, in trees directly above the beach. Restaurant has views of St Malo bay. ROOMS E–F. MEALS E–F. Open early June–early September.

Dunes, rue Primauget (96.41.80.31). Modern, bright; demi-pension midsummer. ROOMS C–E. MEALS C–F. Shut early November–Easter.

Arcades, 15 rue Duc d'Aiguillon (96.41.80.50). Quiet, near the beach; some rooms have sea views. ROOMS E–F. MEALS A–D. Open Easter–end October.

RESTAURANT

Biniou, Pen-Guen (96.41.94.53). Facing sea. Terrace over beach. Good cooking, especially fish. MEALS B–G. Open Easter–early November. Shut Tuesday low-season.

ST-GEORGES-DE-GRÉHAIGNE
[ILLE-ET-VILAINE]

Named after a chapel to St Georges on a hilltop in 1030 and replaced in the 15th century by a church, St-Georges-de-Gréhaigne is just inside Brittany, on the Normandy border. It was 1km from the sea until the polders were created by draining the sands west of Le Mont-St-Michel, the magnificent abbey on the top of a rock which, to the chagrin of the Bretons, is in Normandy.

But Brittany has its own Mont-St-Michel – one fiftieth scale– at Petit Mont-St-Michel, 9km north-west in the direction of Le Vivier-sur-Mer and a road left towards St Marcan. There are also models of Pontorson church, Château de Fougères and other buildings (open daily mid-June–mid-September; weekends 1 April–mid-June, mid-September–mid-November).

ST-JACUT-DE-LA-MER
[CÔTES-DU-NORD]

On a long spit of land to Pointe du Chevet between two deep bays, it is only 8km south-west of Dinard, it looks out to sands, headlands and wild rocks. There are said to be eleven beaches on the point but I have still not counted them. A fishing port as well as a beach resort.

TOURIST INFORMATION rue de Châtelet (15 June–15 September – 96.27.71.91)

HOTEL
Vieux Moulin (96.27.71.02). Old windmill with some rooms shaped like wedges; bathrooms in round turrets. Excellent seafood. Good value. ROOMS B–D. MEALS A–D. Open March–October. No lunches.

RESTAURANT
Terrier, rue des Sciaux (96.27.71.46). Madame Ruellon, chef-patronne, is Dame Cuisinière de France. Excellent meals A–D.

ST-JEAN-DU-DOIGT
[N. Finistère]

Picturesque village (17km north-east of Morlaix by D46) has a delightful enclos paroissial (parish close) with a triumphal arch (16th century) and an exquisite Renaissance fountain with three basins above which are statues of God the Father blessing the baptism of his son by John the Baptist. In the 15th-century church various old treasures include a fine silver gilt processional cross, and a simply magnificent chalice decorated with statuettes of John the Baptist and seven apostles. These beautiful treasures were given to the little village by the Duchess Anne, who used to attend the Pardon when she stayed in Morlaix. She walked the 17km, they say.

But the strangest treasure, carried in procession at the Pardon on Midsummer's Eve, 23 June, is claimed to be the index finger of John the Baptist, hence the name of the village 'St John of the Finger'. The finger is dipped into a small basin fed from the fountain and *dour ar biz*, the water of the finger, is said to be a miraculous cure for eye complaints and even blindness. To this day, people suffering from sight problems attend the Pardon, which includes a bonfire by the village calvary.

The village is built cosily in a deep valley of the river Donant, which widens to the sea 2km from Plougasnou.

HOTEL
Ty Pont (98.67.34.06). Simple village inn where locals eat and drink. Rooms A–C. Meals A–E. Hotel shut mid-October–Easter. Restaurant shut Sunday evening, Monday low-season; 1 October–31 May.

ST-LUNAIRE
[Ille-et-Vilaine]

A still-fashionable and smart resort on a peninsula 4km west of Dinard, with beaches on both sides of the tip, Pointe du Décollé, which is joined to the mainland by a natural granite bridge over a rock fissure called 'Saut du Chat' (Cat's Leap). This was made by the Irish saint Lunaire with his cross when chasing the Devil. From the bridge you can see a fascinating cave Grotte des Sirènes, especially spectacular at high tide for the rush of the sea. The east-facing beach of St Lunaire is most popular, the west beach Longchamp is the biggest.

In the old quarter, the part-Romanesque church has an 11th-century nave. It is the centre for a pardon in July.

It was from St Lunaire that Claude Debussy and his friends sailed across to Cancale (*see* page 92) in a storm to taste the oysters. On his return to St Lunaire he wrote *La Mer*.

ST MALO
[*see* Major Towns, page 30]

ST MARC-SUR-MER
[LOIRE-ATLANTIQUE]

Alas, M. Hulot has gone and we shall only see Jacques Tati's delightfully lugubrious face peering round a rock if they show the great old film on TV, but St Marc has not changed all that much. On the terrace of the Hotel de la Plage overlooking the sea the same sort of solid citizens from the Paris suburbs sit sipping pastis or vermouth before dinner, and the little cannon is still ready to repel English invaders. The brilliant Tati made St Marc part of French folklore but the French guide books, alas, have not caught up with him. Only our old friends Logis de France and Red Michelin remember *La Plage*. St Marc is 12km along the coast east from la Baule on the little D292 along an attractive coast stretch from Pornichet.

HOTEL
La Plage, 37 rue Ct. Charcot (40.91.99.01). ROOMS C–D. MEALS A–E. Shut 5 January–5 February. Restaurant shut Sunday evening, Monday from mid-September to mid-June.

ST-MICHEL-EN-GRÈVE
[CÔTES-DU-NORD]

At the eastern end of the spectacular Corniche de l'Armorique and 10km south-west of Lannion (*see* page 168), St Michel is a charming little resort at the end of Lieue de Grève, a long stretch of flat sand in a bay. The bay runs dry at low tide, with the sea up to 2km away. The sands become so dry that they are used for racehorse training and occasionally for races. This is one of my favourite areas of Brittany. The road round the bay passes through woods where trout streams run through little valleys into the sea. Halfway round the bay a rock, Grand Rocher, rises 80 metres. A steep path takes you to the top, with rewarding views (about half an hour return from the road).

Nearby, a hermit from Ireland, St Efflam, set up a chapel in AD 470. The next village, now a resort, was called after him. Beside the chapel is an ancient domed fountain where pilgrims still gather each year. From St Efflam the Corniche road twists along heavily indented cliffs looking down on savage rocks, then slopes down to gentler scenery at the little fishing port of Locquirec (*see* page 173).

HOTELS
Plage (96.35.74.43). Right on the seashore with views from bedrooms. Old hotel well modernised. Comfortable, excellent value. ROOMS C–D. MEALS A–E. Open all year.

ST NAZAIRE
[LOIRE-ATLANTIQUE]
(*see* Major Towns, page 56)

ST-NICOLAS-DES-EAUX
[MORBIHAN]

A charming little hillside hamlet overlooking the river Blavet, with thatched cottages around the 16th-century chapel. The river does a great horseshoe loop after the hamlet. At the end of the loop is Site de Castennec with a lovely valley view. St Nicolas is 16km south-west of Pontivy on D156. St Nicodème Chapel, 1km east, has a massive tower with granite steeple. Enter the tower by a Renaissance doorway and you can climb it by a staircase. The chapel has a pardon on the first Sunday in August.

D156 and its continuation D142 are attractive roads.

HOTEL

Vieux Moulin (97.51.81.09). A pleasant converted old farmhouse. Logis. ROOMS C–D. MEALS A–E. Shut Sunday evening, Monday low-season; 1 February–1 March.

ST-NICOLAS-DU-PÉLEM
[CÔTES-DU-NORD]

On the river Faoudel, very near the upper reaches of the Blavet and just bypassed by the D790 14km north-east of Rostrenen. Attractive area with pretty side roads and about 9km from Gorges de Toul Goulic, where the Blavet disappears among enormous rocks. St Nicolas has a Gothic church with a superb 15th-century stained-glass window and a chapel with a sacred fountain surrounded by a stone shrine.

HOTEL

Kreisker, place du centre (96.29.51.20). Changed its name from Hotel Bertrand. Excellent value meals of local ingredients and dishes. ROOMS A–C. MEALS A–D.

ST PIERRE–QUIBERON
[*see* Quiberon, *see* page 216].

ST POL-DE-LÉON
[N. Finistère]

Extremely busy market town almost joined to Roscoff. Here the great agricultural auctions are held (*see* Roscoff, page 232), so from January to September there is a near-constant flow of lorries, trucks and tractors pulling huge trailers arriving from the farms to bring in animals, onions, potatoes, cauliflowers, artichokes and many other vegetables and fruit to the markets, then taking them out for transport to anywhere in west and central France as far as Paris, or to Roscoff for shipment to England.

St Pol's cathedral was begun in the 13th century. It has beautifully sculptured choir stalls, a fine rose window with a sort of pulpit above it from which sentences of excommunication from the church used to be read, and also a fine porch. St Pol (St. Paul) was a Welsh monk who founded a monastery on the Île de Batz (*see* page 69), in the 6th century and was later made Bishop of Léon, which took his name when he died. The town's religious houses became so important and rich that they drew many attacks from Norse pirates. It ceased to be a Bishopric in 1790.

The proudest building in the town is the 15th-century Kreisker chapel, whose soaring spire and superb belfry can be seen far away across fields. The belfry is 77 metres high and is in granite. The delicacy of the carving is magnificent. You can climb its 169 steps to its platform for a circular view of Batz isle, the coast to the Breton Corniche and Arée Mountains inland. Kreisker means 'lower town'. St Pol has been called 'Capital of the Artichoke' and you can see field after field of these blue-green vegetables, which the French adore.

Kerouzméré castle (8km south-west) is a granite 15th-century castle known as a fine example of military architecture.

The Tuesday market overflows from the main square into many streets.

MARKET Tuesday
FESTIVALS Third Sunday in July – Fête du Léon

HOTEL

France, 29 rue des Minimes (98.69.00.14). Logis de France. Good value meals. ROOMS B. MEALS A–E. Shut Sunday evening, Monday in winter; 5–20 October; 5–20 February.

ST QUAY-PORTRIEUX
[CÔTES-DU-NORD]

Resort with five good beaches 20km north of Saint-Brieuc. It is popular in midsummer with French families and with amateur sailors using its large harbour, so it can be very busy. Particularly crowded is its main beach St Quay which has a sea-water swimming pool right on the sands and a casino behind it. St Quay is a lively little place, with a good programme of entertainment and discos. It has a sailing school and holds regattas and an international sea-fishing competition. There's a riding school where national show-jumping events are held, international tennis championships, and an international golf course 6km away.

The port of Portrieux at the southern end used to be home to a deep-sea fishing fleet. Now lobster boats go out to the St Quay islands.

St Quay is not for travel snobs. It does not have much style but a lot of family fun.

A 5km coastal walk from Portrieux gives lovely views of St Brieuc Bay. In summer boats run from St Quay to Île de Bréhat.

At Kermaria, 10km north-west of St Quay, past Plouha, is the Chapel of Kermaria-an-Iskuit (House of Mary who Restores Health), scene of a well-known pilgrimage on the third Sunday of September. It was built in the 13th century and has been renovated several times. From its balcony above a 14th-century church the local Seigneur used to dispense justice, if you can imagine a mediaeval Seigneur dispensing true justice. For a chapel also dispensing health, it has strange 15th-century murals of the Danse Macabre, with Death in the form of dancing corpses and skeletons dragging the living into a dance of death. And all classes are represented, a pope, emperor, king, lord, constable, bourgeois, userer, lover, ploughman, monk and many more.

A stony beach just north of Plouha is now called Plage Napoléon. Before the war it was a lonely place called Anse Cochat (Cochat Cove). Now it has a big car park with a tunnel to the shore. An inscription at the tunnel entrance tells how, between January and August 1944, 135 Allied airmen were shot down over France 'embarked in secret for England on dark nights'. There is a clifftop memorial to all who helped them escape. Bonaparte was the operational code name, the Resistance group which organised the escapes was Shelbourne and the code message which the BBC transmitted to announce a lift-off from the beach was *'Bonjour à tous dans la maison d'Alphonse'*. Maison d'Alphonse was a small cottage on the clifftop where the air crews gathered. Later 'La Maison d'Alphonse' was the title of a book on the operation by the great French agent 'Rémy', whose real name was Gilbert Renault, a member of the Renault car family. It is an exciting book told in interviews with the Resistance men and the farmers, peasants, priests and schoolteachers who risked torture and death to hide the airmen. It was Rémy who sent a message about the battleship *Scharnhorst*'s escape from Brest which got me shot down in 1941. He apologised to me after the war and gave me a signed copy of his wartime memoirs!

TOURIST INFORMATION 17bis rue Jeanne d'Arc,
St Quai (96.70.40.64)
MARKETS Monday, Friday
FESTIVALS Summer at St Quai – Music; end of July –
Pardon

HOTELS

Ker Moor, 13 rue Président-le-Sénécal (96.70.52.22). Excellent little hotel beside the beach; balconies with sea views. ROOMS E–F. MEALS B–E. Shut 20 December–4 January. Restaurant shut Saturday lunch, Friday evening.

RESTAURANT

Auberge La Chapelle, 2½km west on D9, route de Lanvollen (96.71.92.52). Good reliable cooking. MEALS A–E. Shut Wednesday except July, August; February.

ST-RIVOAL
[S. Finistère]

Little hamlet east of Le Faou (*see* page 127) in the Arrée Mountains with a park museum showing buildings in different styles of Breton architecture, including interesting 18th-century farmhouse.

ST-SULIAC
[Ille-et-Vilaine]

A very pleasant little village of granite houses down a hillside to a landing quay on the Rance river 9km south of St Malo, named after yet another Welsh monk who killed a dragon. He started a monastery here in the 6th century. The little harbour is used by pleasure craft.

ST-THÉGONNEC
[N. Finistère]

This village 12km south-west of Morlaix has a superb enclos paroissial with a massive triumphal arch built in 1587 representing the Gateway to Paradise. The whole ensemble is left over from the days when the village was a wealthy linen centre. The church is as ornately carved as an Eastern temple, with a magnificent Renaissance tower topped by a graceful domed lantern. Inside, the pulpit carved in wood in 1683 by two brothers is a fine example of Breton church art. The calvary is beautiful. In a small niche below the groups of figures depicting the Passion is St Thégonnec himself with the wolf he harnessed to his cart after wolves had eaten his donkey.

If the village is not quite Paradise, in its attractive old-style auberge opposite the church young Alain Le Coz, son of Manick Le Coz of La Plage at Ste Anne-La-Palud, cooks fresh local ingredients like an angel. I am proud to have been one of three judges who chose his auberge as 'Brittany Ferries' Restaurant of the Year' back in 1984.

HOTEL
Auberge St-Thégonnec, place Mairie (98.79.61.18). Gets better all the time; brilliantly simple, succulent cooking of fine food. Elegant table settings in comfortable dining-room. Very reasonable prices. ROOMS C–E. MEALS B–F. Shut Sunday evening September–June; 1 January–15 February.

ST-TUGEN
[S. FINISTÈRE]

St Tugen was St Eugene or Eoghan (7th century) who was Bishop of Derry in northern Ireland and was regarded as a protector against mad dogs. Perhaps he is needed back in Derry now. His statue stands next to the high altar in the chapel of this little town 6km west of Audierne and a pardon is held on the Saturday and Sunday before the Feast of St John (24 June).

SARZEAU
[MORBIHAN]

An attractive little market town on the Rhys peninsula which is near enough to the beautiful beaches of the Morbihan Gulf to have become a little resort. It was the birthplace of the playwright and novelist Alain-René Lesage (1668–1747), author of *Gil Blas*, a good-humoured satire, and the very cynical and amusing *Turcaret*, a satire on social climbing in which each confidence trickster is duped by another. Lesage's bust is in the market square.

The majestic ruins of Suscinio castle are 3½km south-east. It was begun in 1218 and a century later became the summer residence of the Duke of Brittany until confiscated by François I of France. It had eight towers. During the Wars of Succession it changed hands several times between the forces of Jean de Montfort and Charles de Blois. It was partly dismantled after the Revolution and its lovely staircase, windows and stones sold off, but restoration began in 1966. Great blocks of granite have been brought 55km from Roc-St-André and worked by stone-cutters in the old way of medieval craftsmen. You can see five crenellated towers around a courtyard and some fine fireplaces.

It was here that Duc François II detained Henry, Earl of Richmond, between 1471–83. He had fled after the Lancastrian defeat at Tewkesbury by the Yorkists. Seeking shelter, Henry found a prison. When he got out, he sailed for Milford Haven in Wales, raised an army, defeated Richard III at Bosworth Field and was crowned Henry VII of England.

Earlier, the Lancastrian king, Edward IV of England, had tried to persuade François of Brittany to hand over Henry to him and in 1476 François did in fact take Henry as far as St Malo to ship him to England and almost certain death. But Henry feigned a deadly fever and was taken to a sanctuary. After that Edward paid François to keep Henry imprisoned in France, and François treated him and his followers well. The new English king, Richard III, tried to bribe him to hand over Henry. François' treasurer, Pierre Landois, was plotting to carry out the sale, but Henry was forewarned and fled from Brittany to Anjou an hour before Landois' men came to arrest him.

In Suscinio, Henry fell for a Breton girl, who bore him a son named Roland de Velville. When he was crowned, Henry sent for Roland and in 1497, after the battle of Blackheath, knighted him, then made him Constable of Beaumaris castle in Anglesey. Roland married a Welsh girl and settled down in Wales. (Château open daily 1 April–30 September, rest of year Tuesday, Saturday, Sunday.)

TOURIST INFORMATION Bâtiment des Trinitaires, rue Gén-de-Gaulle (summer – 97.41.82.37)

RESTAURANT

Espadon, at La Grée-Penvins, 8km south-east by D198 (97.67.34.26). True Breton cooking in a delightful, small restaurant with old furniture. MEALS C–F. Shut Tuesday evening, Wednesday in winter.

SCAËR
[S. Finistère]

Market town above the river Isole quite near to Cascadée Forest, which is excellent for picnics, walks and riding. Restful area 35km east of Quimper. Two hotels, two campsites.
Tourist Information Mairie (98.59.42.10)

HOTEL
Brizeux, 56 rue Jean-Jaurès (98.59.40.59). Useful. Good value. Rooms A–D. Shut early January–early February. Meals A–D. Restaurant shut Sunday evening, Monday low-season.

ÎLE-DE-SEIN
[S. Finistère]

This island off Pointe du Raz in the Atlantic Ocean is only one square kilometre in size, with no trees or even bushes. A few tiny fields of barley and potatoes are surrounded by dry brick walls and sometimes the sea covers the land. That happened in 1868 and again in 1896. Sein has just 607 inhabitants. Yet this insignificant isle is a symbol in modern times of French courage. '*Sein est donc le quart de la France*,' said de Gaulle in June 1940. 'So Sein is one quarter of France.' He was reviewing the first Free French contingent of 500 men in the Empire Hall in London. And 130 of them came from the Île de Sein.

On 18 June de Gaulle had broadcast his famous speech to the French: 'Whatever happens, the flame of Resistance must and shall not be extinguished in France.'

The people of Sein held a discussion. The mayor, the priest, the teacher and doctor, the fishermen were all there. They voted unanimously that every man should answer the call to arms. On the Sunday the priest stood in his pulpit at High Mass. 'My brothers – France calls to you from London. Make sure that you answer her call.'

The first boat left next evening, crammed with fifty men, slipping across the Channel to Cornwall. The rest of the 130 followed in two days. When the Germans occupied Sein, they found only women, children, old men, and the priest and mayor, who had stayed behind to look after them. And they helped another 3,000 French soldiers and sailors to go to England. For their fishing boats secretly brought in and took out Allied officers, under the noses of the German boats from Brest. Twenty-nine of the island's fishermen died fighting. Général de Gaulle himself came to give the island the Croix de la Libération – the Liberation Cross.

The fishermen are still lifesavers, rescuing crews of wrecked ships or yachts which mainly get into trouble in the wicked racing waters of the Raz de Sein. The men farm lobsters and catch crabs, langoustines, ray and more recently a lot of scallops. The women work the little fields. The lighthouse, which you can climb (249 steps), is vital to passing ships because of the highly dangerous rocks. It took 14 years to build because of the seas. Its light has a range of 55km.

Once the 'guiding' lights from Sein led ships and men to their doom. Like the people of the Scilly Isles, off Cornwall, the men of Sein were wreckers. They lured ships on to the rocks, killed any surviving crews and looted the wrecks. Even today some of the houses are furnished with the loot. And they still profit occasionally from the bounty washed up by wrecks.

The isles were regarded by the mainlanders for centuries with superstitious dread. Even by the 18th century the few inhabitants lived in almost total isolation, still pagans until converted by the Jesuits. The village, called Le Bourg, is of small white houses and a church in alleys only a metre wide, not so much to save space but for protection from Atlantic winds. The harbour is used as a haven for yachts, much appreciated in bad weather. The passage is well marked with buoys now.

Passenger boats sail all the year from Audierne – Service Maritime Departemental, quai Jean-Jaurès, Audierne (98.70.02.38), with other boats also from June to September.

HOTEL

Rozen-Fouquet (98.70.90.77). Very simple. Nice view. ROOMS A. Shut 1 November–1 June.

RESTAURANT

Auberge des Sénans (98.70.90.01). Good. Famous ragoût of potatoes and lobster. MEALS A–E. Open 15 April–30 September.

SIZUN
[N. FINISTÈRE]

This tiny town on the Elorn river 33km south-west of Morlaix has a parish close with a splendid triumphal gate from 1590 consisting of three round arches with Corinthian capitals and columns. A platform above the arches has a Flamboyant balustrade with lanterns, a small altar and a calvary with figures. The face of the late 14th-century ossuary, the 16th-century porch and 17th-century bell-tower are pleasingly ornate and grand for such a small place.

Inside the church is an ornate organ with balustrading, rebuilt in 1688 by one of the Dallam family (*see* Quimper cathedral, page 219). The interior is all rather riotous, with painted and gilt altars.

Sizun has become a small resort with the expansion of a Centre de Loisirs Milin Kerroch in an old converted watermill. It has a large park with lakes, fishing, pedalos, sports, children's amusements, two restaurants, a crêperie and grill.

TOURIST INFORMATION place Abbé-Broch (15 June–
15 September – 98.68.88.40)

HOTELS

Voyageurs, 2 rue de l'Argoat (98.68.80.35). Simple, cheap Logis. Used by French. Good value. ROOMS A–B. MEALS A–C. Shut Saturday evening in winter; early September–early October.
Milin Kerroch (96.68.81.56). *See above*. Rooms demi-pension. MEALS A–E. Shut Tuesday.

TINTÉNNIAC
[ILLE-ET-VILAINE]

Charming, flowery small town and holiday resort on the Ille-Rance canal 6km north-west of Hédé (*see* page 149) on N137. Port of call for pleasure boats, with adjoining campsite. Church floodlit. Only 24km from Dinan and 27km from Rennes.

Circuit signposted 'Tinténniac-Montmuran' gives a fine tour on minor roads of the whole attractive area past Château du Montmuran, Iffs and Hédé (*see* page 150).

MARKET Wednesday

HOTEL
Voyageurs, rue Nationale (99.68.02.21). Two-star Logis. ROOMS B–D. MEALS B–D. Shut Sunday evening, Monday; 15 December–15 January.

RESTAURANT
Genty-Home (99.45.46.07). Country auberge in Hédé Valley by a wood. Truly classical cooking; very good fish. Wide range of menus. Good value. MEALS A–E. Shut Tuesday evening, Wednesday; 15 days in February.

TRÉBEURDEN
[CÔTES-DU-NORD]

A fashionable family resort from the end of the last century, Trébeurden has survived happily and successfully without changing very much, although its family summer villas are mostly divided into seaside flats and its bigger, elegant villas are hotels. Just 13km from Perros-Guirec. There are seven beaches of superb sands and fine views to countless tiny isles and sandbanks. The only small snag for very small children is that much accommodation is up a hill. Trees add to its beauty and many of the villas have terraces looking out to sea. True, a few small blocks of modern flats have been scattered among the villas and hotdog and pizza stalls are on the front in midsummer. But

Trébeurden keeps its *fin-de-siècle* respectability. There are fine sea views over the isles from Pointe de Bihit 3km south-west. The old castle rock between two main beaches is joined to the town by a thread of land.

The climate is good, thanks to the Gulf Stream and the protection of Île Grande. One beach, Pors Mabo, faces south.

Île Grande, joined to the mainland by a bridge, has a few old fishermen's cottages dotted about, a coast of attractive blue-toned granite and a few megaliths. Joseph Conrad, the writer of the sea, spent his honeymoon here. Now campers have found it. A few fishermen supply little café-restaurants with excellent fish.

Trébeurden is a centre for sub-aqua, windsurfing and riding. The sailing school operates in July, August. Boats give trips in summer around the little isles.

TOURIST INFORMATION place Crech'Héry
(96.23.51.64)
MARKET Tuesday

HOTELS

Ti al-Lannec, allée de Mezo Guen (96.23.57.26). Old granite mansion on a hill with a path to the coast and lovely sea views from its terrace. I have loved it for more than fifteen years and so do my readers, so book ahead. Superb cooking of delicious fresh fish, poultry and lamb. Classical with individual touches. Very helpful family and staff. Good value meals, especially weekday lunch menu. Delicious in May or September. ROOMS E–G. MEALS C (weekdays), E–G. Open mid-March to mid-November. Restaurant shut Monday lunch off-season.

Manoir de Lan-Kerellec, pointe de Kerellec (98.23.50.09). Old manor in trees above the sea transformed into Relais et Châteaux hotel. Beautifully furnished rooms, very pricey. Deserved Michelin star for the cooking of Jean-Luc Danjou, especially his fish. He was trained at Troisgots. ROOMS G. MEALS E–G. Shut early November–mid-March.

Glann Ar Mor, 12 rue Kerariou (96.23.50.81). Down-to-earth but very good cooking; two cheap good value menus. Eight simple rooms B. MEALS A–F. Shut Wednesday; 1–15 October.

TRÉGASTEL
[CÔTES-DU-NORD]

A beach resort and an inland town, only 8km west of Perros-Guirec and 2km west of Ploumanach. It is among those great weird rocks of the Côte de Granti Rose which look as if giants have been stoning their enemies. In fact they have been moulded by nature over the ages into strange shapes to which men have given inadequate names like the Witch, the Corkscrew, the Tortoises.

Beneath the rocks to the right of Coz-Pors beach are caves, and in one of them is a prehistoric museum and a seawater aquarium. The beach itself, inevitably bordered by rocks, is of fine sand. Take a path at the end of the beach as far as Grève Blanche and Grève Rose, beaches of white and rose shingle, close to Île aux Lapins, which can be reached on foot at low tide. You can drive on to Île Renote, an isthmus with a beach and views of sea and islands. Sailing and windsurfing are popular (Club Nautique for hiring craft).

Trégastel village has a charming little Romanesque church and a charnel house with the discouraging inscription '*Hodie Mihi, Cras Tibi*' (I today, you tomorrow!). Hardly encouraging to happy holidaymakers.

TOURIST INFORMATION place Ste-Anne (96.23.88.67)
MARKET Monday

HOTELS

Armoric, plage Coz-Pors (96.23.88.16). Old, comfortable hotel. Restaurant faces sea. ROOMS C–F. MEALS D–E. Shut end September–early May.

Belle Vue, 20 rue des Calculots (96.23.88.18). France Accueil family hotel in Breton house with nice garden. Excellent cooking. Quiet. ROOMS E–F. MEALS C–G. Shut end September–1 June.

Vieille Église, Trégastel–Bourg, 2½km inland (96.23.88.31). Auberge with twelve simple rooms; very good seafood. ROOMS A–B. MEALS A–E. Shut Sunday night, Monday off-season.

TRÉGUIER
[Côtes-du-Nord]

A superb little town terraced up a hill overlooking the meeting of the rivers Guindy and Jaudy where they open into a wide estuary. The port can take biggish ships and has become an important pleasure port, too, with many British and Jersey boats tying up. It is 15km west of Paimpol.

Old houses and cobbled streets surround the superb granite Gothic cathedral, one of the finest in Brittany. Founded by the Welsh monk Tugdual, after whom it is named, it was originally an important bishopric. It has three towers. The intricate, open slatted south spire soars more than 60 metres over place du Martray. The slats and holes were not just for decoration but to lessen the force of the wind. The north Romanesque tower is all that remains of the 13th-century church. The Sanctus tower over the transept crossing is squat, but still 30 metres high.

The cathedral is lit by sixty-eight windows. Medieval glass destroyed in the Revolution has been replaced by modern glass. Forty-six Renaissance choir stalls carry scenes from the lives of St Tugdual and St Yves. Through Porte-St-Jean are lovely cloisters from 1461 with the most graceful Flamboyant twin-arches supported by slender columns. The finest of thirteen side chapels has an 1890 reproduction of the 15th-century tomb of St Yves, patron saint of Brittany and of lawyers all over the world. St Yves was the priest, lawyer and magistrate of the 13th century, 'righter of wrongs', who defended the poor and weak in court against the strong and powerful.

Yves Hélori was born in the manor of Ker-Martin at Minihy-Tréguier, 2km south, in 1253. A church is built over his family chapel there. One of the greatest Breton pardons, 'Pardon des Pauvres', is held on 19 May, drawing thousands of pilgrims, including lawyers from many countries. A huge procession goes from the cathedral to the Minihy church and its cemetery, where his relics are displayed on a 13th-century stone table. Many people are in Breton costume. They march with candles and banners to the music of bagpipes and *bombardes*, and afterwards there is music and dancing.

At midnight local farmers come to have their crops, animals and themselves blessed, for Yves was a farmer, too.

He wore a hair-shirt, soaked his jacket in water to make it less comfortable, and lived on bread and vegetable soup. He slept very little and then on a clay bed. He died aged forty-nine, worn out by overwork and austerity. The local story is that when he appeared before Heaven's Gates the woman in front of him told St Peter: 'I'm a nun.'

'Wait outside,' said Peter, 'We have quite enough nuns in Paradise.'

'I'm a lawyer,' said Yves.

'Come on in,' said Peter, 'You're the first lawyer we've had.'

In the square in front of the cathedral containing St Yves' tomb stands paradoxically a big statue to another local hero – Ernest Renon, the great 19th-century philosopher, historian and freethinker, who scandalised the Roman Catholic church in 1863 with his *Vie de Jésus*, insisting that Christ was a man – incomparable but only human. Just off the square is his timber-framed 16th-century house, well restored and containing a museum of his work and his travels.

4km up the Jaudy estuary is the little oyster port of La Roche Jaune. Pointe du Château, at the end of the estuary, is an odd place with dozens of very strange rocks sticking out of the water.

10km north-west of Tréguier is Port Blanc, a wild but delightful place of battered rocks, tiny mysterious islets and little dry-walled fields which is still a fishing port but a tiny resort, too. A 16th-century chapel has a rustic painting of St Yves between a poor and a rich man. A pardon is held on 8 September.

TOURIST INFORMATION Syndicat d'Initiative, Mairie (15 June–15 September – 96.92.30.19)

MARKET Wednesday (especially pigs)

HOTELS

Kastell Dinec'h, 2km route Lannion (96.92.49.39). Old Breton farmhouse and barns with raftered dining-room; garden in old farmyard. Peaceful. Charming bedrooms. ROOMS D–E. MEALS (evenings only) B–F. Shut Tuesday evening, Wednesday low-season; 12–27 October; 1 January–15 March.

Grand, at Port Blanc (96.92.66.52). Not very grand – 1 star Logis

on boul. de la Mer. Simple rooms B–C. MEALS A–D. Shut
Monday; October–Easter.

TRÉHIGUIER
[MORBIHAN]

One of the little ports in the Vilaine estuary and around the
coast south-west which are shellfish breeding centres.
Tréhiguier breeds mussels. Pleasure craft use it, too, mingling
with motor and rowing boats of the musselmen. Another main
shellfish breeding centre is Assérac, 9km south-east.

LA TRINITÉ-SUR-MER
[MORBIHAN]

More campsites and many more yachts have altered somewhat
this lively port on the river Crach estuary, known long for its
Bélon oyster beds. The village, built on a hill above the port on
Quiberon Bay, has spread down to the port, where pontoons are
lined with boats – seven hundred of them in midsummer, from
ocean racing yachts to family cruisers. Big races are held, with
yachts and yachtsmen well-known in the yachting world competing. A long, sandy beach has lured holidaymakers, so there is
a choice of hotels and restaurants. The long Kerisper bridge
crossing the estuary makes it easy to reach Locmariaquer's dolmens and megaliths, while Carnac is only 5km west.

TOURIST INFORMATION Syndicat d'Initiative, cours des
Quais (March–September – 97.55.72.21)
FESTIVALS International regattas in summer

HOTELS
Rouzic, 17 cours des Quais (97.55.72.06). Livelier than it looks.
On the main promenade. Popular, especially for fresh fish. Well
modernised. ROOMS C–E. MEALS A–D. Shut 15 November–15

December. Restaurant shut Sunday evening, Monday off-season.

Ostréa (97.55.73.23). Good restaurant with eight rooms. Classic cooking. Splendid shellfish. Bar used by yachtsmen. ROOMS E. MEALS C–F. Restaurant shut Tuesday except July, August.

Panorama, at St-Philibert, 2½km by D781 (97.55.00.56). Friendly, quiet Logis. Sensible prices. ROOMS C–D. MEALS A–D. Shut end September–end March.

RESTAURANT

Les Hortensias, place Yvonne-Sarcy (97.55.73.69). Fine position overlooking port, facing yacht club. Attractive and flowery. Charming welcome and service. Extremely expensive for cooking which is brilliantly inventive or over-eccentric according to your taste. Top French guides love it (Michelin star, accolades from Gault-Millau, 'best in Brittany' to Champérard). Superb desserts. MEALS F–G. Shut Tuesday, Wednesday off-season; 2–8 October; 1 December–1 March.

LA TURBALLE
[LOIRE-ATLANTIQUE]

Along Rade du Croisic coast on the edge of the Marais Salants 12km south-west of La Baule, a fishing village with an artificial port popular with pleasure boats. Modern buildings along sea front, modern church, arc-shaped modern fish market.

TOURIST INFORMATION place de Gaulle (40.23.32.01)

RESTAURANT

Maison de la Pêche, terrace of market (40.23.39.49). Splendid fish. MEALS B–F. Shut Tuesday evening, Wednesday low-season.

LE VAL-ANDRÉ – PLÉNEUF-VAL-ANDRÉ
[CÔTES-DU-NORD]

Resort with excellent golden sand beach in the bay of St Brieuc, 11km north of Lamballe. Its promenade runs for 2km from Pointe de Pléneuf in the north-east to Pointe des Murs Blancs in the south-west. Very popular, with all holiday amenities, so crowded in summer. The little port at the south-west end still has a small fishing fleet. A path from here called 'La Guette' leads to a walk with sweeping views over the whole bay and dramatic coastline. At the end is the once important fishing port of Dahouët in a creek between high cliffs – now a charming little resort with a few little fishing boats.

Val-André is virtually joined to the village of Pléneuf and is sometimes called Pléneuf-Val-André. A good sailing school is open much of the year. See also Erquy (page 126) for nearby sites.

TOURIST INFORMATION 1 rue Winston Churchill (96.72.20.55)

MARKET Tuesday; Friday (June-September)

HOTELS

Grand, 80 rue Amiral-Charner (96.72.20.56). Old seaside grand hotel (smaller version) on promenade. Shaded gardens, sun trap, sea view from dining-room. ROOMS E. MEALS C–E. Open early March–mid-November; Restaurant open late March–30 September.

Port, 22 quai Terreneuvas (96.72.96.92). Simple, useful hotel opposite harbour. Good fish. Patron cooks. ROOMS A. MEALS A–D. Shut Wednesday low-season.

RESTAURANTS

Cotriade, port de Piégu (96.72.20.26). Looks like a harbourside café for snacks or aperitives until you enter. Jean-Jacques Le Saout, formerly of Lutece, New York, cooks fish superbly. Michelin star. Cheaper menu with little choice is a bargain. Some carte prices are outrageously high. Try any fish, especially seafood platter. MEALS D–F. Shut Monday evening, Tuesday; January; February.

Biniou, 121 rue Clemenceau (96.72.24.35). Splendid fresh fish at reasonable prices. MEALS A–E. Shut Thursday; mid-November–mid-March.

VANNES
[MORBIHAN]

Vannes has many faces. Attractively placed in an amphitheatre at the north-east end of the great Gulf of Morbihan, it has a lovely old town behind ramparts, with a canalised river leading right into the heart of it. But Vannes becomes an increasingly industrialised, noisy town outside the ramparts. It is an agricultural market town, too, and a tourist centre, with good boat trips round the gulf.

The old town is elegant, dignified and handsome. It was the ancient capital of the Veneti, the brave tribe which lost the vital sea battle to the Roman galleys.

Vannes

In the 9th century Nominoë, made Count of Vannes by Charlemagne, who had conquered all Brittany, defeated the other powerful counts of Brittany and became the first Duke of Brittany. Then he turned on the Franks who had given him power, defeated Charles the Bald, King of the Franks, at Redon and destroyed Frankish power over Brittany. Vannes was his capital.

Vannes escaped major damage in World War II and has kept much of its medieval atmosphere – apart from the droves of tourists in the old town.

The little place Henri IV in the centre is lined with 15th- to 16th-century half-timbered houses with overhanging storeys and tall roofs. The 13th-century Romanesque belfry of the Cathedral of St Pierre looks down majestically from one corner. The cathedral is an interesting if unharmonious hotchpotch of styles from the 13th to 19th centuries. The most interesting is the fine circular granite Renaissance chapel from 1537 on the north side. Delightful niches on the first storey are divided by Doric columns. A Latin inscription goes all round the tower. The second storey has rounded arches and Ionic columns. The interior is a real jumble of styles from different centuries. In the chapel of the Blessed Sacrament is the tomb of the Spanish preacher St Vincent Ferrer, who died in Vannes in 1419. He succeeded in ending the split between Rome and Avignon, which had rival popes, dividing the loyalties of Europe. He travelled most of western Europe and arrived in Vannes in 1416, refusing to stay with the Duke in Château d'Hermine. He stayed with an ordinary citizen in a house which you can see but which was remodelled in the 16th century (No. 17 place Valencia).

The well-preserved ramparts are set in charming French formal gardens. Three gateways remain, a powder tower and Château d'Hermine, built in the 14th century by Duke Jean IV of Brittany.

A 17th-century house now contains the Tourist Office (Hôtel de Limur, rue Thiers). Château Gaillard, a 15th-century building in the old rue Noë, was the seat of the Breton parliament, and now contains an archaeological museum (shut Sunday).

At the exit of the pleasure-boat harbour, the large Aquarium has fifty pools with waterfalls and thousands of fish from all round the world. It has a scientific and technical laboratory. It is highly imaginative and very interesting. You can see what happens in the seabed and follow water-life from the Morbihan Gulf to the Amazon, African lakes and Pacific coral reefs (open daily).

Vannes is an excellent centre for visiting the Morbihan and its big gulf. The little port of Séné, 5km south, in a very sheltered inlet, was until recent times the home-port of the *sinagots*, two-masted fishing boats of the Morbihan. It still has fishing boats and pleasure craft. Follow the road to the point of the inlet for Bellevue and Port Anna, another old fishing port now used a lot by pleasure boats.

Largest island in the bay, Moines, (6km long) is reached by motor boat from Vannes in five minutes. (*see* page 183).

Arz island is only 3km long and less visited. It has several megaliths and a church left over from the days when it was owned by an abbey.

There are many boat trips around the Gulf in season, including a gastronomic tour from Vannes round the Gulf and up the Auray river in a boat with a restaurant (*Vedettes Vertes*, Gare Maritime – 97.63.79.99).

Boats also go to Port-Navalo, Arzon, Auray, Locmariaquer, Îles-aux-Moines and Arz.

TOURIST INFORMATION 1 rue Thiers (97.47.24.34)
MARKET Wednesday, Saturday
FESTIVALS 15 August – Fête d'Arvor; September – Commercial Fair

HOTELS

Aquarium et Restaurant Dauphin, parc du Golfe (97.40.44.52 – Restaurant 97.40.68.08). New; shaped like a ferryboat. Garden. Good restaurant. ROOMS E. MEALS C–F. Hotel open all year. Restaurant shut Sunday evening.

Le Roof, at Conleau, island ferry port 3km south (97.63.47.47). Lovely view of Gulf. Modern. Good simple cooking. Superb shellfish. Popular – book. ROOMS D–F. MEALS B–G. Shut mid-January–mid-February.

Escale on Île d'Arz (97.44.32.15). Hotel on the embarkation quay. Pension or meals only high-season. ROOMS B–E. MEALS A–D. Shut mid-October–end March.

RESTAURANTS

Richemont, place Gare (97.42.61.41). Régis Mahé is back from Paris and from Negresco in Nice and Le Richemont's cooking is superb again. Not cheap but worth the francs. MEALS C–G. Shut Sunday evening, Monday; mid-November–end November; mid-February–end February.

Pressoir, at St-Avé, 5km north-east (97.60.87.63). Some of the best cooking in the area; classic but not heavy. Good wide choice of menus. MEALS D–G. Shut Sunday evening. Monday; 6–20 March; 3–10 July; 9–23 October.

Vénètes at Arradon (9km south-west) (97.44.03.11). Hotel right by the sea with excellent fish. ROOMS D–F. MEALS C–E. Shut 1 October–end March.

Chez Charlemagne on Île aux Moines (97.26.32.43). Reasonable restaurant. MEALS C–E. Shut Tuesday except mid-summer; 1 November –1 April.

VITRÉ
(ÎLLE-ET-VILAINE)

A delightful old town. There is a lovely view of it as you enter on D178. Then you step into the Middle Ages, with a maze of narrow streets, often arcaded or lined with medieval houses with projecting upper storeys and the great castle on the point of a high spur. Only the girls in jeans and clothes displayed in shop windows destroy the illusion that you have gone back four hundred years. The city is usually described as one of the best preserved in Brittany. Yet a great part of it was destroyed to build the Paris–Brest railway last century.

Vitré was part of Brittany's defence line against the French, who coveted the Duchy constantly. First built around 1080, its castle was reconstructed in the 14th and 15th centuries in a triangular shape in granite and was a fine piece of military architecture. It stood out against French attacks and against many English attacks in the Hundred Years War. Its greatest siege was in the Wars of Religion when its owner, the Protestant commander Coligny, held it against the Duc de Mercoeur and the strong forces of the Catholic League. The men of Vitré through the ages dined with their swords ready in the scabbard as the guards vigilantly paced the great ramparts.

The English occupied the north part of the town below the castle. The people of Vitré became so tired of having them there that they paid them to go away. The area is called 'Rachapt' – bought back.

The entrance to the castle is most impressive, flanked by two massive towers supporting a redoubt. Its massive outer walls are grey chequered with brown, and its pepper-pot capped bastions and machicolated towers make it fit for a fairy story.

Inside the walls it has a lighter, more Renaissance look, though rather ruined by a completely misplaced pseudo-Gothic

La rue Poterie, Vitré

town hall added early this century. The town bought the castle in 1820 for 8500 francs and restored it. Now it houses in three towers a small museum of wood carvings, pictures, tapestries and prints, but the greatest pleasure is to walk its ramparts and look down on the town.

Vitré was one of the most prosperous cities in Brittany from the 16th to 18th centuries, exporting woollen cloth and cotton stockings all over France and western Europe, and to America and the Indies.

Among the streets of old houses, the rue Beaudrairie leads to the 15th-century Flamboyant church of Notre-Dame, which is rich in gables, pinnacles and sculptured gargoyles. From its fine stone pulpit outside the church, the Catholic priests preached to the crowds and debated heatedly and publicly with the Protestant followers of Coligny, whose family owned the town. They preached from a house opposite.

From Rachapt a high path called Chemin des Tertres Noirs takes you to a fine panorama of the city and the château below.

Château des Rochers-Sévigné 7km south-east, is a literary shrine to the French. Built in the 14th century and altered in the 17th, a picturesque manor house on a hill surrounded by trees, it was the country home between 1654 and 1690 of Madame de Sévigné, beautiful, witty and bitchy chronicler of French life in Louis XIV's reign.

Widow of a dissolute marquis who was killed in a duel, she wrote her comments on the court, on life, on the bourgeoisie of Vitré and on her own garden at Château Rochers in letters to her daughter, Françoise, who was married to the governor of Provence. Their style and composition show that she had intended them for publication. She had plenty of good material in the 'Sun King's' court, of course. Her husband had among his mistresses the famous Ninon de Lenclos, who became mistress to his son, then his grandson – a remarkable record of family service and a tribute to her lasting charms. Among her lovers were the great Condé, the Duc de la Rochefoucauld, a great writer, two marquises, two Marshals of France and several abbés of the church. She was so cultivated that aristocrats sent their daughters to her to be taught etiquette, manners and the graces.

When Louis XIV took as one of his multitude of mistresses

Mademoiselle de Fontanges, Madame de Sévigné called her 'beautiful as an angel, stupid as a basket'. And on her death in childbirth at the age of twenty, Madame wrote that she had died 'from wounds received on active service'.

Madame was forced to leave Paris several times after upsetting the king and settled finally in Rochers, partly for economy and partly to avoid more royal disfavour. She inherited Rochers from her uncle, Abbé de Coulanges, who built the interesting octagonal chapel here. Her main contribution was the garden, designed for her by Le Nôtre, designer of Versailles gardens. She watched and recorded the growth of little trees until they were 12 metres high, and she personally planted flowers and laid out alleys in the park – a remarkable hobby for a woman of her class in those days. You can see the chapel, decorated in gold, grey and blue, with furniture she designed, and visit her room, Cabinet Vert, with her furniture, books and papers (open mornings except Saturday and Sunday and afternoons mid-February–mid-November).

TOURIST INFORMATION place St Yves, Vitré
(99.75.04.46)
MARKET Monday

HOTEL

Petit-Billot, 5 pl. Mar-Leclerc (99.75.02.10). Best rooms in new wing. Outstanding cheap regional menus. ROOMS B–D. MEALS A–C. Shut 15 December–15 January. Restaurant shut Saturday lunch. Hotel shut Friday, Saturday off-season.

RESTAURANTS

St Yves, 1 place St-Yves (99.75.05.11). New, charming; fresh local products freshly cooked. Outstanding value. MEALS B (weekdays), D. Shut Saturday lunch, Wednesday.

Taverne d'Ecu, 12 rue Beaudrairie (99.75.11.09). In a 17th-century house with 17th-century dining-room, meals balanced between ancient and modern. Good grills from open grill. MEALS A–F. Shut Sunday evening, Monday; end July–10 August; 1–15 February.

Pichet, 17 boul. Laval (99.75.24.09). Traditional cooking; good value. Garden. MEALS B–E. Shut Sunday evening, Monday; middle fortnight August; part February.

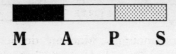

M A P S

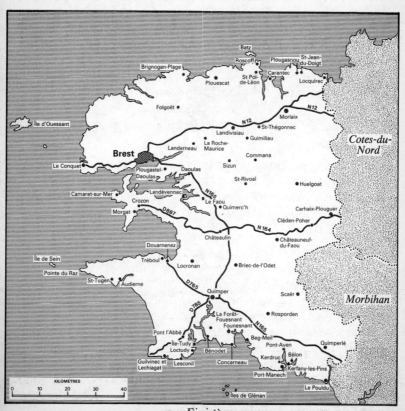

2 *Finistère*

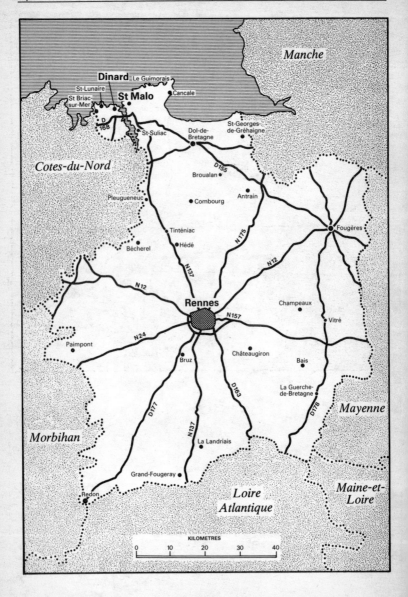

3 *Ille-et-Villaine*

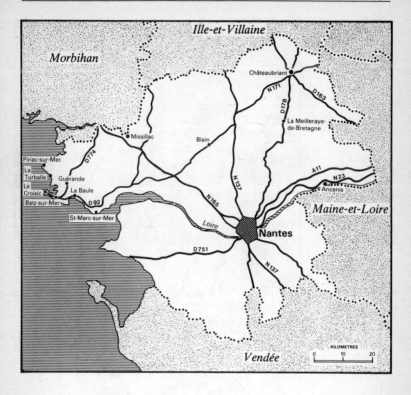

4 *Loire-Atlantique*

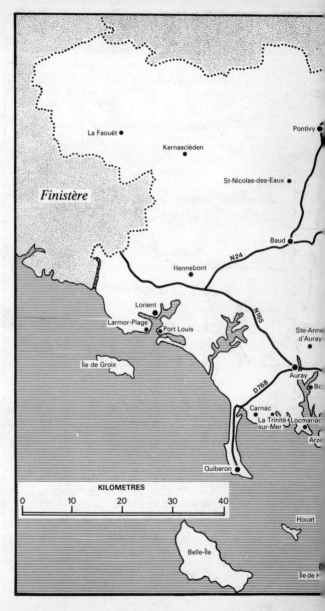

5 *Morbihan*

MORBIHAN

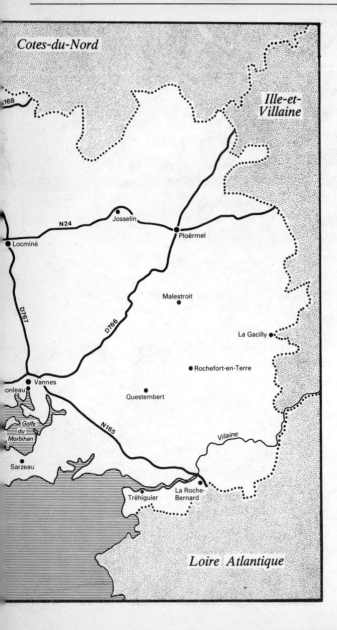

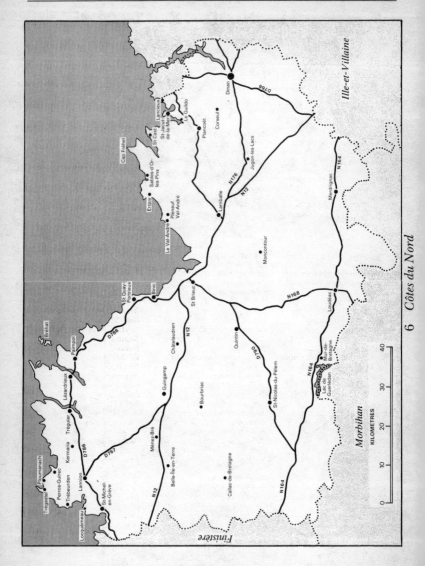

INDEX

Names of hotels and restaurants appear in *italics*.

Abbaye, Auray 68
Abbaye de Villeneuve 62
abbeys
  Abbaye de Bon Repos 144
  Abbaye de Campénéac 14
  Abbaye de la Meilleraye 14, 181
  Abbaye de Langonnet, La Faouët 129
  Abbaye de St Anne-d'Auray 14
  Abbaye de St Michel-de-Kergonan, Carnac 99
  Abbaye de Ste Anne-de-Kergonan, Carnac 99
  Abbaye de Ty-Madeuc 14
  Beauport abbey, Paimpol 192
  Daoulas abbey 117
  Landévennec abbey 166
  Paimpont abbey 195
Abers, Les 63
agriculture 27, 179, 232–3, 245
Aiguillon, Duc d', Governor of Brittany 22, 38, 74, 139
Ajoncs d'Or 207
Alain-le-Grand 214
Albret, Alain d' 19
Alexander VI, Pope 21
Altaïr 52, 55
Amadeus 238
Amandier 166
An Triskell 154
An Ty Korn 189
Ancenis 63–4
Ancre de Marine 81
Angleterre 164
Angoulême, François, Duc d' 20, 21
Ankou 73
Anne, Duchess of Brittany 19–20, 21, 34–5, 45, 56, 58, 64, 134, 148, 158, 241
Anne, St 5–6, 67
Anne de Beaujeu, Regent of France 18–19, 20
Antrain 64
Aquarium 264
Ar Falz movement 4–5
Ar Maner 234
Ar Men 213
Ar Moor 212
Ar Reder Mor 88

Ar Vro 239
Arcades 239
Arcouest 192
Argoat 173
Argoat 3, 153
Arguenon river 198
Armada 93
Armel, St 200
Armor 3
Armor, Guingamp 149
Armor Vilaine, La Roche-Bernard 230
Armoric, Trégastel 256
Armorique, Fouesnant 132
Aron, Robert 25
Arthur, King 104–5
Arvor 132
Arz island 264
Arzon 64
Astéries 179
Astor, Joseph 176
Atlantic, Lesconil 171
Atlantide, Batz-sur-Mer 70
Aubergade 103
Auberge, Ste Anne-d'Auray 68
Auberge Bretonne, La Roche-Bernard 229
Auberge Bretonne, Questembert 214
Auberge de Kerland 207
Auberge de Kervéoc'h 125
Auberge de la Hardouinais 182
Auberge de Poher 97
Auberge de Toul-Douar 152
Auberge de Toulfoën 224
Auberge des Chiens du Guet 30
Auberge des Sénans 253
Auberge du Moulin Neuf 231
Auberge du Poteau Vert 228
Auberge Fouesnantaise 125
Auberge Grand'Maison 190
Auberge La Chapelle 247
Auberge La Taupinère 208
Auberge Moulin du Boël 89
Auberge St-Laurent 131
Auberge St-Thégonnec 249
Auberge Vieux Château 232
Audierne 65
Aulne river 103, 105, 106
Auray 5, 66–8
Avel Vor 212
Avenue 168
Azou 202
Bader, Wing-Comm.

Douglas 40
Baie 131
Baie des Trépassés 227
Baie des Trépassés 226
Bains 213
Bais/Bais church 68–9
Balzac, Honoré de 134
Barbe-Torte, Alain 17
Barbu, Le 192, 193
Bart, Jean 187
Batz, Ile de 69
Batz-sur-Mer/Batz-sur-Mer church 70, 114
Baud 71
Baule, La 7–8, 71–3
Beau Rivage, Larmor-Plage 170
Beau Rivage, Mur-de-Bretagne 190
Beau Rivage, Quiberon 217
Beau Séjour, Landévennec 166
Beaumanoir, Jean de 157
Beauséjour, Erquy 126
Bécherel 73–4
Beg Rohu 216
Beg-Meil 3, 74–5
Belle Etoile 112
Belle Vue 256
Belle-Île 75–9
Belle-Île-en-Terre 79
Bellevue et Terrasse 86
Bélon 79
Bembrough, Richard 157, 200
Bénédiction de la Mer, Beg-Meil 75
Bénodet 3, 80–2
Bernhardt, Sarah 76, 77
Berry, Duchess of 60
beurre blanc 11–12
Binic 82–3
Biniou, Le Val-André 262
Biniou, St Cast-Le-Guildo 239
Bistro de la Tour 224
Blain 83–4
Blavet 145
Blois, Charles de 18, 48, 66, 110, 140, 151, 157, 250
Blot 159
Bocher 193
Bogue, La 228
Bois d'Amour, Pont-Aven 206

INDEX

Bon Accueil, Châteaulin 104
Bon Accueil, Sables-d'Or-les-Pins 235
Bono/Bono river 84
Borgia, Cesare 21
Botrel, Théodore 206
Bouillon, de, family 95
Bourbriac/Bourbriac church 84–5
Bourg, Le, Île de Bréhat 85, 252
Bourhis 234
Bousquet, Jean-Baptiste 219–20
Branhoc, Le 68
Brantôme, Pierre de Bourdeilles, Seigneur de 21
Bréhat, Île de 192
Brélévenez church, Lannion 168
Brest 39–44, 191
Bretagne, Belle-Île 78
Bretagne, Dol-de-Bretagne 123
Bretagne, Gilles de, 238–9
Bretagne, Le Croisic 115
Bretagne, Pont l'Abbé 210
Bretagne, Questembert 214
Breton language 4, 23, 24
Breton War of Succession 18, 42, 48, 110, 137, 140, 148, 151, 157, 224, 249–50
Briec-de-l'Odet 87
Brigantin 126
Brignogan-Plages 87–8
Brittany, Roscoff, 234
Brizeux 251
Brosse, Salomon de 45
Broualan 88
Bruz 88–9

Cadoudal, Georges 67
Caldecott, Ralph 206
Calèche 143
Callac-de-Bretagne 89
Camaret-sur-Mer 89–91
Cancale 91–3
Canterbury, Sir Thomas 119
Cap d'Erquy 126
Cap Fréhel 136–7
Cap Horn 38
Cap-Coz 132
Capucin Gourmand 222
Caradeuc de la Chalotais, Louis-René de 74
Carantec 94
Caravelle, Dinan 120
Caravelle, Plouescat 202
Carhaix-Plouguer 95–7
Carnac 6, 24, 97–100
Carnac Plage 97–8, 99
Carré, Corentin 128
Carrier, Jean-Baptiste 23, 56–7

Cartier, Jacques 33, 35
Casanova de Seingalt, Giovanni Jacopo 92
Cassard 56
Cast 103–4
Castel Clara 78
Castel Marie-Louise 73
Castel Régis 87
castles *see* châteaux/castles/manor houses
Catell-Gollet (Catherine the Lost) 147
cathedrals *see under* individual names
Catholic League 22, 33, 58, 97, 103, 124, 140, 162, 211, 266
Celtique 132
Celts 4, 16–17, 105, 113
Central, St Malo 38
Centre, Guilvinec 146
Centre, Hennebont 152
Centre de Loisirs Milin Kerroch, Sizun 253
Champeaux/Champeaux church 100
Chandouineau 227
Chapelle de l'Espérance 122, 127
Charlemagne, King of the Franks 17
Charles V, Emperor of Austria 21
Charles V, King of France 18
Charles VIII, King of France 18, 19–20, 45, 148
Château, Combourg 108
Château, Josselin 159
Château de Coatguélen 193
Château de Locguénolé 151
Châteaubriand, François-René de 36–7, 102, 106, 107
Châteaubriant 101–2
Châteaubriant, Geoffrey de 102
Châteaugiron 22, 102–3
Châteaulin 103–4
Châteauneuf-du-Faou 104–5
Châteaux/castles/manor houses
 Branféré château, Le Guerno 229
 Brest castle 40–1
 Château Careil, Guérande 140
 Château de Blossac, Bruz 88
 Château de Bonne Fontaine, Antrain 64
 Château de Bourbansais, Pleugueneuc 199
 Château de Bretesche, Missillac 182–3
 Château de Caradeuc,

 Bécherel 74
 Château de Cléray 16
 Château de Comper, Forêt de Paimpont 194
 Château de Kergrist 169
 Château de la Groulaie, Blain 83–4
 Château de la Hardouinais, Moncontour 239
 Château de la Hunaudaie, Jugon-les-Lacs 160, 198
 Château de la Motte Beaumanoir, Pleugueneuc 199–200
 Château de la Noée-Sèche, Quintin 225
 Château de la Touche-Trébry, Moncontour 184–5
 Château de Landal, Broualan 88, 122
 Château de Lanrigan, Combourg 108
 Château de Maillé, Plouescat 201–2
 Château de Montmuran, Les Iffs 150
 Château de Robien, Quintin 225
 Château de Rocher Portail, Saint-Brice-en-Coglès 64
 Château de Trécesson, Forêt de Paimpont 194
 Château de Vaux-le-Vicomte, Belle-Île 77
 Château des Basses Fosses, La Roche-Bernard 229
 Château des Ducs, Nantes 57–9
 Château des Granges, Moncontour 184
 Château des Ormes, Epiniac 122
 Château des Rochers-Sévigné, Vitré 267, 268
 Château du Taureau, Morlaix 187
 Château Gaillard, Vannes 263
 Château Léhélec 229
 Château Roche-Jagu 231
 Château Vauban, Camaret-sur-Mer 90
 Châteaubriant castle 101–2
 Châteaugiron castle 102–3
 Combourg castle 107
 Dinan Château 119
 Fougères castle 133–4
 Guingamp castle 148
 Josselin castle 156–9
 Kergornadeac'h Château 201
 Kerouzméré castle 245
 Le Lupin Château, Le Guimorais 147

INDEX

Les Salles Château, Etang des Salles 144
Manoir de Kerazan-en-Loctudy, Loctudy 176
Manoir de Tronjoly 201–2
Manoir du Stang, La Forêt-Fouesnant 130–1
Font l'Abbé castle 210
Pontivy castle 208–9
St Malo castle 33, 34–5
Suscinio castle 249–50
Tonquédec castle 169
Vitré castle 265–7
Châtelaudren 106
Chaudron 68
Chaumière 149
cheese 14
Cheval Blanc, Loudéac 180
Cheval Blanc et Château, Châteaugiron 103
Chez Charlemagne 265
Chez Crouzil, La Gare 198
Chez Jacky 208
Chez Mélanie 207
Chez Robic 209
Chouans 23–4, 66–7, 134, 216, 229
Chouin 52
churches *see* under individual names
cider 132
Clair de Lune promenade, Dinard 53
Claude of Brittany 21, 45
Cléden-Poher/Cléden-Poher church 106
Clemenceau 73
Clisson, Olivier de 66, 83, 157–8
Clos de Vallombreuse 125
Clos du Pontic 166
coastline of Brittany 2, 3
Cobh 201
Coetanlem, John der 187
Colbert, Jean Baptiste 4, 22, 49, 176, 211
Coligny, Gaspard de 266, 267
Collégiale 141
Colline de la Clarté, Perros-Guirec 197
Colombière 127
Colvert, Le 62
Combourg 106–8
Commana/Commana parish close 108
Commerce, Fougères 136
Commerce, Josselin 159
Commerce, Port-Louis 212
Commerce, Quintin 226
Common Market 28
Comorre, Count of Cornouaille 152–3, 224
Conan IV, Duke of Brittany 18, 133
Concarneau 3, 11, 75, 109–12, 137

Conleau 112–13
Conquet, Le 113
Conrad, Joseph 255
Continental 93
Contre Quai, Le 79
Coquille 112
Corentin, St 218
Cornelius, St 98
Cornic, Charles 187
Cornouaille, La 105
Cornouaille folklore festival, Quimper 222
Corret, Adèle 95
Corsaire 234
Corsairs 31–2, 187, 232
Corseul 113
Côte de Granti Rose 256
Côte Sauvage 70, 78, 215
Cotriade 261
cotriade 11
Cottet, Charles 220
Couëdic, du 43
Coureaux channel 170
Coypel family 46
Coz-Pors beach, Trégastel 256
crêpes 8, 13–14
Croisic, Le 70, 114–15, 139
Croix Blanche 68
Crouesty, Le 115
Crozon 89, 116–17
Crozon-Morgat 185
Cruaud 201
culture, Breton 4–5, 26–7

Dahouët 261
Dahut, Princess (Marie-Morgane) 125
Dallam, Robert 219
Daoulas 117
Daoulas river 144
Dauphin 264
D'Avaugour 120
De Bricourt 93
Debussy, Claude 92, 125, 242
Des Carmes church, Pont l'Abbé 210
Deux Magots 230
Diana 99
Diben Point 202
Dinan 7, 54 117–21
Dinard 4, 7, 52–5
Dol-de-Bretagne 121–3
Domaine de Kereven 82
Domaine d'Orvault 62
Douanne 112
Douarnenez 123–5
Dourduff 203
Dreyfus, Alfred 46
drink 15–16
Druids 5, 138, 226
Du Guesclin 51
Du Phare 78
Duchesse Anne, St Malo 39
Duchesse-Anne, Sables-d'Or-les-Pins 235

duck 12
Ducs de Lin 104
Duguay-Trouin, René 32, 187
Dunes, Dinard 55
Dunes, Lesconil 171
Dunes, St Cast-Le-Guildo 239
Dupont D'Anjou 143

Edict of Nantes 58
Edward IV, King of England 250
Elizabeth 38
Elizabeth I, Queen of England 116
Elorn 168
Elorn river 165
Enclos, Lampaul-Guimiliau 147
Enclos, Landivisiau 168
Enclos de Rosveign 211
Eon, Col. 25–6
Epiniac 122
Erquy 126
Escale, Locmariaquer 172
Escale, Vannes 265
Escu de Runfaô 51
Escurial 126
Espadon, La Baule 73
Espadon, Sarzeau 250
Espérance 131
Estrées, Gabrielle d' 163
Étables-sur-Mer 127
Eugene, St 249
Euromer 155
Europe 188

Falaise 94
Faou, Le 127–8
Faouët, La 128–9
Farmer, George 43
Ferme du Letty 81
Ferrer, St Vincent 263
Ferrière 102
Fête de Locmaria, Belle-Île-en-Terre 79
Fête des Filets Bleus, Concarneau 110
Fête des Pommiers, Fouesnant 132
Feu Sainte-Elme 126
Feux des Îles 197
'Finisterre' 3
fish 9–12, 91–2, 105, 110–11, 114
Flaubert, Gustave 98
Fleur de Sel 141
Foix, Françoise de 101
Foleaux 229
Folgoët 129–30
Fontaine de Barenton, Forêt de Paimpont 194
Fontaine de la Pompe, Guingamp 148
Fontaine de St Brieuc 237
Fontaine de St Thivisiau,

INDEX

Landivisiau 167
food 8–14
forests *see* below, or under individual names, e.g. Hardouinais forest
Forêt de Carnoët 213, 223, 224
Forêt de la Guerche 143
Forêt de Paimpont (Brocéliande) 194–5
Forêt de Quénécan 143 189
Forêt d'Escoublac 72
Forêt-Fouesnant, La 130–1, 132
Forge 164
Forges-des-Salles, Les 144
Fort de Penthièvre, Quiberon 216
Forte National, St Malo 34, 37
Fouesnant 132
Fougères 133–6
Fougères, Raoul II, Baron de 133
Fouquet, Nicolas 58, 76–7
Fowles, John 194
France, Camaret-sur-Mer 91
France, Combourg 108
France, Josselin 160
France, La Gacilly 137
France, Nantes 61
France, Plougasnou 203
France, St Pol-de-Léon 246
François I, King of France 4, 45, 101
François II, Duke of Brittany 19, 56, 158, 250
Franklin, Benjamin 66
Frère Jacques 44
Fret, Le 116
Frobisher, Sir Martin 116
Fulton, Robert 90–1

Gabriel, Jacques-Ange 45
Gabriel, Jacques-Jules 45, 46
Gacilly, La 137
Gai Logis, Châteauneuf-du-Faou 105
Gai Logis, Rosporden 235
Galion, Le, Binic 83
Galion, Le, Concarneau 112
Galopin-Gourmet, Le 52
Gambetta 210
Garnier 89
Gauguin, Paul 50, 111, 205, 206, 213
Gaulle, Gen. Charles de 251, 252
Genêts d'Or 170
Genty-Home 254
Geoffroy, Gustave 188
Georges V 55
Gildas, St 152–3
Giscard d'Estaing, Valéry 26
gîtes 28

Glacier 65
Glann Ar Mor 255
Golfe de la Bretesche 183
Gouarec 143
Gouët river 225
Goulet de Brest 190
Goursen 217
Gourvennec, Alexis 27, 232–3
Goyen, Le 65
Gradlon 97
Gradlon, King 124–5, 166, 218–19
Grand, Dinard 52, 55
Grand, Le Val-André 261
Grand, Tréguier 258
Grand Bé island 30, 34, 35–6, 37
Grand Phare, Belle-Île 77–8
Grand' Rue, Morlaix 186–7
Grande Fontaine 160
Grandes Grottes, Morgat 185
Grand-Fougeray 137
Grand-Rue des Stuarts, Dol-de-Bretagne 121
Grands Sables, Belle-Île 78
Grève de Goulven, Brignogan-Plages 87
Griffon 237
Grotto du Diable, Huelgoat 154
Guénolé, St 166
Guérande 139–41
Guerche-de-Bretagne, La/Guerche-de-Bretagne church 141–3
Guerno, Le 229
Guesclin, Bertrand du 4, 18, 48–9, 66, 110, 118, 119, 137, 150, 224
Guesclin, Olivier du 199
Guildo, Le 238–9
Guillou, Julia 205
Guilvinec 145–6
Guimiliau/Guimiliau parish close 146–7
Guimorais, Le 147
Guingamp 148–9
Gulf Stream 234
Gwel-Kaër 81

Hardouinais forest 182
Hédé 149–50
Hennebont 150–2
Henri 73
Henri IV, King of France 58, 83, 124
Henry II, King of England 18, 133, 157
Henry VI, King of England 238, 239
Henry VII, King of England 250
Henry VIII, King of England 42–3, 187
Hermitage 72

Hermitage et Manoir de Kerroch 224
Hervé, St 181
history of Brittany 16–29
Hoche, Gen. Lazare 216
horses 151, 163
Hortensias, Les 260
Hostellerie de la Mer 117
Hostellerie de l'Abbaye 145
Hôtel de Ville, Rennes 46
Hôtel des Ducs de Bretagne, St Brieuc 237
Houle 236
Houle, La 92
Hubert, St 104
Huelgoat 153
Hugo, Victor 134

Iffs, Les/Iffs church 150
Île aux Moines 183–4, 264
Île Béniguet 86
Île de Bréhat 85–6
Île de Groix 138
Île de Hoedic 152, 153
Île de Houat 152–3
Île de Tristan 22, 97, 123, 124
Îles des Landes 92–3
Île d'Ouessant (Ushant) 43, 190–1
Île Grande 255
Île Tomé 196
Île-de-Sein 26, 226, 251–3
Îles 153
Îles de Glénan 132, 137–8
Île-Tudy 155, 176
Institut Thalasso Thérapie, Quiberon 215
Intra Muros, St Malo 30, 33
Is, mythical town of 124–5, 218, 226

Jacob, Max 220–2
James II, King of England 114–15
James V, King of Scotland 233
Jardin Anglais, Dinan 118–19
Jean II, Duke of Brittany 18
Jean III, Duke of Brittany 18, 37
Jean IV, Duke of Brittany *see* Montfort, Jean de (later Jean IV, Duke of Brittany)
Jeanne d'Arc 82
Jeanne d'Arc 57
Jeanne de France 18, 20–1
Jesuits 22, 38, 74
John, King of England 122
Josselin 156–60
J.-P. Delaunay 39
Jugon-les-Lacs 160

Kador 186
Kastel Roc'h 204

INDEX

Kastell Dinec'h 258
Kastel-Moor 81
Ker Izel 237
Ker Moor, Bénodet 81
Ker Moor, St Quay-Portrieux 247
Ker Noyal 217
Kerdruc 161
Kerfany-les-Pins 161
Kergonan, Île aux Moines 183–4
Kermaria 246
Kermaria-an-Iskuit chapel, Kermaria 246–7
Kernascléden/Kernascléden church 129, 161–2
Keroman 178
Klots, Alfred and Trafford 230
Kreisker 244
Kreisker chapel, St Pol-de-Léon 245

La Chalotais family 74
La Fontanelle, Guy de 22, 97 124
La Noué ('Bras-de-Fer') 163
La Rouerie, Marquis de 134–5
La Tour, Georges de 59–60
La Tour d'Auvergne-Corret (Théophile Malo Corret) 95–7
La Trémoille, General Louis de 19
Lac 108
Lac de Guerlédan 143–5, 189
Lacs des Mottes 142–3
Laënnec, Dr René 46
Lainé, Célestin 26
Laïta river 213, 224
lamb 12
Lamballe 162–4
Lamennais, Félicité Robert de 35
Lampaul 190, 191
Lampaul-Guimiliau/Lampaul-Guimiliau parish close 147, 167–8
Lancelot du Lac, Sir 194–5
Lancieux 165
Lande St-Martin, La 61
Landerneau 165–6
Landévennec 166–7
Landivisiau 167–8
Landois, Pierre 250
Landriais, La 168
language, Breton 26
Lann Roz 100
Lannion 168–70
Lannion, Pierre de 71
Lanvallay 119
Larmor-Plage 170, 212
Lauberlac'h 203
Lautram 172

Laval, Jean de, Count of Châteaubriant 101
Laval, Jeanne de 151
Law, John 177
Le Coz, Alain 248–9
Lechiagat 145–6
Légué 237
Lemenager family 52
Lemordant, Jean Julien 50
Lenclos, Ninon de 267
Lesage, Alain-René 249
Lesconil 171
Letty 80
Lézardrieux 171–2
Lieue de Grève 243
Lion d'Or, Bais 69
Lion d'Or, Rochefort-en-Terre 231
lobster à l'Armoricaine 9–10
Loch, Le 68
Locmaria, Belle-Île 78
Locmariaquer 172
Locminé 172–3
Locquémeau 169
Locquirec 173
Locronan 173–5
Loctudy/Loctudy church 3, 155, 176
Logis de la Bresche Arthur 123
Lorient 170, 176–9, 211
Loti, Pierre 191, 192
Loudéac 179–80
Louis, Duc d'Orléans (later Louis XII, King of France) 18–19, 20–1, 58
Louis IX, King of France 102
Louis the Pious, Duke of Brittany 17
Louis XI, King of France 18
Louis XIV, King of France 4, 22, 49, 58, 92, 140, 176, 267–8
Louis XV, King of France 45, 74
Louis XVI, King of France 74, 163
Louis-Philippe, King of France 37, 60
Louthebourg, P. J. de 50
Louvigné-de-Bais 143
Lusignan, Guy de 234

Madeleine 182
Mainotel 136
Mairie 166
Maison de la Duchesse Anne, Morlaix 187
Maison de la Pêche 260
Maison des Marmousets, Ploërmel 200, 201
Maison du Sénéchal, Carhaix-Plouguer 95
Malestroit 180
Malestroit family 16
Manoir de la Comète 62
Manoir de Lan-Kerellec 255
Manoir de Moëllien 175

Manoir de Vaumadeuc 198, 199
Manoir des portes 164
Manoir du Stang 131
Manoir du Tertre 195
Manoir Le Cardinal 141
manor houses *see* châteaux/castles/manor houses
Maraîchers, Les 62
Mare aux Sangliers, Huelgoat 154
Marée Bleue 189
Marguerite 120
Marie-Antoinette, Queen 163
Marine 100
Mark, King of Cornouaille 123
Mary, Queen of Scots 233
Maximilian, Emperor of Austria 19, 20
megaliths *see* menhirs/megaliths
Meilleraye-de-Bretagne, La 181
Mélusine tower, la, Fougères 134
Ménage de la Vierge, Huelgoat 154
Ménez-Bré 181
menhirs/megaliths 6, 16, 97–9, 122, 142, 172
Mercoeur, Philippe de Lorraine, Duc de 58, 103, 162, 211, 266
Merdrignac 182
Mère Pourcel 120
Merlin, magician 194
Merveilles des Mers 120
Midi 87
Milin Kerroch 253
Miln, J. 99
Minaret 81
Minihy-Tréguier 257
Missillac 182–3
Moderne, Crozon 117
Moderne, Île-Tudy 155
Moderne, Quimper 222
Moncontour 184–5
Monet, Claude 188
Mont Dol 122
Montagnes Noires 104–5, 128
Montfort, Jean de (later Jean IV, Duke of Brittany) 18, 42, 48, 66, 110, 130, 140, 151, 157, 224, 250
Monts d'Arrée 153
Mont-St-Michel 121
Moreau, Jean-Victor 188
Morgat 2, 89, 185–6
Morlaix 186–9
Moulin de Belle-Isle 180
Moulin de Via 228
Mur-de-Bretagne 143, 189–90

INDEX

Muscadet wine 15–16, 61
museums
  Aquarium, Vannes 264
  Aquarium and Marine museum, Dinard 53
  Aquarium Charles-Pérez, Roscoff 233
  Archaeological museum, Vannes 263
  Belle-Île museum 77
  Binic museum 82
  Brest museum 41
  Exposition d'Oeuvres en Coquillages, Concarneau 110
  Gauguin museum, Pont-Aven 207
  Jules Verne museum, Nantes 59
  Maison de la Culture, Rennes 50
  Morlaix museum 188
  Musée Automobile de Bretagne, Rennes 50
  Musée d'Art Populaire Regional, Nantes 59
  Musée de Bretagne, Rennes 49–50
  Musée de la Mer 191–2
  Musée de la Pêche, Concarneau 110
  Musée de la Vilaine Maritime 229
  Musée de Préhistoire J. Miln-Le Rouzic, Carnac 99
  Musée de Vieux Brest 41
  Musée des Beaux Arts, Nantes 59–60
  Musée des Beaux Arts, Quimper 220
  Musée des Beaux Arts, Rennes 50
  Musée des Marais Salants, Batz-sur-Mer 70
  Musée des Poupées, Josselin 158
  Musée des Salorges, Nantes 59
  Musée International du Longcours Cap Hornier, St Malo 37–8
  Naval museum, Brest 41
  Pont l'Abbé museum 210
  Quimper museum 219
  St Malo museum 35
  St-Rivoal museum 248

Nantes 11, 12, 17, 19, 23, 45, 55–62, 102
Napoleon Bonaparte 35, 36, 59, 67, 96, 188, 208
Napoleon III, Emperor 35, 208
Neptune 217
Nominoë, Duke of Brittany 17, 121, 263

Normans 17
Notre-Dame basilica, Folgoët 129–30
Notre-Dame chapel, Carantec 94
Notre-Dame church, Lamballe 163
Notre-Dame church, Vitré 267
Notre-Dame-de-Bon-Secours basilica, Guingamp 148
Notre-Dame-de-Kroaz-Batz church, Roscoff 233
Notre-Dame-de-la-Paix chapel, Le Pouldu 213
Notre-Dame-de-Larmor church, Larmor-Plage 170
Notre-Dame-de-Paradis church, Hennebont 151
Notre-Dame-de-Rocamadour chapel, Camaret-sur-Mer 90
Notre-Dame-de-Roscudon church, Pont-Croix 219
Notre-Dame-de-Victoire church 177–8
Notre-Dame-du-Haut chapel, Trédaniel 184
Notre-Dame-du-Roncier church, Josselin 159
Notre-Dame-du-Tertre chapel, Châtelaudren 106
Nouveau Port 124
Novotel-Lorient 178

Océan, Concarneau 111
Océan, Le Croisic 115
Odet river 80, 176, 218
onions 12–13
Ostréa 260
oysters 11, 63, 79, 84, 91–2, 191

Paimpol 2–3, 191–3
Paimpont 195
Paineau, Georges 214
Paix 55
Palais 51
Palais, Le, Belle-Île 76, 77, 78
Palais de Justice, Rennes 45–6
Palmeraie, La 73
Panorama, La Trinité-sur-Mer 260
Panoramique, Le Pouldu 213
Paramé 38
Parc 204
Parc Régional de Brière 140–1
Pardons 5–6, 17
  Batz 69
  Carnac 99
  Châteauneuf-du-Faou 105
  Folgoët 129
  Fouesnant 132
  Guingamp 148–9

Josselin 159
La Faouët 128–9
Locronan 174–5
Pont-Aven 206
St-Jean-du-Doigt 241
Tréguier 257–8
Patton, Gen. George 25
Pélican 159
Pencran/Pencran church 165
Pen-Lan Point 94
Pension de Famille 217
Penthièvre 216
Penthièvre, Jeanne de 18, 42
Perros-Guirec 2, 196–8
Petit Mont-St-Michel 240
Petit-Billot 268
Phare 93
Pic 179
Picasso, Pablo 220, 221
Pichet 268
Pierre du Champ-Dolent, Dol-de-Bretagne 122
Piré 51
Piriac-sur-Mer 198
Place des Lices, Rennes 48
Plage, La, St Marc-sur-Mer 242
Plage, Locronan 175
Plage, Quiberon 217
Plage, St Michel-en-Grève 243
Plage et Fréhel 136
Plage Napoléon 247
Plancoët 198–9
Pléhérel-Plage 235
Pléneuf-Val-André 261
Pleugueneuc 199–200
Pleumeur-Bodou 169
Pléven 198
Ploërmel 200–1
Ploubalay 165
Ploubazlanec 192
Plouescat 201–2
Plougasnou 202–3
Plougastel-Daoulas 117, 203–4
Ploujean 188
Ploumanac'h 204
Poêlon d'Or 102
Pointe de Bloscon 233
Pointe de Hock 92
Pointe de l'Arcouest 192
Pointe de l'Armorique 203
Pointe de Penhir 90
Pointe de St Cast 238
Pointe des Espagnols 116
Pointe du Castelli 198
Pointe du Grouin 93
Pointe du Raz 226–7, 251
Pointe du Van 226
Points *see* above, or under individual names, e.g. Diben Point
Poisson d'Or 179
Pol, St 69, 167, 245

INDEX

Pont 172
Pont de Recouvrance, Brest 41
Pont l'Abbé 210–11
Pont-Aven 205–8
Pont-Aven school of painters 50, 111, 205–6, 220
Pontivy 208–10
pork 9, 12
Pornic 115
Pors Pol 94
Pors-Even 192
Port, Blain 84
Port, Le Val-André 261
Port, Lechiagat 146
Port, Locquirec 173
Port Blanc 258
Port Donnant, Belle-Île 78
Port du Goulphar, Belle-Île 78
Port du Rosmeur 124
Port Navalo 64
Porte de France 170
Porte Saint-Pierre 38
Port-Haliguen 215
Port-la-Forêt 131
Port-Louis 211–12
Port-Manech 206, 212
Portrieux 246
Port-Tudy 138
Portzmugeur, Hervé de 43
pottery 219–20
Pouldu, Le 213, 223
Président 51
Pressoir 265
Prieuré 175
Primel-Trégastel 202
Printania, Binic 83
Printania, Perros-Guirec 197
Printania, St Brieuc 237
Pullman-Beaulieu 61

Questembert 214
Quiberon 3, 214–17
Quimerc'h 217
Quimper 11, 218–23
Quimperlé 223–5
Quintin 225–6

Rabelais, François 15
Rabine, La 88
Raguerel, Tiphaine 119
Rais, Gilles de 57–8
Rance river 53–4, 117, 119–20
Redon 227–8
Relais Brenner, Lézardrieux 171
Relais Brenner, Paimpol 193
Relais de Breocéliande de Paimpont 195
Relais de la Forêt 71
Relais de la Place 128
Relais de l'Argoat 79
Relais du Porhoet 160

Relais du Roch 224
Relais du Roy 149
Relax 217
Remparts 141
Rémy (Gilbert Renault) 247
Rennes 19, 27, 44–52 56
Renon, Ernest 258
Repaire de Kerroc'h 193
Resistance, Breton 24–6, 180, 211, 247
Retz, Cardinal de 57
Revolution, French 23–4, 56–7, 66–7, 96, 134, 135, 216
Richard II, King of England 42
Richard III, King of England 250
Richelieu, Armand, Duc de 83, 158, 163, 169, 176, 211
Richemont 265
Riec-sur-Bélon 207
Rielle, Hervé 115
Roche Jaune, La 258
Roche Tremblante, Huelgoat 154
Roche-aux-Fées, La 142
Roche-Bernard, La 228–30
Rochefort-en-Terre/ Rochefort church 230–1
Rochelle, La 39, 40
Roche-Maurice, La/Roche-Maurice parish close 231–2
Rochers 204
Roches-Douves 123
Rock Tregnanton 190
Rohan 209
Rohan, de, family 83–4, 148, 158, 161, 208–9
Roi Gradlon 65
Romans 3, 16–17, 45, 70, 76, 113, 114, 123, 139, 262
Ronan, St 174
Roof, Le, Conleau 112
Roof, Le, Vannes 264
Roof, Morgat 186
Roscanvel/Roscanvel church 116
Roscoff 13, 27, 201, 232–4, 245
Rosporden 234–5
Rothéneuf 147
Rouzic 259
Rozen-Fouquet 252
Ruellan, Gilles 64

Sables-d'Or-les-Pins 136, 235
saints, Breton 3–4, 5–6, 17; *see also* under individual names, e.g. Ronan, St
Salaun 129–30
salt 139–40
Samson, St 6, 121
Sarzeau 249–50

'Saut du Chat' (Cat's Leap) 242
Sauvion family 15–16
Sauzon, Belle-Île 78
Scaër 251
Séné 264
Sept-Îles 196, 197
Serpolet 170
Sérusier, Paul 105, 206
Sévigné, Marie, Madame de 267, 268
shellfish 9–10, 65, 171, 259
SICA (Societé d'Intérêt Collectif Agricole) 232, 233
Sirène 153
Sizun/Sizun parish close 253
slave trade 56, 57, 59
smuggling 140, 187–8
Sofitel 216
Solidor tower, St Malo 37–8
Source 199
Sphinx 197
St Aignan 144
St Anne-d'Auray 5–6
St Armel church, Ploërmel 200–1
St Aubin church, Guérande 139, 140
St Briac-sur-Mer 236
St Brieuc 82, 236–8
St Cast-Le-Guildo 238–9
St Cornély church, Carnac 99
St Effiam 243
St Etienne cathedral, St Brieuc 236
St Fiacre chapel, Le Faouët 129, 161
St Gilles church, Malestroit 180
St Gilles-Vieux-Marché 145
St Guirec bay 204
St Hervé chapel, Ménez-Bré 181
St Hubert church, Cast 103–4
St Jean-de-Béré church, Châteaubriant 102
St Joseph church, Pontivy 209
St Laurence church, Le Puy 118
St Louis church, Brest 41
St Malo 3, 7, 11, 13, 27–8, 30–9
St Marc-sur-Mer 242
St Mathurin church, Moncontour 184
St Maurice 224
St Mélaine church, Rennes 49
St Mériadec church, Stival 209
St Michel chapel, Île de Bréhat 86
St Michel church,

Quimperlé 223
St Nazaire 57
St Nicodème chapel, St-Nicholas-des-Eaux 244
St Nicolas, Îles de Glénan 138
St Nicolas chapel, La Faouët 129
St Pierre cathedral, Nantes 59
St Pierre cathedral, Rennes 46–7
St Pierre cathedral, Vannes 263
St Pierre-Quiberon 216
St Pol cathedral, St Pol-de-Léon 245
St Pol-de-Léon 232, 245
St Quay-Portrieux 246–7
St Ronan church, Locronan 174
St Samson cathedral, Dol-de-Bretagne 212–2
St Sauveur basilica, Dinan 118
St Sauveur church, Redon 227
St Sauveur church, Rennes 47
St Servan-sur-Mer 37
St Sulpice church, Fougères 135
St Tugdual cathedral, Tréguier 257
St Vincent cathedral, St Malo 35
St Yves 268
St-Antoine 189
Ste Anne-d'Auray 64, 67
Ste Barbe chapel, La Faouët 128–9
Ste Croix church, Quimperlé 223
Ste Marine 80–1
Ste-Anne-la-Palud chapel 175
Steir river 218
Sterne, La 68
St-Georges-de-Gréhaigne 239–40
Stival 209
St-Jacut-de-la-Mer 240
St-Jean-du-Doigt/St-Jean parish close 241
St-Lunaire 241–2
St-Michel-en-Grève 243
St-Nicholas-du-Pélem/St-Nicholas church 244
St-Nicolas-des-Eaux 209
St-Rivoal 248
St-Suliac 248

St-Thégonnec/St-Thégonnec parish close 248–9
St-Tugen 249
Styvel 91
Sully, Maximilien de Béthune, Duc de 83
Surcouf, Robert 32–3

Tati, Jacques 242
Taverne d'Ecu 268
Temple de Haut-Bécheral (Temple of Mars), Corseul 113
Temps de Vivre 234
Térénez 202
Terminus et Gare 178
Terrasses 120
Terrier 240
Thabor gardens, Rennes 48–9
Thalamot 75
Thermes 38
Ti al-Lannec 9, 255
Tinténniac 254
Tour d'Argent 164
Tour d'Auvergne, Pont l'Abbé 211
Tour d'Auvergne, Quimper 222
Tour Tanguy, Brest 41
tourism 7, 28–9
Touristes 145
Tournemine, de, family 160
travel to Brittany 1
Trébeurden 254–5
Tréboul 2, 124, 125
Trédaniel 184
Trégastel 256
Tréguier 5, 257–9
Tréhiguier 259
Tréhorenteuc 195
Trestraou 197
Trestraou beach, Perros-Guirec 196
Trinité-sur-Mer, La 259–60
Tristan and Iseult 123
Tritons 223
Trou du Serpent, Batz 69
Truite 155
Tu-es-Roc 126
tumuli 98–9, 202
Turballe, La 260
Ty Douz 155
Ty Pont 241
Ty-Gwechall 225
Ty-Mad 138

Univers 182

Vache Enragée, La 224

Val de Loire 63
Val-André, Le 261–2
Vallée, Le Bourg, La 145
Val-sans-Retour 195
Vannes 262–5
Vauban, Sébastien Le Prestre de 77, 90, 109
vegetables 12–134, 232, 245
Velville, Roland de 250
Vendome, César de 163
Venétes 265
Vénus de Quinipily, Baud 71
Vieille Auberge, Hédé 150
Vieille Auberge, Île de Bréhat 86
Vieille Eglise 256
Vieille Renommée 127, 128
Vieille Tour, Paimpol 193
Vieille Tour, St Brieuc 237
Vieux Moulin, Hédé 150
Vieux Moulin, St-Jacut-de-la-Mer 240
Vieux Moulin, St-Nicholas-des-Eaux 244
Vikings 115
Vilaine river 7, 88, 228, 229
Ville Close, Concarneau 109–10, 111
Ville d'Ys 186
Villefromoy, La 38
Vitré, 265–8
Viviane, enchantress 194
Vivier 178
Voile d'Or 235
Voltaire, François de 56, 74
Voyageurs, Brest 43
Voyageurs, Fougères 136
Voyageurs, Loudéac 179
Voyageurs, Sizun 253
Voyageurs, Tinténniac 254

Wars of Religion 21–2, 33, 140, 162–3, 266
Whelpton, Eric 192
wine 15–16, 61
World War I 24
World War II 24–6, 30, 39–40, 150–1, 177, 178, 180, 211, 247, 251–2
wrestling 5, 79
Wylie, Robert 111, 205

Yaudet, Le 169
Young, Arthur 121
Yves, St (Yves Hélori) 5, 257–8

Zoo du Moulin de Richard, Binic 82

Index compiled by Peva Keane